SOME OF MY
FRIENDS
HAVE TAILS

Other titles by Sara Henderson

From Strength to Strength
From Strength to Strength (audio tape)
The Strength in Us All

SARA HENDERSON

SOME OF MY FRIENDS HAVE TAILS

Illustrations by Marlee Ranacher

MACMILLAN
Pan Macmillan Australia

First published 1995 in Macmillan by Pan Macmillan Australia Pty Limited
St Martins Tower, 31 Market Street, Sydney

National Library of Australia
cataloguing-in-publication data:

Henderson, Sara, 1936– .
Some of my friends have tails.

ISBN 0 7329 0817 5.

1. Henderson, Sara, 1936– . 2. Women ranchers—Northern
Territory—Bullo River Station—Biography. 3 Domestic animals—
Northern Territory—Bullo River Station. I. Title.

636.0092

Typeset in 12/14.5 Sabon by Midland Typesetters
Printed in Australia by McPherson's Printing Group

Dedicated to Danielle, Martin and Natalie

The unconditional love of 'man's best friend'
The bravery of the noble horse
The soft wet caress of a friendly dolphin
The many marvels and miracles of the
Kingdom of Animals...
If you have never experienced any of these things
Then you, my friend, have never truly lived...
Have missed some of the real, true pleasures of life.

CONTENTS

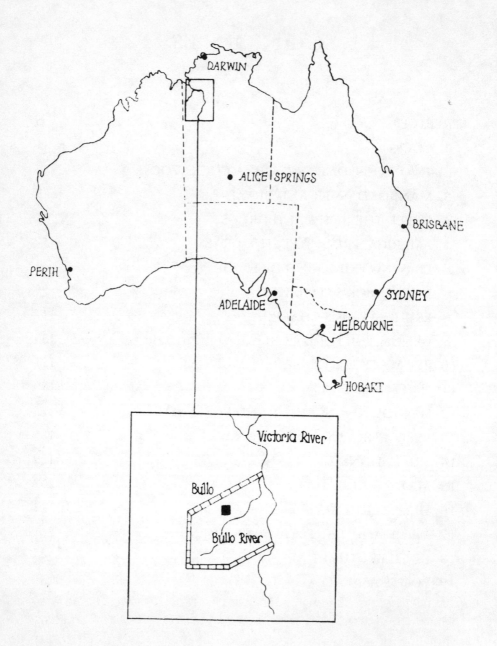

PREFACE

I am fortunate to have been associated with the world of animals since I was a very young child.

The love of my dogs.

The brave and faithful horses I have known.

The gentle nudge or soft caress of a loving cat.

The trust in the knowing eye of an injured wild creature.

All these experiences I firmly believe have given me a better balance to my life. And certainly given me remarkable memories and endless pleasure.

Journey with me through these pages and I hope I can show you another world.

If you too are fortunate enough to know the Kingdom of Animals, still come with me on a smiling, head-nodding journey, whispering—'Yes, my dog does that!', 'My cat is just like that!', 'This could be my horse, my poddy calf, my milking cow, my cockatoo!'

Although animals take up a good portion of the book, there are more stories about the characters in the other books and a few new characters.

This is a truly international book. I started writing at the beginning of the 'wet' season on Bullo, in temperatures of forty degrees Celsius. It then travelled with me to Darwin, then London, ten days around England for the launch of my first book and then to Austria for a holiday in the snow, minus fifteen degrees!

Well I did have to write seven hours a day to finish the second half of the book, so I wrote from 5 a.m. to lunchtime and then I had the day off.

Together we travelled through a snow blizzard to the airport in Munich, Germany, then off to Frankfurt and on to Johannesburg, South Africa for another book tour. On to Durban, Cape Town, back to Johannesburg, then to Perth, Sydney, Darwin, Bullo where it was finally corrected and, in finished manuscript form, travelled with me to Sydney. The manuscript was read by my editor while I toured Sydney, Melbourne, Wagga, Brisbane, Toowomba, Brisbane and ended up in Caloundra. The book and I were reunited again in Caloundra where I did the final corrections and it departed for Sydney and typesetting and I flew to Darwin. Marlee met me in Darwin with a suitcase of photos and the next day was spent choosing the photos. They went to Sydney and Marlee and I flew back to the station where the final touches, dedication, preface, and epigraph were written and faxed to Sydney, and there you have book number three!

So much for the quiet log cabin in the mountains and uninterrupted thought!

I hope you have some of the enjoyment reading this book that I had writing it.

1

COCKO

The telegram read:
SENDING BABY COCKATOO OVERNIGHT MAIL
STOP YOURS CENTRAL MONDAY 7:30 AM.
'Good Heavens,' said Mum. 'Your Aunty Nin
is sending a baby cockatoo on the mail train
from Canberra!'

Most of the weekend was spent preparing for the little Ford
Anglia to make the horrendous journey to Sydney's Central
Railway Station.

Mum said to Poppa, 'I can drive you into the city to work
on Monday; you won't have to take the train.'

There was a long pause before Dad replied. Then he said
very quietly, 'No, I'll take the train. Two destinations on one
trip might be too much for you to handle.'

Mum, completely lost in her battle plan of venturing out
onto the major highway to town, did not take offence to
Dad's unspoken suggestion that the journey would be a disaster from go to whoa.

Monday morning at six o'clock saw us, Mum and me,
ready for the big journey. I was around five-and-a-half-years-
old, so not much help to Mum on this great navigational feat.

There were many 'pull overs' to the side of the road to
study the map 'to town'... well-l-l-l, we didn't have to pull

over far. Mum never drove over fifteen miles per hour, and with two wheels almost in the gutter, she had to actually go around a few parked cars we encountered along the way. This involved a complicated procedure, and took up endless time.

Mum would wait behind the parked car until the traffic cleared. The definition of 'cleared' was, not a vehicle in sight... in either direction. Mum would then propel herself out the window, at least up to her waist, with right arm fully extended, index finger ramrod straight, and pointing towards heaven as she struggled to engage the clutch, whilst still hanging half out of the car. With a terrible noise issuing from the abused gearbox, the valiant little car would lurch and hop around the parked car to once again continue the journey to town, via the gutter.

The car did have a cute little indicator that popped out of the upright between the front driver's door and the back door. It was, if my memory serves me correctly, a yellow indicator light. But it was too chancy that the indicators might not work, and Mum never left anything to chance.

There was another indicator on the left side of the car, but Mum helped it along too. To inform the driver in the car behind that she was turning left, she would again propel herself out the window up to the waist, but instead of the ramrod arm and index finger pointing to the heavens in the direction of right, the arm would now assume a graceful pose, straight out of *Swan Lake*'s opening scene, giving the illusion you were about to witness the ballet. The illusion, soon to be destroyed by the ramrod pointed finger and the repeated jerking of the whole upper body, indicated that the car, and indeed Mum (if she didn't fall out the window and could engage the clutch far enough) were about to kangaroo around to the left.

Mum always maintained the automatic indicators were too small for a following car to see, hence the elaborate procedure to make her intentions clear to anyone behind. Of course, if some car did happen to get close enough to see even the car, let alone the indicators, this would throw Mum into complete panic, and reduce the whole operation of turning anywhere to utter confusion. Everything would stop, including the engine, until the car passed and was out of sight. Then we would begin again.

This is why we left home at six o'clock in the morning to be in the city at seven-thirty, when the city was only a twenty-five minute drive away... by normal driving standards.

When we got close to the industrial area, there were many more parked cars and trucks, and it took forever for Mum to navigate around them. It got to the point where there were so many cars and trucks parked, Mum was forced to stay in the main stream of traffic. But, at the first possible chance, she went through her *Swan Lake* routine and left the highway by this unusual method, leaving the traffic at a standstill!

After wandering around the suburbs and inner city for an inordinate length of time, we finally stumbled across Central Station. The mail train from Canberra was already in, and was standing huffing and puffing, slowly reducing its steam and having a breather after its long journey. It was pretty exciting journeying to town with Mum in the little black car, but to stand on the big platform at Central, and look at the Canberra Express billowing steam everywhere, flexing the mighty power it still had in reserve after a long cross-country haul, well, at five and a half, a long-drawn-out 'w-o-w' about sums it up.

The scene is still very clear in my memory; early morning, no direct sunlight had yet broken through the city buildings, yet sunlit steam swirled up high above the roof of the station enveloping the entire scene in sparkling grey, ghostly, mist-like obscurity. The bustle of people, people hurrying off the train, people rushing to meet them, people saying good-byes, ready to board the train. Porters everywhere, removing luggage and freight, pushing large trolleys weighed down with luggage, disappearing into the luggage van. It was turning into the most exciting day of my very short life.

Mum marched up to a porter on the goods wagon and demanded a box addressed to her. He looked at her with a tired, impatient expression and told her in a very dead monotone voice, that all cargo was dispatched through the goods freight office: he pointed to the other end of the platform. With an expression of complete disapproval, Mum wheeled around and, with me in tow, marched off down the platform.

The man's manner had displeased her; I knew this because he had not been given her normal courteous 'thank you'. In my few short years, I had seen the scenario many times; indeed, on a few... many... occasions, I had caused that very same expression.

We arrived at the correct counter, only to be told there was no box addressed to Mum. Waving the telegram as proof didn't help, the clerk patiently told Mum. The telegram didn't prove the bird was on the train; he needed a dispatch number.

Mum argued that surely they would keep a live bird separate from the general cargo. The man must have been a twin to the porter on the train, and he got the same look from Mum as she departed in a storm of protest, with me still in fast tow.

We disappeared down the ramp to street level, leaving dreadful visions of what was about to befall the staff of goods freight, when Mum got into gear, on the phone.

We started the long journey home, which didn't take as long as the morning journey, because Mum had her mind on hanging and quartering most of the freight staff at Central Station.

We were having lunch when another telegram from Aunty

Nin arrived stating dispatch number of one live cockatoo. The rest of the day was spent on the phone gathering her troops for war, after being told the parcel still wasn't there. She was most upset; somewhere in the cavernous confines of Central Station was a few-days-old cockatoo, and if she didn't find it soon it would be too late.

The next morning very early, the way Mum rammed the hats on my head, then hers, made me pity the poor clerk at the freight office. With the all-important dispatch number in her hand, we were heading for war, and I had no doubt who would win.

Mum's driving, for one thing, changed dramatically. We stayed on the road, and the speed increased to twenty miles per hour; we were flying—for Mum, that is.

She had rallied together everyone she knew working in the railways, even my sister's current boyfriend who worked in the offices upstairs from the freight office. They met us outside freight, and we descended as a delegation.

It was actually Jack, Sue's boyfriend, who was responsible for finding Cocko and saving his life. He took Mum back into the enormous freight warehouse, where the public were forbidden to venture, and as they prowled up and down the endless rows of freight, Mum heard a feeble but penetrating squawk issuing from a mound of boxes.

She had the clerk moving the pile of freight at an alarming rate; if he dared to pause, she yelled, 'Faster!'

He complained it was the porter's job to move freight, but one murderous look from Mum, and he was working at top speed.

The box was at the bottom, and in the middle of the pile. A panting and perspiring clerk handed Mum the box. Clearly written on all sides were the words:

LIVE BIRD. GIVE WATER IF NOT PICKED UP IMMEDIATELY (in smaller print).

With our escort carrying the box, we walked to the parked car, after Mum had 'dressed down' every clerk and porter in the vicinity and the poor bird had been given many drinks of water and a large quantity of the clerks' morning tea biscuits.

Mum thanked, then dispersed, her war troops, and we started our triumphant journey home. Straight down the highway like a conquering hero, at speeds that would amaze anyone who knew Mum's driving style.

2

TWO DOGS, ONE CAT AND A COCKATOO

It had been quite a campaign, one and a half days of intense combat. I had managed a few catnaps along the way, but Mum had gone at full steam.

By the time she had had the regulation cup of tea and a Bex and the bird had been made comfortable and fed something more substantial than biscuits, it was the end of the day. Our evening meal was a simple affair of baked beans on toast, rolled oats with sugar and milk for the bird, and that was how 'Cocko' came into our lives.

For those readers thinking, What a memory for a five-and-a-half-year-old! Not so. I listened to Mum tell that story again and again, to any captive audience, for at least the next ten years.

As Cocko developed into a beautiful bird, and the greatest character 'in feathers' you could ever hope to meet, the story of how Cocko nearly died became an integral part of my childhood, as did Cocko himself.

Cocko did not start out as a beautiful bird. When Mum opened the box in the freight office, there in one corner was this scrawny, squawking, mostly featherless, purple-skinned, bug-eyed... thing. A few downy, fluffy feathers here and there. After Mum encouraged it to drink some of the clerks' warm tea, with lots of sugar and milk, and eat their morning tea biscuits, this funny-looking apparition snuggled up against her and went sound asleep in her hand. Unfortunately, it had to go back in the box for the drive home, and it screeched and squawked the whole way home, only stopping when Mum picked it up again.

It squawked all night; we thought it would never stop. The only peace was when Mum was stuffing food down its throat, or holding it. Cocko was without a doubt Mum's bird; he adored her. This is understandable, I suppose: after spending the first days of his life in a box, a pair of gentle hands took charge and changed his life for ever. Along with the hands, there was a kind voice, and he soon learned about all the other parts that made up the wonderful person called 'Mum'.

It would be a normal reaction to stay close to such a person, and Cocko did, for the rest of his life. In Mum's capable hands he blossomed into a splendid bird, and a lively character. He grew up with six kids, two dogs and a cat.

Although he was one hundred percent Mum's pet, everyone loved him, and he in turn paid attention to the whole family. I dressed him in doll's clothes and wheeled him around in my doll's pram. Cocko took it all in his stride. On his back, with two scrawny claws up in the air and a bonnet on his head, he would lie patiently as I wheeled him around the garden and up and down the street. Luckily for Cocko, I soon gave up dressing him as my doll as my interest in tennis grew. Which was fortunate, because his reaction to seeing me approaching pushing my doll's pram was to let out a loud squawk and fly off his perch to land on top of the highest tree he could find. No amount of coaxing would get him down.

Mum played competition tennis during the week on our courts in the garden, and so I spent a lot of time on one of the vacant courts playing. Cocko followed Mum everwhere; he would be climbing the wire netting, or the light poles, or doing trapeze highjinks, screeching and squawking until Mum would finally have to scold him for making too much noise. He soon learned to settle down and watch tennis.

The ladies' mid-week competition, as well as the weekend tennis, was A-grade top district tennis and all sets were umpired. Cocko grew up over the years watching and listening to these very competitive tennis matches. Perhaps it was inevitable that he would pick up tennis lingo.

Sitting on top of the netting, he called the score, or called a ball out. He was so good at voice imitation that no-one could tell it was a bird. He didn't have that 'Polly want a cracker' type of parrot sound at all. As he grew up, everyone spoke to him in a normal voice, not a 'parrot' voice, and he responded the same. He could imitate male and female voices. In the family, he was so good at different people's voices you couldn't tell him from that person, especially Mum.

His best trick was to sit in the plum tree right next to Court Number One, and have his fun. A point would be in progress and a very clear and official voice would break the silence of play. 'Out!'

All hell would break loose. 'What do you mean out, it was in by a foot!' All eyes would be on the umpire waiting for an explanation.

'I didn't call,' would be the feeble reply.

'Then who did?'

Cocko got away with this for quite a while. He had the competition in an uproar.

'Oh, good shot!' would ring out, when the ball was two feet over the base line, causing bedlam, until the umpire would set the record straight by calling the ball out.

Things would just settle down, and play would continue, then loud and clear, 'Fault!' would be called in the middle of a rally. Play would stop while the players argued with the umpire about calling a fault three strokes into a rally. The poor umpire would struggle to convince everyone he or she hadn't called.

The point would be replayed, the match would resume until, 'Oh, bad luck, just missed!' would be called on a ball six feet in the court; which would send all players on both sides into a riot.

Cocko came undone during the mid-week ladies' competiton, when he slipped up and called out a remark in a man's voice.

'That was a man's voice!' was the outcry. Mum was playing that day, and she immediately knew the culprit.

'Cocko, where are you! Come here this instant!'

Cocko sheepishly walked pigeon-toed down a branch of the plum tree, out from the cover of the leaves and into view. Putting a scrawny claw up to his beautiful crest, and unfurling it into a brilliant yellow fan, his head on the side, and one beady eye cocked in her direction, he asked, 'How about a beautiful boy, then.'

With the mystery of the phantom caller of Court Number One solved, competition tennis at Halcyon returned to normal. To achieve this, I was assigned the duty of locking Cocko in his cage on the sunporch every time competition tennis was on. This made us instant enemies. I was well and truly into my tennis career, and when I was supposed to be leaving for a match away from home, I would be up a tree or crawling over the roof trying to catch Cocko, who knew what day it was, and was not going to be caught.

It became impossible to trap him; he would just fly away in the morning, and return when play was about to begin. To solve this problem, he was not let out of his cage on the mornings of competition tennis until play was over. When it was just social tennis with no umpire, he was quite a hit, sitting sometimes on the arm of the umpire's stand, calling scores, making his remarks and laughing: 'Oh, bad luck, old boy!', or 'Jolly good shot!', or 'I say, what a smash!' and endless other remarks.

Another problem developed when he started using some unsavoury expressions he picked up along the way. But a few well-aimed balls whenever he came out with a four-letter word soon made him realise that every time he said these words he would be knocked right off his perch. Eventually he was encouraged to drop them from his repertoire.

He would yell, 'Oh, sh—!' and a white missile would knock him clean off his perch, or whistle close by. He would ruffle his feathers, then settle back after he regained his feet and his composure, and remark, 'Oh, goodness!' in a very alarmed voice.

Cocko's antics were not restricted to the tennis court area; he was very definitely a people's bird and sought out company whenever and wherever possible.

One of his favourite spots was the front garden at sunset, when all the people coming home from work would pass by. He would sit under the roof eaves, and as people passed, in the most friendly of tones, he would say, 'Hullo, how are you!'

The person would turn around searching, but find no-one.

Sometimes Cocko wolf-whistled, and if a girl was passing, she would be mystified; if a man was walking behind her, he received a glare.

Sometimes Poppa sat in the sun, and Cocko got him into

embarrassing situations with a few wayward whistles. People just did not believe Poppa's explanation: 'It was the cockatoo!'

After a few confrontations with irate mothers or fathers of girls whistled at, Poppa stopped sitting in the sun, or else made sure Cocko was locked in his cage.

Because he roamed free and was always friendly, Cocko was stolen many times. But we always got him back. He set up an unholy, endless squawking screech, and would not stop night or day. Mum would advertise on the radio or in the local newspaper, offering a reward for information, and a sleepless neighbour usually dobbed in the culprit.

The rescues followed a similar pattern. Mum arrived at the address, often with me in tow, sometimes with a brother or two. At the front door, the person would immediately say they thought the bird was wild, and had no idea it belonged to anyone.

Then Mum would ask, 'How could you think the bird is wild, when it talks like a threshing machine?'

'Oh, this bird doesn't talk, so it can't be yours.'

I would then call out, 'Is that you, Cocko?'

And he would start calling, 'Sara, is that you, Sara, is that you, Sara,' on and on non-stop.

Mum then insisted we see the bird. On one occasion he was in a canary cage, and could hardly turn around; had to stand on the floor of the cage to have enough headroom. When he saw us, he went crazy. The door was so small my brother had to bend the bars so we could get him out. He latched onto my arm so tightly his claw marks drew blood. Mum was the only one he would release his grip for.

The man actually had the hide to ask for money for the damage to his canary cage. When he was told by my brother that he was lucky he wasn't wearing it on his head, he didn't press the issue.

Sometimes the person would insist it was their bird. But again, Mum just said, 'Well, let him out of his cage and let's see what he does.' Every time, Cocko headed for Mum, ran up her arm, sat on her shoulder and kissed her cheek.

Mum always ended the little charade by asking the person to take Cocko. If they were still fool enough to approach, Cocko would raise his comb, spread his wings, open his beak and make a hissing sound by sucking in air. He gave very clear and menacing signals that he would latch onto anything he could sink his beak into. After such performances we were free to take Cocko home. He soon realised he couldn't go into any garden, and after being locked in canary cages, aviaries and toolsheds, he learned to stay high in the trees where he knew he was safe; but mostly he stayed in the trees in our garden, or only flew around the close neighbourhood where everyone knew him. Or he spent the day finding parts of the house he could chew.

He always sought out Mum. This was done by going to the window of different rooms, and knocking on the glass, calling her; if the window was open, he would just walk in looking for her. He usually started with the kitchen; and there was one place other than the kitchen where he knew he could often find her: on the phone.

Mum was president of the district Red Cross branch, and she spent a good deal of the day on the phone, arranging charity functions to raise money, or just organising and running the branch. So Cocko's favourite pastime was to sit on the window near the phone and mimic Mum.

He would loudly jabber non-stop, then pause and say some words like, 'Oh really?', in a very clear, animated voice, then back to the incoherent jabber, only to pause again and say, 'Oh I agree,' or 'She didn't!', or 'We'll see about that!'

Finally he would break into his song-and-dance routine. Mum had taught him to dance right from a young bird, and he was quite good. With wings spread, and raised crest, he tapped one foot while swaying his head back and forth, chanting a very flat, unmelodious 'Da-Da-Da-Da' up and down the scale, completely out of tune. It was very distracting, and made it impossible for Mum to carry on a normal conversation, and it wouldn't be long before she threatened Cocko with terrible things, hand over the mouthpiece so the person on the other end of the phone wouldn't be shocked. But it usually had to be physical action, and she'd eventually have to chase him with the broom. Cocko didn't like the broom; when it appeared he headed for the trees.

It was at these times, just before the broom-swinging, that I would ask Mum's permission to do something she usually wouldn't allow. Almost always the reply would be, 'Yes, but take Cocko with you and go away. I'm busy talking on the phone.' I would wander off down the garden with Cocko sitting on my shoulder, still jabbering.

He ruled the roost with the dogs and cat. They were not allowed in the house, and at mealtimes all stood at the door on the verandah waiting for their dinner. Sometimes the anticipation was too much, and one or all would quietly edge closer into the breakfast room, heading close to the kitchen. There they would sit and patiently watch Mum preparing their meal.

Cocko sat on his perch, not moving a muscle until the dogs had passed him, then he swung into action. He was off the perch in a flash and in his peculiar pigeon-toed gait, he would advance across the floor, wings out, comb up, saying, 'Get out! Naughty dogs! Out!' He'd run his beak along the lino, and when he managed to come in contact with a paw, he would give it a sharp nip.

Just the sight of him approaching sent the dogs and cat into a frenzy. There would be leaping and bounding, dancing on the spot, and some very nifty footwork to avoid the dreaded beak. But he was fast, and eventually a paw would land in range; the beak would pounce, and dogs and cat would head for the door in a tangled, yelping, yowling heap, finally realigning themselves at the door. Cocko would strut up and down the room in command until Mum carried the bowls outside.

He tried the same game outside. But it was a different story there; that was their domain and many a time Cocko came through the door in a whoosh, half flying, half running, barely ahead of snapping teeth or flashing claws. It was a great game, and Cocko couldn't wait for it to start every day.

He also nipped any bare feet that happened to be walking around, and he had great fun with the boys. But the boys always got him back. They were often in trouble with Mum when they were young because of the pranks they played on Cocko.

One year on Guy Fawkes Day, they gave Cocko a string of bungers, and while he curiously held the crackers in his scrawny claw and investigated with his beak, the boys lit them. Poor Cocko got such a fright he couldn't let go, and stood there on one leg with the string of firecrackers going off in his beak and claw, jumping and squawking every time one went 'bang'. Everyone was in stitches, even Mum, he looked so funny dancing up and down. He wasn't hurt, but he was a very nervous bird for weeks after; he would just start jumping and squawking at any time of the day, sending everyone in fits of laughter again.

The boys were punished and told never, ever again. So firecrackers were off-limits. The next time they got Cocko for toe-nipping was at Christmas. While Mum was busy preparing the turkey, they filled Cocko's drinking glass with whisky. He liked the taste and in no time at all was rolling drunk. He was the night's entertainment. Every time he lifted a foot to walk he fell over. He jabbered constantly, breaking into his song-and-dance routine, then he'd overbalance and roll right over on his back, then stagger to his feet again, only to repeat the whole routine. Mum put him on his perch and he fell off, rolling around on the floor, singing an even more unmelodious and off-key scale than usual, and squawking. You couldn't shut him up. He went on for hours, and eventually perch and Cocko had to be moved out onto the porch so we could eat dinner in peace. He finally collapsed and fell asleep on the ground, leaning up against his perch.

When Mum found out what the boys had done, they were in trouble again, big trouble this time. The vet told Mum, after examining a groaning, moaning cockatoo with a hangover, that he could have had a heart attack and died. All his antics that entertained us could have been a fit. The boys were punished suitably, and alcohol joined firecrackers on the forbidden list.

Cocko was a great fundraiser. I spent my early childhood with Mum collecting money from door to door for the Red Cross. Mum would go down one side of the street, and Cocko and I, the other. We always got the most money.

Cocko would say, 'Hello', and things like, 'How about a bit of a scratch?', and raise his wing; or, 'How about a drink?', which always got a good laugh. All in all, a professional performance; he would captivate the people and they, in turn, would donate generously to the Red Cross.

When Cocko was around two years old, our Irish Setter had puppies, and although Mum called in the vet when things were not going along as normal, we lost her, and all the puppies except two. The vet said it was near impossible to raise Irish Setter puppies from birth without their mother, but we were willing to try, and all the children pitched in under Mum's guidance. With Mum in charge of the formula, we all took turns at the night feedings which, in the first month, were hourly.

There were a lot of bleary-eyed children walking around for weeks, but the puppies lived, includng Lucky, who was the first puppy born under the house, and was there alone for two days before we found her and put her with the rest of the litter.

We had the puppies in a box lined with warmed housebricks under covers, and hot water bottles wrapped in woollen material, so the puppies could snuggle up to something warm during the night, along with a ticking alarm clock to keep them company. One night they set off the alarm on the clock and scared the daylights out of themselves, and the whole household, in the early hours of the morning. It took hours to stop them yowling and to settle them down to sleep again.

Cocko was very interested in the puppies, and a few times we found him in the box with them, gently stroking them with his beak. It was such a sight. At the time the pups were born, the tabby cat next door had kittens, yet again, and the kittens, yet again, were taken away—to homes elsewhere, all the children were told.

The tabby cat's name was Timmy: our neighbours thought their kitten was a boy, until she grew up and presented them with a litter of kittens. Despite being female Timmy's name was never changed.

When Timmy lost each litter of kittens, she would spend days wandering around meowing and looking for them. Mum suggested putting Timmy with the puppies. She took one look at the box of puppies and fled. But the next morning we found her squeezed in the box with the two pups, with them happily sucking away at breakfast, and Timmy eyeing off

Cocko, who considered he was the puppies' guardian and was perched on the side of the box, wings out, comb up, beak open, hissing. Timmy had her ears flattened, eyes large black holes, teeth bared, and was growling just loud enough for Cocko to hear, and keep his distance, but not loud enough to scare the pups.

This Mexican standoff mellowed into a friendship as the days passed, and cat and bird came to accept each other. Cocko would climb onto the side of the box each morning with a hearty 'Hullo', and Timmy slowly came to accept him. After a month or so we actually found him in the box— puppies, cat and bird, all as happy as Larry, together.

The *Telegraph* heard about a tabby cat raising two pedigree Irish Setter puppies with the help of a cockatoo, and sent a photographer out, and next morning there they all were on the front page of the newspaper.

Within a few months, the pups were bigger than Timmy, and because they were only drinking from her back teats, she had such a bust it was difficult for her to walk. The pendulum effect of her large bosoms would knock her off her feet. She appeared punch-drunk when she tried to walk anywhere, and she couldn't run fast enough to get away from the pups.

The pups were so big by now that one would sit on Timmy so she couldn't move, while the other pup had a drink. You could hear Timmy's yowls, as the naughty pups waylaid her somewhere. Eventually Mum made her a bra to keep her bosoms from dragging on the ground, and to stop the pups from drinking. This tiny little tabby cat with a thirty-six-inch bustline strutted around wearing a green bra, or sometimes a floral one. But the situation became serious when her nipples got sore and were starting to split, it was even painful for Timmy when Mum rubbed on the healing ointment. So the floral and coloured bras saved the day, and became a permanent fixture until the pups were weaned. Timmy's bosom slowly reduced in size until she could walk in a normal fashion. The pups were soon lapping milk from a saucer.

They grew into enormous dogs, and the amazed look on Timmy's face as her offspring towered over her never faded. She cleaned them daily, but by the time they were six months old Timmy would work all day and she would still be only halfway down the side of one pup. When they were fully grown, their grooming consisted of licking their eyes and around their mouths; even that took most of her day.

By this stage, Timmy was well and truly our cat. Each night you would find her curled up between the paws of one of her babies, purring proudly, with the dog's head resting on her back. Even after years, you could look into the garden and see her cleaning Lucky's face, with the other dog patiently waiting for its turn to be groomed.

I often wondered what Timmy thought of her two 'babies'. They would romp down the lawn to greet her, and you could see her cringe, expecting to be crushed, but even though they were awkward and gangly they never hurt Timmy. They loved her dearly, and she was clearly amazed at what she had produced, but also extremely proud. You could often see Timmy, Cocko and the two dogs sitting on the lawn, having a quiet moment together.

One of the dogs eventually went to my uncle's farm outside Canberra. The dogs had rapidly grown very big indeed, and needed lots of room for exercise, so Mum thought it best only to keep one. Of course all the kids were heartbroken, but Mum was right. So we kept Lucky, the first puppy born under the house.

Of course, Cocko was a long-time resident, twenty-four years in all, and he continued his outrageous behaviour, always destroying or demolishing something or up to some kind of mischief. One of his favourite pastimes was scaring Mum's visitors.

Guests would be taken into the lounge room. This room was off-limits to children, Cocko, dogs and cat, so, of course, we all spent our time trying to get in there. Cocko almost always succeeded, I came second; the dogs and the cat never had a chance.

The lounge chairs were enormous. I could sit in a chair with my legs straight out in front of me, and my feet just reached the edge of the seat. If I put my knees at the edge and leaned back, I disappeared—all that remained in sight were my knees, shins and feet. My eyes, when I sat up, were level with the armrests. Even when grown-ups sat in the chairs, it was quite difficult to get out of them. They were covered in heavy damask, embossed with a raised velvet pattern. At the end of the enormous armrests were fairly large, flat, wooden squares with ornate wood supporting them, and continuing down to the floor. The chairs were the closest thing you could get to a throne (outside a throne room).

Guests would sink into them and be held captive, with Cocko lying in wait. While Mum served tea and biscuits, Cocko hid behind a chair ready for his big chance. Finally the signal came: the phone ringing. Mum would excuse herself and leave the room, and Cocko would swing into action.

As the unsuspecting guest sat with a cup of tea and biscuits, Cocko would climb up the outside of the chair and suddenly appear over the edge of the arm, scaring her half to death. But he would be friendly and open the conversation with, 'Hullo, how are you?'

Most guests recovered quickly, having heard about Mum's cockatoo, and realising he was friendly they would start chatting with him. Cocko would then waddle along the arm, quickly take a biscuit from the plate with his beak, transfer it to one scrawny claw and start nibbling it, while asking the shocked guest, 'How about a bit of a biscuit?' and, 'How about a drink?', as he slipped his beak into the cup of tea and took a drink. If Mum returned at this point, he would let out an 'Oh goodness!', drop the biscuit and head for the nearest escape route as Mum threw at him anything she could lay her hands on.

If the phone call was longer, Cocko would finish his snack, climb down from the chair and disappear out the door, leaving Mum to return to a very stunned guest. One look at the biscuit crumbs all over the chair, and the guest's expression, would soon tell Mum what had happened. After calming her guest, she would guard as another cup of tea and another biscuit were peacefully consumed. Mum would bid her still slightly dazed guest goodbye, and set off in hot pursuit of Cocko, who by then would be perched on the top of the highest tree, knowing full well he was in for it.

Mum would try to coax him down, and he would respond with an endless string of replies like, 'How about a bit of a good boy?'

'You'll be in bits when I get hold of you!' she would say.

He would sense Mum's anger and talk faster, non-stop, 'How about a beautiful boy then, how about a r-e-e-e-a-a-a-ally beautiful boy, how about a drink, how about a driscuit (a drink and a biscuit), how about a scratch?' A loud, 'Oh!' would stop the flow, as a missile whizzed close by. Then, even faster, 'How about a boy, a biscuit, a drink, a driscuit! A bit of a-a-a g-g-g-o-o-o-o-d b-o-o-o-o-y!' would all come tumbling out as he ducked brooms, buckets and mops.

Cocko got away with that little game many, many times.

Sometimes, though, he found himself in situations that he definitely didn't like. One I remember vividly was 'The Great Car Trip' up north, along the old coast road, for our yearly holiday.

Mum's driving never improved over the years. Nearly everyone who knew her wondered why she ever bothered to drive, it was such a trial for her just to get into a car. She was a nervous wreck the whole trip, and often would have to go to bed to recover from the ordeal. But regardless of the horrors ahead, it was Mum who had to drive because Poppa only ever drove a car once.

When they were newly married, Dad went out and bought their first car, and started his driving lessons. They came back after the first hour, and the driving instructor told Mum if she wanted to keep her husband, and the car, then she should learn to drive quickly. Poppa, it seemed, had no depth perception, or any other driving perception, and would just drive into the back of anything in front of him. He didn't improve with age, because he was not much better at steering a boat, as Charlie found out when he was trying to teach Dad, in the Philippines, in the 1960s.

Charlie showed Poppa how to keep the wind in the sails, and left him at the wheel. The wind changed, but Dad stuck to the course, never moved the wheel; he jibbed the boat, the main boom swung to the other side of the boat and knocked Mum overboard. Dad obviously never developed a steering ability; well, it appeared he never had it to develop, even in the early days.

So Mum reluctantly became the driver of the family, and although she was the slowest and most nervous driver in creation, at least she never ran into the back of anything. My brothers said it was because she never went fast enough to get near anyone to run into them.

I was around age eleven when we started up the north coast

on our holidays. Dad packed the little Ford Anglia. Mum and Dad were in the front, and I shared the back seat with some of the luggage. The boot was open with a suitcase lying flat, and strapped to the top of the suitcase sat Cocko's cage.

It was a three-hour drive. That meant Mum would take about five and a half hours or more, depending on how many parked cars we encountered along the way. We left at daybreak. Cocko set up a squawking wail the moment the little car turned out of the driveway. They say birds are psychic; if he knew what was ahead of us on our holiday, I can understand why he was carrying on.

Progress was slow in the suburbs, but we sped up to fifteen miles per hour once we were out in the rural area, and the drive was uneventful—that is, if you could eliminate Cocko's continuous screeching. The trip went along pleasantly enough until we came to the mountain. The road began to weave up a long, steep incline, and ahead we could see cars and lorries struggling up the zigzag slope.

We were approaching the beginning of the climb, and all the other cars and traffic were actually going as slowly as Mum! Mum took one look at the heavily loaded lorry in front of our little Ford Anglia, and refused to drive up the mountain behind it. No amount of persuasion from Dad could convince Mum its brakes wouldn't fail; she had visions of it rolling back onto the little car and squashing us all. So we pulled off on the side of the road, waiting for a lull in traffic, which Dad rightly explained would never come as we were on the main interstate highway. I could see this was true, because for the half hour he spent talking to Mum, the traffic had gone past at a regular flow.

Dad finally convinced her to pull in behind a few cars; if they rolled back on us, he reasoned, the damage would only be to the car, not to us. She agreed to go. I had to look back down the road and shout a report, indicating what was coming. When Dad heard three cars in a row, followed by a slow truck, he shouted to Mum to go in after the third car. 'Go! Go!'

Mum hung halfway out of the window, giving her extended arm signal with ramrod index finger to the truck driver, then kangarooed back onto the highway in front of the truck.

Dad said it was good to be in front of the truck because it had a big load, and would travel slowly once we hit the steep grade. Mum gripped the wheel in a deathlock, and giving the appearance of someone driving at one hundred miles per hour, she faced the road ahead. One eye was on the road, and the other on the ever-increasing cliff that was appearing on the other side of the road. The higher we climbed, the slower the little car climbed. The closer the truck came, the louder Cocko screeched. Along with Mother's fear of the mountain she was climbing, the other reason we were slowing to an almost engine-failing halt was that Mum wouldn't change gear. Dad kept telling her to change down, but Mum was terrified of rolling back, or rolling over the cliff, even though it was on the other side of the road.

The truck's bumper was inches from Cocko's cage; he was screeching, the truck's horn was honking, the clear road stretched out in front of us as far as you could see, and the traffic down the mountain behind us was at a standstill. The little car was barely crawling, starting to show stalling symptoms, when Mum told us to get out and push!

By this stage she was crying, and Dad knew there was no way he could convince her to change to a lower gear. The little car made the next decision by giving a few feeble coughs and stalling. Dad and I jumped out under the glaring eyes of the truckie. We held the car from rolling back, while Mum got it going again.

She put the car into first gear, took off and didn't look back; Mum had her eyes firmly glued to the top of the mountain, and that's where she was heading. We watched as the little car disappeared around the next bend, the last sight being Cocko, comb up, flapping his wings and still screeching. It was at least another mile to the top of the mountain. The traffic was stacked up behind the truck for as far as you could see down the mountain.

The truck driver shook his head in disbelief as Mum disappeared around the corner, and without saying a word he opened the passenger side door. Dad thanked the driver at the top of the pass, and we walked over to the little car sitting in a parking space outside a lookout restaurant that served Devonshire teas. We found Mum hunched over the wheel, crying her eyes out.

It took many pots of tea, and a Bex, before Mum had the courage to get in the car and drive on down the mountain. We reached the bottom in one piece, although the brakes were very much the worse for wear. Mum had her foot clamped on the brake pedal, and we crawled at a rubber-burning snail's pace down the mountainside with traffic banked up behind us for as far as the eye could see. It was fortunate that there was not another mountain between us and our destination, because there was no way Mum would go off the 'flat and straight'.

The holiday was a back-to-nature thing; Dad had hired a caravan on a camping site, right on the beachfront. Thank heavens the caravan was already set up there; the mind just cannot comprehend Mum towing a caravan with screeching Cocko on the back. The place was so back-to-nature, we didn't even have electricity.

Tragedy struck the first night. Mum asked Dad to light the Tilley (a pressure hurricane lamp). Pressure lamps are designed to withstand high winds. I suppose the designers never dreamed people like my Dad existed; the lamp couldn't withstand Poppa. Mum thought it was a simple operation, to light the lamp, so when it started to get dark, she gave it to Dad with all the bits and pieces for him to start it. No-one, not even Dad, knows what he did, but one moment he was sitting at the table, glasses on, reading the instructions with an innocent-looking unlit lamp in front of him. He turned a few knobs, poured some metho into a small ridge at the base of the glass, did a bit of frantic pumping on a handle, put a match to it—and ended up with a bonfire. The ceiling of the caravan was quickly turning black, and so Poppa grabbed the lamp and rushed out into the open.

We were just about to get into the car to take Dad to the hospital for treatment for his burns, when more smoke started billowing out of the caravan. Mum had forgotten she was cooking dinner, and it was now on fire.

We came back from the hospital with Dad's hands wrapped. The doctor said the burns were not serious, and in a few days his hands would be okay for the bandages to come off.

It was late; the inside of the caravan was black and smelt terrible. The meat for dinner was ruined, so we had tea and sandwiches by candlelight.

Mum, now paranoid about fire, would not let the candle be moved from the table. Much time was spent groping in the dark. My bed was at the far end of the caravan, behind a sliding door, so I couldn't see a thing. We did get torches the next day, and the evenings passed playing cards, eating, writing and everything else by torchlight. Poppa wasn't allowed a second go at the pressure lamp. We finally adapted to living by torchlight, but we were all pleased to pack and head for home, especially Cocko. He had not been allowed out of the cage. Mum thought he might fly off and never be seen again, and Dad, quite rightly, was worried about the destruction of the area if Mum unleashed Cocko.

Driving home was similar to the drive there, a little better but not much. Mum stopped at the bottom of the mountain, and again we waited for the right spot to charge into the traffic. She leaned so far out of the car for the hand signal that the approaching driver thought she was climbing out of the window onto the road, and quickly put on his brakes, giving Mum loads of time to kangaroo into the traffic lane. She stayed in low and crawled up the hill, oblivious to the horns honking behind her and to Cocko screeching.

We had the compulsory cups of tea, and Mum had a Bex, at the top of the mountain, then we went down the other side in low, riding the brakes all the way. The rest of the journey home was child's play, except that Cocko didn't stop screeching until we turned into our driveway.

That was my last long holiday away with Mum and Dad. I became so committed to my tennis career and there were never three weeks I could be away because of tournaments. So when Mum and Dad ventured off on their yearly jaunt, I stayed at home with my sister, Sue, and had a wonderful time. The only drawback was we had to look after Cocko! At least he didn't screech twenty-four hours a day, but he sulked a lot because he missed Mum.

I was in Manila, in the Philippines, in 1964, when Mum wrote to say Cocko had laid an egg. What a crazy mixed-up bird! Didn't know he was a she until he—she—was twenty-three years old!

I think growing up with Cocko, Timmy and Lucky gave a very solid foundation to my love of animals. It also taught me valuable lessons, other than care of animals. It was wonderful to watch three animals, traditional enemies, living in such harmony. A dog, a cat and a bird cared for and looked after each other lovingly. Yet society said they were not supposed to like each other.

With the love of all animals firmly established in my early years, my Mum and Dad completed my training by giving me a few golden rules to live by, then set me free to sail the sea of life, out in the big world. Learning fast, but still terribly naïve, I sailed right into the arms of Charlie, one of the world's greatest characters. A different 'cut of the jib' altogether from the people and characters I had shared my first twenty-four years with. It took me quite a while to work him out... while I struggled with that task, he exposed me to a new world full of all types of people.

3

MANILA, DASHER AND BLAZE

 After living in Hong Kong for a few months, from June to September 1960, Charlie and I sailed for Manila, where we lived for the next four and a half years. After living first on the boat in the harbour, then in a friend's apartment, we finally rented a top-floor, four-bedroom apartment, in the suburb of Paco. (Our apartment was actually the upstairs floor of a big house; the owners lived downstairs.) Paco had once been an attractive area of big homes with big gardens, just on the outskirts of downtown Manila. But the city had overgrown the quiet tree-lined streets and rolling lawns. The houses gradually lost their rambling gardens as more and more houses were built, until the big old houses sat with no land around them at all, just small patches of lawn, a driveway; ugly high walls surrounded them, topped with broken glass, or embedded barbed wire, or both. Because along with more houses and people, came crime.

The streets of Paco were a curious sight, if you took the time to stroll and observe. There would be an imposing two-storey stucco mansion with elaborate wrought iron lace trimmed windows and glass doors standing regally beside a small wooden house, jammed against the fence on the other side of the drive. You never knew what the next step would bring.

In fact it was on our street in Paco that I came face to face with my first Brahman bull—never realising that in the years to follow I would be breeding these beautiful regal creatures. And it was indeed a very regal creature I walked straight into that day as I came around the corner.

The Indian Ambassador lived across the street from us in another large Spanish mansion of bygone years, now squeezed in amongst all the smaller houses. It was so squeezed, in fact, that when the maid cleaned the ground-floor apartment where the Ambassador's pet Brahman bull resided, she tied the bull to the telegraph post, outside the gate on the street.

So you can imagine my shock when I came face to face with two thousand pounds of massive bull in the heart of downtown Manila. The maid, a tiny girl, assured me he was as quiet as a lamb, and proceeded to brush his already shiny, satin black coat. He was the quietest, fattest, most docile bull I had ever seen. You could hug him and sit on him, and crawl all over him, as the Ambassador's children did most of the day. He lived downstairs with the maids, and the Ambassador and family lived upstairs, and on the day when his apartment was cleaned, he stood out on the footpath and was patted by all the local people, who knew he was harmless. New people in the area took one look and disappeared at high speed back around the corner, especially if he decided to let out a deep long-drawn-out bellow.

He was not the only animal of distinction in the district. Friends at the end of our street had a Bassett hound. He was unbelievably spoilt, and extremely overweight, so much so that the middle of his long torso bowed under the great bulk, and touched the ground. This was distressful for the dog, because his small garden was a cement courtyard, and when the maids took him for a walk, the footpath was cement too. His poor tummy and other unmentionable parts rubbed on the cement and the skin was rubbed raw, causing infection, not to mention how uncomfortable it must have been. So the dog wouldn't exercise, and became even fatter, which accentuated the problem. Finally a small platform on four tiny castors was made and fitted under the long expanse of torso; two straps went up and around the wide expanse of tummy and two buckles secured the contraption snugly to his midriff.

He lived upstairs with the family, and a wide staircase separated him from the busy world below. He did not need to wear the platform in the house, because the floors were polished parquet with lots of scatter rugs, and he could move around in comfort. But he couldn't walk down the stairs, they were too steep; so when he wanted to go down into the courtyard he would stand at the top of the stairs and bark, and two maids would carry him down in a basket. But the funniest sight was when he went for his daily constitution, on his leash, with platform strapped to the sagging parts, accompanied by children or maids.

When he wanted to mark his territory, he would stand by the light pole waiting; the maid would unstrap the platform, he would complete his task, then wait for his platform to be buckled back in position before he headed for his next pole. There were some very funny situations when he met another dog in his territory, and wanted to fight. He was very nifty at skating around on his platform, and would thoroughly confuse the other dog. But, of course, at times he was a bit too cocky, and would challenge a large dog who was too much for him, even with his trusty platform. On these occasions you would see maids or children struggling down the street carrying the dog on his platform with some dog snapping at him, as he carried on the fight from an elevated position. They were very patient people, because they took him walking every day!

I settled comfortably into this animal-loving environment

and I no sooner had the house furnished and the last vase of flowers in place, than I wanted a dog. The next December I found a beautiful German Shepherd puppy under the Christmas tree. I named him after one of the reindeer, and called him Dasher. He soon grew into a very large dog, and because of the lack of garden space, I joined the 'walking brigade' every afternoon up and down the street. We would end up in a little walled park at the end of the block, and Dasher loved to play ball with anyone willing.

Marlee was toddling around at this stage, and had great fun with Dasher and Rita, her amah. I was very pregnant with Bonnie, so we all took a regular daily constitutional in the park. Midway through my pregnancy, Mum and Dad arrived from Australia aboard a P&O liner. Dad enthusiastically took over the daily parade to the park and started Dasher's obedience training. I am not too sure who was in control, or who was training whom, but by the way the dog and everyone bounded in the door each day, they all enjoyed the dog-training sessions. The few times Mum and I went along, it was certainly entertaining. Dog, child, maids and Dad all had a wonderful time, and it was never decided if Dad was training the dog, or Dasher was training Dad. Still, Dad must have been doing something right, because they came back one afternoon with a prize. Dasher had won a silver cup in a dog show. Mum said when they arrived in the park, a dog show was about to start, so Dad entered Dasher. Mum was convinced they gave Dad the cup for prancing, not Dasher. Dasher only wanted to play ball, and was not the least bit interested in prancing around in circles on his leash with a lot of other dogs.

So Dad put the ball in his pocket, and Dasher followed the ball, watching Dad's every move, waiting for him to take the ball out of his pocket and throw it. What impressed the judges was this young dog's attentiveness to his owner, eagerly awaiting his next command. I wonder if they would have awarded the prize if they knew Dasher was just watching and waiting for Dad to throw the ball. Mum said it was really Dad who got the prize because his prancing was far superior to Dasher's. After this achievement Dad had to rest for the next few days, so Dasher had to be content going to the park with the maids and Marlee. It was only a few days, though, before Dad was back to normal, and he and Dasher bounded off again with the ball each afternoon. Dasher was certainly well named, at least after Dad came into his life.

Mum and Dad stayed for six months on that visit, and it was very much enjoyed by everyone. Dad was keen to participate in everything—well, not *quite* everything: he did steer clear of sailing after Charlie gave him his first lesson.

Dad loved going to the office with Charlie. I am not sure Charlie was too pleased, though he thought the world of my Dad and wouldn't dream of doing anything to upset him. So when Dad showed interest in the business side of the shipping company, Charlie included him wherever possible.

Dad's days then were divided between going to the office with Charlie in the mornings, and dashing around the park with Dasher in the afternoons. His afternoons were full of physical activity, and he soon had his mornings following similar lines. He organised the office staff to do exercises, to get them 'stimulated' (was Dad's favourite expression). As disruptive as this was, Charlie allowed Dad to continue his exercise breaks.

In the 1960s, the office girls, like any women in Manila, were not too keen on physical training. They all wore complicated attire, lots of make-up, beehive hairdos, stiletto heels, and flashed long, bright red talons; none of which was conducive to Dad's energetic work-out routine. But they all thought the world of Dad, and went through the motions in a superficial way that did not crack the perfectly groomed façade that the era demanded of them. Dad finally had to accept that his physical training class was not living up to his expectations. These stiletto-heeled, tight-skirted, beehive-haired females, who collapsed into a near faint if they even chipped their nail enamel, finally wore Dad down, and his visits to the office were not as regular. Soon, however, he had another distraction.

Even though Marlee was only approaching two years old, Charlie gave her her first pony, a tiny little native pony not much taller than a Great Dane in height. He was spoilt, well fed, and so fat that when she sat astride him she was actually doing the splits. He was called Blaze (Porky would have been more appropriate); but a better child's pony one could never wish for. I think Marlee's love of horses developed from that first association with Blaze; they developed a great bond. And so my Dad redirected his morning energies from the grateful office staff to leading Blaze and Marlee around the polo club. They were a sight: Marlee in full riding attire and black velvet riding hat, perched regally, if precariously, on top of Blaze, and Poppa striding alongside.

By the time Mum and Dad caught the southbound P&O liner out of England for Australia, Marlee could walk Blaze without someone leading him. But on my insistence a groom took over Dad's duties and walked with Marlee. They would not be out of hearing range before I would hear Marlee telling the groom not to hold the bridle, in a very polite but authoritative manner. They would disappear down the riding track, groom and three-year-old, arguing this point. By the time she was three and a half, she was a very good rider, and looked forward to riding each afternoon with her Mum and Dad and occasionally her baby sister sitting up with Dad.

We were setting out one afternoon, Marlee in full regalia, astride Blaze, proudly riding alone with no groom in sight. It was polo practise day, so I had a tight rein on my horse (a recently retired polo pony, who didn't look kindly on being retired and tried to join any polo match, regardless of what I wanted). But I relaxed my grip when I saw the horses walking back to the stables: practise was over.

There was a break in the stream of horses, then a bit further along the path we approached the top polo player for the Philippines, who was slowly riding back to the stables. We had seen him and his beautiful Andalusian stallion many times on the riding path. He was a gruff man, very stern and serious, a Spanish aristocrat, quite unapproachable.

This afternoon, he was in the process of giving one of his personal grooms one hell of a dressing-down. The Spanish aristocrat, on a perfectly formed, perfectly groomed black stallion, with a long flowing wavy mane, and swishing an equally elegant tail, came abreast of a very beautiful three-and-a-half-year-old American girl, perfectly attired, astride a ridiculously overweight but very healthy, well-groomed native pony. The man was still in full verbal attack when Marlee looked up from her mount, her face about level with the man's stirrup, and said in a very clear, haughty child's voice, a strange combination of Australian, English and American accents, 'That is a beautiful cwee-chur.'

She stared up at the Spaniard with such an air of supreme confidence that it stopped him mid-word. He stared down at this tiny, long-haired, blue-eyed beauty on a ridiculous pony, and gave her a rare smile.

'Thank you, and you, too, have a beautiful creature,' he replied.

She gave her reins a slight jiggle to move Blaze into a slow walk, touched her riding cap to bid him good day, and rode on, leaving the self-assured reply of 'I know!' hanging in the afternoon air.

Charlie was quick to take up the opportunity his daughter had created, and introduced himself, but the face of the

Spanish aristocrat had lost the smile bestowed upon the child, and resumed its severe mask. After telling Charlie, in very few words, that he had an unusually gifted child, the conversation was terminated as he rode away, leaving Charlie still conversing.

Whenever we met after that, he would always exchange a few pertinent words with Marlee, and she would respond in the same manner. Be it about horses or weather, she would seriously agree with his statement, add a few sage words of her own, then touch her riding hat with her crop and ride on regally. A performance of such calibre any grown actor would dearly love to emulate.

It obviously impressed the aristocrat, because he always made a point of greeting her. I think he was fascinated that a child so young had such panache. Adults clambered for his approval, business connections, judgment, advice, or just a smile, and he went to extreme lengths to avoid them. I think the man was amazed that a three-year-old held the formula to penetrate his severe façade, when hordes of businessmen and social climbers failed miserably, including her father. This relationship continued with the exchange of a smile, and brief, astute observations, each time they passed: Charlie and I, following, only ever received a curt nod.

When Marlee was four, Charlie hired a riding instructor to teach her the finer points of equestrianism. He was a retired British Colonel, who never seemed to stop shouting orders. He didn't faze our four-year-old, didn't even make a dent in her composure. Marlee followed the instructions, and ignored most of the other shouting.

When Bonnie was born, Rita, Marlee's amah, took over the newborn baby, and Bobby, one of the housegirls, became Marlee's amah. This was a smooth transition, because Marlee loved Bobby as much as she did Rita, and so she didn't feel left out of the new baby celebration; rather it was an expansion of her group, she now had Bobby and Rita full-time, plus a new baby. The baby fascinated her no end, and she took part in the daily routine: with me when it was feeding time and playtime; with the amahs at bathtime, and any time they had her while I was busy with work for Charlie.

Marlee would lie on the bed watching me breastfeeding Bonnie, and would have her usual sage, worldly-wise conversations. I told her the baby was drinking milk, which contained the same food as she ate, but because she was so small she had to have it in the form of milk. I would get questions like, 'What is she having now? Is she up to her vegies? Is she having peas yet?' and, 'When does she have apple and custard? Can I taste it? When does she get to ice-cream? What flavour is it?' She sat in on most of the feeding times, and she referred to my breasts as 'feeding sisters'.

One day, the maid sent Marlee to my bedroom to tell me someone from the office had brought papers for me to sign. I had just taken a shower, and was dressed in a bathrobe ready for a nap. I didn't want to dress again, so I asked Marlee was it the regular girl who brought the messages. She replied, 'No, Mummy. She's new and she's got the biggest "feeding sisters" I have ever seen.' I slipped on a dress, went into the library to sign the papers, and met the new office girl ... and Marlee was right.

Another time, at an Embassy afternoon tea party, she struck up a conversation with a very terse, older British woman, and shocked her to the core during their conversation about her new baby sister. When asked did she help her mother care for the baby, and what did she feed her baby sister, Marlee replied, 'Oh no, I don't have to do that; the meat, potatoes, peas, carrots, apples and custard and icecream she eats, Mummy has all stuffed up her jumper; my sister gets it all out of Mummy's "feeding sisters"!' She paused for a few seconds and added, 'They're stuffed up her jumper, too.'

The English lady quietly placed her teacup on the side table and mingled with the crowd.

When Bobby moved into the nursery to help Rita, we needed a new housemaid; Bobby said she had a sister in the province, who could come to the city to work if I wanted her. Bobby was such a gem, and thinking her sister would be more of the same, I immediately hired her. Bobby was a small and fine-boned, very tiny girl, so I was not prepared for the half gorilla, in size only, who walked in the door. I couldn't believe she was Bobby's sister: they were in fact half-sisters, different fathers. Maria had Bobby's lovely nature, but there the similarity ended. She was much taller, and about four times the width—definitely front row forward material; when she walked, even the floor vibrated. Hardworking, and a very sweet pleasant girl, she had one problem: no matter how many times a day she washed and changed her uniform, she could not get rid of a very overpowering body odour. After she cleaned a room it had to be aired for hours. I didn't know how to solve this; I certainly couldn't fire her, but couldn't think where she could work without leaving lingering evidence.

Her big test was helping serve drinks and dinner, her first meeting with Charlie. She had many showers, Bobby informed me, and to be on the safe side I doused her in perfume, so the body odour was temporarily held at bay. We just had to get through dinner without Maria dropping anything or colliding with the furniture. We didn't get as far as dinner.

Charlie arrived home, plonked himself down in his favourite chair, and shouted for some service. Bobby pushed Maria into the room. She was bright and clean and starched, and still smelling like a rose. She approached Charlie as if approaching the jaws of death, she stood next to his chair, and gave a slight bob.

He looked up at the towering girl with a shocked expression, then barked an order. She could follow slowly spoken English fairly well, but didn't understand Charlie's drawl. I quickly repeated his request for a cold beer, and she scurried away. He wanted to know when I started hiring the house help at the zoo. I told him to behave, saying that she was Bobby's sister. This he flatly refused to believe, even by a different father.

Maria reappeared balancing a bottle of ice-cold beer and a frosted glass on a tray. So far so good, I thought. Charlie reached up to take the bottle of beer and glass off the tray, then noticed the beer had not been opened. He looked at her, held up the bottle, and said, 'What am I supposed to do, open this with my teeth?!'

Maria saw the beer bottle, heard 'open' and 'teeth' and took the bottle from Charlie; then she put the beer cap to her back teeth, snapped it off, and handed the open bottle back to Charlie. There were very few times I ever saw Charlie completely speechless; this was one of them. He finally regained his composure, slammed the abused bottle down on the table, and stormed out of the room. His only comment later was, 'Get rid of her.'

I didn't, but I solved the problem by moving her down to the laundry, after Bobby told me Maria had always been a wash amah before. She had wanted to move up in the world, but both of them had to admit in discussions in the following days that working as a housemaid was impossible. She remained my wash amah for many years. A year or so after the beer-opening episode, Maria was upstairs collecting the washing out of some of the guest rooms, when Charlie just caught a glimpse of her disappearing down the back stairs. He came rushing into the bedroom, saying he had just seen that terrible girl who opened the beer bottles with her teeth. I told him he must have imagined it, and he promptly forgot the matter, quite confident I had followed his orders and sacked her on the spot. Maria worked for us until we left the Philippines in 1965. Charlie never knew she was downstairs in the laundry, though he remarked one day, not long after she moved down to the laundry, that I had finally found a good wash amah; and I replied, yes, I had.

When I first arrived in the Philippines, the wives at the American Embassy took me under their wing and told me all the 'dos' and 'don'ts' of living in a tropical environment away from civilisation.

Most of the Americans and other Europeans lived in the Forbes Park compound, with a wall around the entire suburb, and sentries at the entrance gates. It was quite different from how Hong Kong was run, and very foreign to me after Australia. I was told nothing could be taken for granted, and given endless procedures and safety rules. All water had to be boiled, and even then it was advisable to drink imported bottled water. All meat was brought in frozen, on the President Line boats, from the west coast of America, and supplied to Americans in the Philippines, Hong Kong and Japan. In fact, the Embassies had their people so brainwashed about disease that everyone waited for the ships to bring everything from America, including fresh food, which wasn't exactly fresh by the time it was finally in our hands. Charlie's secretary told me this was nonsense, that I would have to be careful about water and seafood, but the markets were full of beautiful fresh fruit and vegetables in abundance, and very cheap. Those from America were all of three weeks old by the time we saw them, and also extremely expensive.

So I ventured to the markets with Elvie, and a whole new world opened up to me. The fruit included a wonderful range of things I had never seen before; I had an amazing time buying and trying. But then I entered a nightmare world, when I stumbled upon the local meatworks. It forced its presence on me when my path was blocked by a stream of blood running across the dirt road while I was picking my way along behind Elvie. I looked up and saw my first dead steer in the flesh, so to speak. There were dirty-clothed men with knives mulling around the hanging beast, some cutting, some shouting orders, some just waving hands and knives in a dangerous manner.

The meatworks was an open tin shed with a dirt floor. The carcass was hanging there, in intense heat and humidity, while thousands of flies swarmed over it, and the men and their knives. Underneath the hanging beast was a pack of mangy, starved dogs waiting for the animal's guts to be dropped to the floor. Well, a few weren't waiting; they were jumping up and grabbing at the intestines as a man hacked away at the carcass. Knives whizzed close to dogs' jaws and necks with each slash.

I stood transfixed as the entrails finally came away, more as a result of countless snarling, fighting, tugging dogs than by the butcher's knife. A few quick kicks from the men sent a frenzied mass of dogs, entangled in endless lengths of entrails, snarling and growling out into the street. Leaving the muddy, dirty area clear for ... whatever came next. It was enough for me; skirting around the snarling pack, I hurried to catch up with Elvie, remembering the large print on one page of the Embassy instructions:

'DO NOT, UNDER ANY CIRCUMSTANCE, EAT LOCALLY KILLED FRESH BEEF.'

I hurried past pigs tied to posts, squealing because they could smell their fate, and chickens sitting in bamboo cages stacked on top of each other, so high they leaned at dangerous angles. The chickens were so hot they couldn't even raise a cackle in protest. I raced away from that living hell, and added pigs and chickens to my memory bank along with the Embassy's beef warning. Just on cruelty grounds alone, I would not buy their food, not to mention the health risk.

The Embassy instructions also said if I did purchase salad vegetables locally they had to be washed very carefully as the growers used human manure to fertilise their gardens! I dreamed longingly, every night, of Australia. My many advisers told me it was all right to use local lettuce as long as it was washed very thoroughly. The first time I handed a lettuce over to the cook, I explained in detail to her that a careful washing was essential to prevent us from getting sick. I was served a salad that night with the lettuce leaves limp and flat, in a glucky mound in the bottom of the bowl. Vilma, my cook, had followed my instructions enthusiastically; for washing she had used hot water and washing detergent to clean off all the germs.

So we survived without contracting any terrible tropical mystery bug. Charlie also made life more interesting by often finding a business reason to fly to Hong Kong for a weekend; we would pig-out on such things as Sydney rock oysters, flown in fresh by Qantas, followed by exotic dishes such as Peking duck and shark's fin soup. We would waddle onto the plane back to Manila, stuffed to the eyeballs with food that hadn't been treated with washing detergent.

As the years wore on, my panics over the Embassy's food

instructions faded, and we could eat lettuce in a salad that actually looked like lettuce. But this didn't stop the mistakes due to language problems. I showed Vilma how I liked cabbage steamed in butter and nutmeg, and the next time I asked for coleslaw, it was made with cooked cabbage. But her greatest *faux pas* was on her first day with me. I asked for a cup of tea. She had always worked for Americans, who drank percolated coffee. I had made the mistake of saying tea was similar to coffee, and so I got percolated tea!

She filled the percolator with tea-leaves and percolated them for about thirty minutes. With about twenty teaspoons of tea-leaves in a six-cup percolator, it was so strong even the smell was repulsive. I never did taste the percolated tea, but it could be a new craze waiting to be discovered.

One of the greatest and nicest characters in my life to date is a Filipino, but we first met in Hong Kong. The first morning after my wedding, Charlie left me on the boat while he went to the office. That wonderful, cheerful face appeared over the side of the boat every day and said, 'Hullo, Mummy!' For the three months we stayed in Hong Kong on a supposed honeymoon, Charlie at the office, me on the boat, Ernesto would appear each morning after Charlie had left and make sure I came to no harm until Charlie's return from the office at the end of the day.

Ernesto was very much a part of our life, trials and tribulations during our time in Manila. We lost contact with him when we left to come to Australia and the station in 1965. Then he came to Bullo to visit us in the mid-seventies. By then he had made his fortune, and Charlie had well and truly lost his. Ernesto was shocked that Charlie allowed the children and me to live in a tin shed, as he put it, 'only used for chickens'.

Charlie didn't bother to contact him after that remark, and indeed, did not speak to him again.

Ernesto contacted the station a few years after Charlie's death, wishing to speak to him, and was sad at the news of his death. Since he found out we were carrying on alone, he has been a constant friend, always there to help, never asking anything in return. The rarest of gems in a jewel box of friends. Like Uncle Dick, I could write a whole book about Ernesto, and our friendship over the years.

4

SMELL THE ROSES
AND DRUGS

I thought Manila was behind the times, barbaric in some ways, but little did I realise I was about to arrive in a place that was a thousand times more remote and barbaric. When Charlie deposited me in the far north-western Outback, I went into deep shock for a year. Even the Manila meatworks looked modern compared to the systems out there—though not cleaner. Everything was clean in the wilderness, except for the flies which equalled Manila downtown. But over the years I have come to discover that the Outback has more characters per square mile than anywhere else.

When we landed on a million acres of nothingness, it created more than one problem. Up to that point in our five years of marriage, Charlie would rise at four o'clock in the morning, plan his day, and that of everyone in his office. He would write reams of instructions for the entire office staff, and also instructions for me, the children, the maids, the chauffeur, even the gardener! Once he started, it was hard to stop him!

Every morning at six o'clock I would have to 'front and centre', to be issued all the work orders for the household, and the boat crew. After a quick breakfast, he would finally be whisked away by the chauffeur, and the staff and I would breathe a long sigh of relief, and go about our day without the aid of Charlie's pages of instructions.

We would have a peaceful day until five o'clock in the afternoon, when the car would bring him back into our midst, and we would be issued with constant orders until he had had his requisite number of cocktails, been fed, and finally he would slowly wind down from the day's hype and promptly fall asleep around eight-thirty each night, to snore loudly until four o'clock the next morning. This was the Manila routine. However, on our million-acre wilderness I suddenly went from seeing Charlie on an average of five hours a day, to seeing him all his waking hours. All day, every day!

From thirty-plus staff in the Manila office, and hundreds of crew members on ships all around the world, Charlie was reduced to having only the children, me, and the Aboriginals to control. It didn't take our stockmen long to work Charlie out, and they soon became very good at the disappearing act.

In Manila, Charlie had four full-time secretaries and an administrative secretary to organise all the other secretaries and his appointments. So guess who was expected to take over *all* those jobs, plus the switchboard operator, plus the household staff, plus the cook, plus new positions like the station nurse, or doctor (whichever was required), plus the baker, gardener, bookkeeper... I'll give you two guesses and Charlie isn't one.

This adjustment caused some contention from the working ranks. Charlie couldn't see my problem: I only had to organise myself, he said. My problem was I was not organised, he said. I won't write what I said.

Suddenly, from having a maid in every room, a chauffeur, gardener, two baby amahs, a cook, a laundress, spending my days entertaining clients' wives, playing tennis, and playing with my children, I went to being 'The Missus'. Which as far as I could see incorporated every living action on earth, except maybe answering God's telephone! And all Charlie could say was I was disorganised when I couldn't stop doing the three things I was doing, and do his bidding.

It didn't take long for me to decide to strike back whenever the opportunity arose. And I have to give Charlie credit, when I did catch him out, he conceded defeat and took note of my point. But if I didn't make an issue of each injustice, he would get away with it until I did challenge him. One of his most annoying habits was the constant remark it should only take me fifteen minutes to cook a meal. Every time he wanted me to do something for him, I was always in the kitchen cooking. This annoyed him! The fact that I was cooking now for thirty people (including the abattoir staff) and teaching three different grades of school, plus the few hundred other jobs that seem to be the personal responsibility of 'The Missus' in the Outback, annoyed me no end. The fact that all this effort—my days stretched from four o'clock in the morning to ten o'clock at night—wasn't even recognised, let alone appreciated, also irritated me.

One particularly bad day he made the remark, 'You're just not organised' once too often. It was the straw that broke the camel's back. It was one of those days when nothing was going right, you want to down tools, tell everyone who approaches to 'get lost', just walk away from it all, change your name. A bad day! So I thought, what the hell. I left the kitchen, went into the classroom, brought order back to the chaotic scene there, and quietly spent the rest of the morning with the children.

At one second past twelve, the ravenous horde of workers would charge in the door, expecting to devour a few tonnes of food for lunch. So, at eleven forty-five I walked into the office. Charlie was industriously devouring a box of Jatz crackers and a block of cheese, washing it down with beer, while reading a paperback about pirates. These activities, eating, drinking and reading, usually occupied ninety percent of his time when at the station; in town it was a different situation altogether... well, I'm not sure if he ate cheese and crackers during his town activities! His excuse when I interrupted him, on the station, that is, was always that he was waiting for an important phone call, and because he always sat at the desk next to the phone, this somehow in Charlie's mind vindicated his outright laziness. This day was no different: 'Just waiting for an urgent call, darling.' Not one twinge of guilt showed through the glib statement.

'Charlie, I must stop and smell the flowers.' It came out in a voice that indicated I was off with the fairies. That certainly changed his expression, and even stopped the hand stuffing cheese and crackers into his mouth.

Before he could splutter any words at me, I went on: 'It's a quarter to twelve, and as you have said many times to me, it should only take fifteen minutes to throw a meal together. Be a dear, and throw lunch together for me today.'

I started out the door, but paused. 'Oh yes, and if the children have any problems in the schoolroom... solve them, there's a dear. I'm off to smell the flowers.'

Before he could recover from the shock, I put on my sun-hat, walked out the door and headed across the front lawn for the distant paddock and the river.

As his voice faded into the expanse of the Outback wilderness, I would hear it going from commands: 'Return at once' to requests: 'Let's talk about what has upset you' to outright begging: 'I'll agree to anything, please come back!'

I just kept walking.

I walked back into the kitchen at four o'clock. A scene of devastation told the story. Forty-plus opened cans of baked beans scattered everywhere, various frying pans with remains of eggs in stages of putrefaction littered the stove, open packets of sliced bread were strewn around the counters. The havoc continued, spilt cooking oil spread across the floor, open jam jars were scattered over the counter, various containers of melted liquid butter were dotted with drowning flies. Open tins of fruit, saucepans with burned peas and carrots stuck to the blackened bottoms. Every surface in the room was covered with some sticky substance of something spilt, all mixed in with dirty plates, knives, forks, spoons and cups of a ravenous horde bent on getting their fill.

I remember thinking, Was it worth it? when I faced the mess. But I had gone that far, so I wasn't about to quit.

I found Charlie sitting in a lounge chair, a strange expression on his face, a look of sheer disbelief, as if a herd of wild animals had charged over him and he couldn't understand why he was still alive and in one piece. The abattoir staff arriving for lunch could be described in such a way.

A big smile came out of the dazed expression when he saw me. It was so genuine I almost felt sorry for him. But I quelled the emotion and charged on into the campaign. 'How was the fifteen-minute lunch?'

He gave me one of his charming, yet wistful smiles, and simply said, 'I'm sorry.'

I didn't relent. 'If you want dinner cooked, I want that kitchen restored to normal.'

He was so glad I had offered to cook dinner, he actually came out to the kitchen and cleared the mess away while I cooked. But Charlie's idea of cleaning was to wipe everything off the counters and into the garbage. So I did have to stop him, and under my instructions he quietly picked out the jars of jam, bread, knives, forks and cups and plates, and put things away, wiped counters and started washing the dirty dishes.

He completed his charm programme by complimenting me

on how quickly I had put the meal together. When I replied I still wasn't up to his fifteen-minute standard, he replied, '*Touché.*'

His baked beans and whatever had taken a few hours, plus his cleaning, another few hours, and he knew the staff went back to work very grumpy, late and still hungry, and what's more he knew I knew. I never heard about fifteen-minute meals again, and to make sure I wouldn't go off and smell the flowers again, he returned from Darwin with two girls to help in the kitchen and with the housework.

I had a long, long line of house help characters; some I have already written about, but I forgot one who particularly stands out, an unusual girl. She was all of sixteen; I repeatedly told Charlie not to bring back young girls to do housework as they were never any good. He assured me this one was from a large family and was used to loads of housework. Her friend, not much older, was going to work in the meatworks. I showed them to their room. The next morning, bright and early, she skipped in the door ready to start. I thought, well, at least she's cheerful.

I explained what she had to do. Took her through the house step by step, explained the washing machine, the vacuum cleaner, showed her all the brooms and mops and left her to it, saying if there were any questions I'd be in the kitchen cooking.

She cleaned all day, regularly asking me questions, and keeping up the cheerful attitude. She bobbed around the house humming and da-da-da-ing her way through endless unrecognisable songs all day. Apart from the terrible sounds she made, I had to admit Charlie just might have found a gem.

My hopes were dashed the next morning when she bobbed in the door, still da-da-da-ing and asked me what I wanted her to do that day. For a moment I thought she was joking, then I realised she wasn't. So I told her that she would have to repeat the things she did yesterday. Unfortunate as it was, the laundry had to be done, the dishes washed, and now the horde of thirty people had departed down the flat to the abattoir, the house had to be dusted, swept, floors mopped, put back in order for another day.

She looked at me in horror and said, 'Oh f... that!' and walked out the door.

After recovering from shock I called her back, told her to keep her remarks to herself, and explained some painful truths: that a job as a domestic entails cleaning, daily, so if she didn't do that, she didn't have a job. She went about her work but didn't sing one note, which was okay by me. But the good work of the first day had disappeared for ever. As soon as I was out of sight she downed tools, so I had to check on her constantly. I finally told her I didn't have time to chase her all day; she had the house to clean, and I didn't care if it took all night, she would stay at it until it was done satisfactorily. So she started cleaning again, but I asked Charlie to start looking for the next domestic. He complained I was too hard to please, said it was very hard to find new girls all the time and I should be more tolerant. The events of that night had him agreeing with me.

Loud thumping on our bedroom door brought me out of a deep sleep; Charlie still snored on soundly. It was my house-girl: her friend was very sick, could I come quickly. One look at the girl made my heart sink to the floor. She was a white/grey tone, her skin was cold and clammy, her eyes rolled back in her head and she was unconscious. I quickly put her in the recommended position for an unconscious person, made the domestic hold her head forward and down, told her to watch the girl in case she swallowed her tongue. Then I raced to the emergency button on the radio. My heart was in my mouth; I knew very little about first aid, but could tell this girl seemed close to death, though for what reason I had no idea. The bleary voice of the doctor came over the radio from the hospital. I apologised for getting him out of bed at . . . I glanced at the clock . . . at three o'clock in the morning, to which I got a very uncivil response. Ignoring his rudeness, I gave all the information I could about the sick girl, and waited for his questions and help.

Well he said quite a lot and I was so shocked at the language coming over the radio from a doctor that I couldn't repeat or remember most of it, but it more or less boiled down to, 'Why in the f... did I have the f...... hide to get him out of his f...... bed in the middle of the f...... night for a f...... heroin junkie!'

I dropped the microphone and jumped back in shock as if the voice had physically struck me. Apart from being insulted by his language and manner, the word 'junkie' rattled my brain. A dope addict! On Bullo! In the middle of nowhere?

My brain came back to the problem with a jolt when I realised my charming doctor had turned off his radio! Now I was mad! I put my thumb on the emergency button and kept it there for an inordinate length of time. When I lifted the button, his irate voice greeted me again. Before he could get out more than one word, I launched my attack.

I told him to never speak to me in that foul manner again, and I didn't care if I had a f...... heroin junkie or a f...... green man from Mars. As a doctor, he took the Hippocratic oath which obliged him to conduct himself in a proper manner, dedicate himself to the saving of lives and didn't mention any f...... office hours. So would he stop wasting my f...... time and give the instructions to help me keep the patient alive until the medical plane arrived at f...... dawn!

He was very humble the next morning when he stepped out of the plane; he didn't have to say he was my radio companion of the night before, it was written all over his face.

The girl lived, but did not return to Bullo, at my request. I packed off her friend the domestic and all their belongings on the next trip to Darwin. I found out she was only on marijuana, but the nineteen-year-old was well and truly on heroin. They had no idea how remote the meatworks and the station were, and thought they would get supplies from the nearest town. They had just arrived in Darwin from Melbourne the day Charlie offered them the jobs. It seems that wonderful first day of cleaning was a marijuana-induced high! I gratefully sent her on her way, and hoped for a less 'out of this world' type domestic the next time around.

However, it wasn't the end of the story. About a month later Charlie's business partner's secretary, Kelly, called me to ask if there was a package addressed to my ex-domestic in the mail Charlie had picked up from our mailbox in Darwin that weekend. I checked through the mail and found a small brown paper package. I told Kelly that it was there; I was asked the size and replied it looked and felt like a paperback book. Kelly said that was what the girl was looking for and was quite upset when it wasn't there in the mail on Monday morning. Could Charlie bring it to Darwin on his next trip.

After hanging up the phone, the conversation wouldn't go away. Questions kept coming into my head... what was my ex-domestic doing still picking up mail from our box number well over... I looked up the wage records... six weeks after she had left Bullo?

I called Kelly back and she confirmed that the girl met her at the postbox every Monday morning and weekly received a parcel. I didn't like the sound of it. I kept remembering a movie I had seen a few months before where drugs were hidden in a book with the middle cut out.

I called a friend on the police force in Darwin and said I thought someone was using our postbox as a drug delivery service, and I just happened to have a package in my hands that I thought might contain drugs. I was sworn in over the phone and authorised to open Her Majesty's mail, on behalf of the police. My hands trembled as I undid the string wrapped around and around the unassuming package. The police said to open the package carefully so it could be re-wrapped with no evidence of tampering. I finally had the book in my hands with the paper wrapping almost in original condition on the desk. Charlie said I had been watching too many movies, but he was right next to me waiting for the big moment. I lifted the cover. The first twenty or so pages lifted easily, and there, nestling in the centre of the book, was a row of plastic packages filled with white powder. I don't know who was more amazed, Charlie or me!

The police arrived by plane and took over the proceedings. We gave the whole story and the girls' names from the wage records, and the police told me they wanted to catch the girls in the process of receiving the goods. So the package was carefully rewrapped and taken back to our Darwin mailbox to be the centre of the trap. It was put in our mailbox and Kelly was to hand it out the next Monday along with, they hoped, that Monday's delivery in another book. The police were all staked out around the mailbox section of the Post Office. Both girls turned up, our ex-meatwork heroin addict looking a much better colour now she was on a regular supply. The police arrested them, with drugs in their hands, as they were stepping into a car.

The girls were new to this drug thing and very frightened, so they gave the police all the information they could, including a valuable list of contacts in each state. It turned out to be a big concern, with outlets like the two girls receiving drug-laden books all over Australia. The police thanked me for my invaluable help in cracking one of the most lucrative drug rackets operating in Australia in the 1970s. Charlie said I just fell into it... and he was right.

The Darwin officer's departing words were about the very grumpy officer standing off to the side near the plane, hands jammed in his pockets, head down, kicking up the dirt. It seems he had been on the case for years, trying to get a breakthrough. When Darwin called through to Melbourne he was on the first plane up. His remarks were along the lines of, 'Bloody years of work to crack this bloody case and some bloody female out in the middle of nowhere does it for me!'

The next domestic was not nearly as colourful or unconventional, didn't sing, wasn't bopping around on a marijuana high, but nonetheless was quite good at housework.

5

AMERICA, PRINIE
AND THE CRABS

In his usual manner Charlie announced, out of the blue, we were going to America to visit his family. I was packed in a flash!

We had been in America for four months and were living with Mrs Henderson at Lloyds Landing in Maryland. It certainly was a wonderful old house, and we were enjoying living in the high degree of normality after eighteen months in a caravan parked in a tin shed out in one million acres of dusty wilderness in outback Australia.

Well, I know I was enjoying myself immensely. Waking up in a comfortable bed, in soft sheets that smelt fresh, was an exquisite sensation, compared to my last year and a half on the undersized sofa-bed in the caravan, with a dip in the middle. Charlie managed to sleep in the dip in the middle of this miserable excuse of a bed, all night, while I clung to the high edge up against the wall. Many a night I disappeared down the gap between bed and wall into the mysterious workings that, with the heave of a lever, miraculously turned the bed back into a sofa, and allowed you to sit or get out the door. Other nights if he turned over with a thump, the spring lever would activate itself and I would be straddling the back of the now-in-place sofa, or if he thumped hard enough I would catapult over the top of him and end up on the floor.

The padding on top of the springs was nonexistent (twenty years of occupancy before us). So I walked around with a strange circular pattern on my back and buttocks. There was no way you could keep a mattress protector on the stupid thing, or a bottom sheet. Everything disappeared into the dip, with Charlie, who snored peacefully no matter what the night might bring. Often I awoke clinging to the raised edge, pillow and sheet down in the dip with Charlie, just the grimy green sofa cover making patterns on my cheek, or the springs making more patterns on my back.

Yes, I was definitely enjoying our new sleeping arrangement. I could lie there in comfort and bliss and look out the dormer windows at the snowflakes and the snow-covered fields and trees. I couldn't get the girls out of the bathroom: after bathing in cold water, in a cut-off forty-four-gallon drum at Bullo, to have a normal bath again was wonderful; they would steam up the room and play in the hot water for hours.

Of course, this didn't please their grandmother, who saw it as a wilful waste of water. Never in a million years could she understand what hardships these two little girls had endured living on Bullo those first years, and I felt a few weeks of hot baths was a small gift to them. But their grandmother was seventy-five years old and very set in her ways, so bathtime had to be reduced to what was deemed acceptable.

But it wasn't only the length of the bathtime that was the problem. Trying to keep five- and three-year-olds quiet was near impossible. Telling them they must walk, not run, sit, not pounce, speak, not yell, and just about everything else. In short, having two little girls behave like their grandma, in order to keep the peace, was a bit more than I cared to agree to. The problem was solved when we moved into one of the little farmhouses on the property. Alone at last! The children ran and screamed and jumped and played non-stop inside and outside for at least a week, until all their pent-up energy was expended. Then they worked through endless long baths, and finally settled down to normal.

The girls started school. I bought furnishings. The house was partly furnished but had no children's things, and we needed a few extras to make it a comfy home. We settled in for the winter, it was almost perfect, but something was missing. I didn't have a dog. It was the first time in my life I had been so long without a dog. My birthday was just around the corner, so I told Charlie I wanted a dog. A few weeks later he said we were going to visit some old friends. When we arrived at their house he took me into the garden and there was a Chesapeake Bay Retriever with a litter of puppies running everywhere.

I had never seen that breed of dog before and knew nothing about them. But looking at the mother, the breed filled my requirement; big, solid, intelligent and playful. Charlie told me they were bird dogs, they retrieved ducks from the water. He had already picked out his bird dog and was handing it to me saying it was my dog. It wriggled and squirmed in my arms, straining to get free.

All the other puppies were racing around and playing, except one. He was sitting in the middle of all the activity, watching. All the pups were light brown, with a wiry, curly, wavy coat; this pup looked as if he had been put through a blond rinse, his coat was not as wiry or wavy and he was twice the size of all the other pups. He tried vainly to join in the play but his feet were so big he kept falling over them. He had a big broad head and beautiful eyes. The moment he looked at me it was love at first sight.

'I want that one.'

'What!' said Charlie.

He took me over to the corner of the garden to talk me

out of my decision. The dog was so clumsy it couldn't walk, would never be able to hunt! It wasn't even the right colour! So it was decided we would take his choice.

'It's that one or forget it' was my stubborn reply.

Even the owners had to admit that my choice, although from pedigree parents, was a strange-looking pup. True it was healthy, but they had to admit it didn't even look like a Chesapeake. They were sure he would grow out of his clumsiness. But sometimes even established pedigree dogs had throwbacks, they conceded. They weren't sure what this one had thrown back to exactly, but they were sure they had a throwback on their hands. The standoff continued. Charlie wasn't going back to tidewater country on the Chesapeake, the heart of the duck-hunting world, with a Chesapeake Retriever that didn't look like one, or more precisely, that didn't look like a pedigree. Even the farmers there had pedigree dogs.

I wouldn't budge; it was the funny big puppy for me. I explained I wasn't going to show the dog and I wasn't going to hunt; if Charlie wanted to hunt, the dog was pedigree and what he looked like wouldn't affect his retrieving skills, so what was the problem? I wanted a big dog to protect the children when they were playing out in our woods, I wanted a family dog. When I accused Charlie of conforming to what everyone else thought a Chesapeake should look like, that did the trick. Charlie couldn't bear to be referred to as average; he immediately warmed to the idea that he would have the only different Chesapeake on 'the Shore', the name used for the area where we lived.

And so I walked happily out the door just barely able to carry the nine-week-old puppy. The girls had his box for travelling ready and we all three sat in the back of the car and cooed to the puppy the whole way home, much to Charlie's disgust.

And that's how Prince London of Lloyds, his pedigree name, we called him Prinie, Charles called him Prince, came into our lives. And what a brilliant dog! He lived up to the size of his paws and grew into a huge dog, all of one hundred and forty pounds (or sixty-three kilograms), all muscle. From an early age he ran for miles, the girls couldn't wait until he was big enough to pull their little red wagon, so they could explore deep into the woods and pine forest that were part of the farm.

Lloyds Landing, the property, consisted of four farms totalling around one thousand two hundred acres (or just under five hundred hectares). The main house, called Lloyds Landing, was built in 1720 on the banks of the Choptank River. In the 1700s, English sailing ships sailed up the Choptank River and loaded grain to take back to England. The ships brought out finished goods like silks, satins, furniture, machinery, light cargoes; for ballast on the way over the holds were loaded with house bricks; these were taken out and the hold filled with grain for the return. As a result, all the lovely old homes along the Choptank River are built out of English brick. Lloyds Landing is a wonderful English-style cottage with low doors and dormer windows and a shingle roof. Mr and Mrs Henderson restored the original house, I think some-time in the 1950s, when they retired to 'the Shore' to live. The present living room was once the big functional all-purpose kitchen/living room. The big fireplace was used for cooking and the smoking of hams was also done there. When we were there in the 1960s, on a cold winter's night with the open fire roaring, the beautiful old original wall panelling released the secrets of the past and you actually smelt, just faintly, a hint of smoked hams in the air.

During the restoration the original building was doubled in size; the old stairway with doors top and bottom was taken out and a whole section of entrance foyer and staircase added in between the old part and a completely new part; the original low front door was now the door into the dining room. A new kitchen, outside porch, double garage and the quaint outdoor smokehouse were added. The barn in the distance, nestling amongst the cornfields with pine woods bordering the property beyond the cornfields, and long sloping green lawns edged with box bushes rolling down to the wide Choptank River, made Lloyds Landing a very beautiful historic country residence.

The other three farmhouses were just farmhouses, made of weatherboard, or clapboard as it is called in America. Their names were Rigby's Marsh, Warehouse and Whitewash. We were living in Rigby's Marsh.

As the name suggests, the farm was on a marshy part of the river, so there was no sloping lawn down to the water's edge, just very thick reed growth along the waterfront, lots of mosquitoes, and no view at all. It was a quaint little house, all closed in and tucked away in amongst the pine forest and cornfields. After the corn was harvested, there was a view across the ploughed fields: you could see Lloyds Landing about three miles away, and the other farmhouses off in the distance. Such a contrast to the wild, empty wilderness of the Australian Outback.

Prinie grew daily and it wasn't long before I could say yes to the question the girls had asked almost daily: 'Is he big enough to pull the red wagon yet?'

Soon they had him in a harness of ropes and straps, with their Dad's help, and they were off exploring. Charlie installed a long stick rigged to the wagon with a piece of red fabric flying at the top, so when I wanted to know where they were I could look out the upstairs window and see the little red flag going up and down the rows of tall corn. Some days Prinie would go on strike and just sit down on the job, and they would finally go off and explore without him. But if I needed them, I would send him off and he would track them down. The children would only come back if he let them hitch him to the wagon. They had some great rides home, clinging to the wagon and squealing with delight, as Prinie trotted home at a fast clip.

Charlie was almost always in Washington, so the girls and I were alone most of the week, another reason why I wanted a big dog. The house was a mile off the road, through a pine forest, so we were quite isolated, and during winter the phone would be out of order quite a bit of the time when snow or pine branches caused trouble with the line.

Charlie called again one night to say he was staying in Washington. It was Friday and he usually came home early for the weekend, but he called to say he had to finish some business, missing the last train, but he would catch the first train in the morning and see us for lunch. I had just put down the phone, knowing full well what 'business' Charlie was up to, when a knock at the door interrupted my sober thoughts.

The girls and Prinie were in the living room watching a loud cowboy movie, but I thought it strange Prinie hadn't barked at the lights when the car came down the drive. I opened the door but left the glass snow-door (keeping the warmth in the house) locked.

A man was standing there; he shouted through the door he was from the phone company and was there to fix the phone, he'd had a report it was out of order. It was nine o'clock at night. I told him the phone was working, I had just finished a call. He said well he may as well check it seeing he had come all the way.

Something was nagging at the back of my brain but I couldn't put a finger on it. I looked out at the vehicle, it was a van like the repair vans used by the telephone company, but finally I knew what was worrying me: it did not have a company name on the side of the van.

The situation just did not feel right, so I called Prinie; he came bounding up to me, tail wagging. When he saw the man standing outside the glass door all his hair stood on end; he stood on his hind feet with his great paws on the steel reinforcement bar across the glass door. Standing as tall as the man, staring eyeball to eyeball, he slowly raised his top lip to reveal massive fangs. The man backed away at such a pace he fell backwards off the edge of the porch, missing the step completely. He shouted he would not come into the house if that dog was there and said I had to lock him up. I just shook my head in a very definite 'no'. He hurried back to the van and drove away. I called the phone company to check on him; they had not sent anyone at that time of night. I called the state troopers on the highway seven miles away and they acted at once. It seemed there had been several cases around the country where a man posing as a repairman had gained entrance to the house and there had been robberies, and in some cases more serious offences. I was informed I was a lucky woman. I told them I had a very good dog. The troopers came the next day and when they were met by Prinie they agreed that indeed I had a very exceptional dog. When Prinie locked those yellow eyes on you there were very few people who didn't react with extreme caution. The man was caught a few months later.

Prinie was a hero for life in my eyes. We told him that night how wonderful he was, and as a special treat he was allowed to sit on the sofa. He had an expression of 'I know, I know' on his face; Prinie took guarding his family seriously.

In the summer Charlie wanted to have a party for the people in Washington he had been working with; they were coming to 'the Shore' for the weekend. He also thought it a good idea to include local friends that he hadn't had a chance to catch up with, being so busy in Washington.

I pointed out that I could not entertain forty people in such a little house. So after much discussion Charlie decided I could manage if the party was outside on the lawn in the late afternoon, and after cocktails, a crab salad buffet dinner.

His nephew was trapping crabs to make money for his university fees, so we could get a lot of crabs for a reasonable amount of money. Charlie went ahead and invited everyone to the party, despite my protests. These days I would call in a caterer, but for some reason, in those days, I always seemed to have to prove myself. The other deciding factor in doing the work myself was that we never had any money to spare.

We had been living quietly for a year, so this was the big coming-out party, a chance for many people to meet Charlie's Australian wife. Americans in the 1960s didn't know much about Australia except they thought all Australians played world-grade tennis and could swim like fish. The few Australians that I met in the States said they had a hard time explaining that every Australian didn't play tennis like Rosewall and Hoad, or swim like a fish. Americans just could not accept that there were Australians who actually didn't play tennis and some who couldn't swim. The other popular notion was that Australia was somewhere in the middle of Europe.

The day of the party arrived. I had really worked hard and was quite nervous. The crabs were to be delivered that day; I had cooked and prepared everything else. So except for the last-minute finishing touches we were ready. It was a lovely day with no sign of clouds, so people could be outside. I borrowed some outside chairs and tables from Mrs Henderson and hired the rest, along with extra trestle tables.

I was very pleased with myself. I was ready at ten o'clock in the morning; I had the space and plates ready in the fridges for the crabs to arrive. I was sitting having a cup of tea, still congratulating myself, when Charlie's nephew drove up and eventually staggered into the kitchen with a plastic garbage bin which he dumped in the middle of the kitchen.

'What's that?' I asked as he disappeared out the door.

'Hang on,' came the reply over his shoulder.

He returned with a second bin identical to the first and dropped it next to the first one. 'Crabs!' he said in a puffed reply.

'Crabs?'

'Yes, your crabs!'

He whipped off the lids and a mass of squirming, floundering, squeaking crabs greeted me.

'They're alive!'

'Yep. How else could they be?'

'How about cooked and ready to eat?'

It was then I was told that everyone on 'the Shore' definitely cooked their own crabs. There was jealous competition over recipes and everyone, I was informed, would be judging mine tonight. He jammed the lid back on, told me to be careful to keep it on, then left a dazed me sitting in the kitchen with two garbage bins full of squirming crabs. I called Mrs Henderson and told her my problem; she told me I could borrow her crab steamer. She went on to say there would also be one in the kitchen somewhere. No home on 'the Shore' was without a crab steamer, I was to learn later; it was standard equipment. After I was told what to look for, I found two in the storage cupboard in the basement. I drove over to Lloyds Landing, had a quick lesson in steaming crabs properly, then raced back to the house, now desperately out of time. Of course, cunning Charlie was arriving with some of the guests coming down from Washington, so I had the children and Prinie as assistants. The woman who helped me during the week didn't work on Saturdays, it was against her religion. I raced back to the house with the instructions, put all the steamers on with water and all the flavourings to make the crabs real 'Shore' crabs, and clutching the recipe which I was reverently told had been in the family for over one hundred years, I started.

The water was boiling, steam was whistling out everywhere it could; it was time to move. Prinie was watching the bins, pricking up his ears and turning his head on the side, intrigued by the funny sounds he could hear. Each boiler could hold about five crabs on the steaming shelf. One look at the bins and I knew I was going to be cooking for quite a while. I gingerly lifted the lid off the bin and with difficulty managed to get five crabs out, one at a difficult time, with long-handled tongs, putting them in a bowl ready to tip the lot into the steamer together. I was feeling uneasy about having to do this but I had no choice, and I reasoned with myself that they would die anyhow if I left them in the bins. I took off the steamer lid, poured them in quickly, and slammed the lid back. No-one had told me about the locking device for the steamer lid. I turned to the plastic bin to fish out the next five, and the five crabs in the steamer catapulted out of the steamer, sending the lid flying. They were hopping all over the stove, understandably, I suppose; if I was sat on a shelf in a boiling hot steamer, I would jump like hell, too. That was what the locking device did, it prevented the crabs jumping out, but the locking device was still in the cupboard.

I dropped the basin of crabs I was holding and they started crawling around the floor while I tried to catch the escapees on the stove, now also dropping on the floor. I put them back in the pot, only to have them leap out again, so I had to hold the lid down until they died. By now I was crying, feeling for all the world like an executioner, realising I would have to keep doing this for the rest of the afternoon.

Prinie was fascinated with the crabs and before I could stop him, he sniffed one heading his way. It latched onto his nose, then all hell broke loose. I let go of the lid to go to his rescue; again the now-half-dead crabs staggered over the edge of the steamer, collapsing on the floor, making terrible noises. The children were sitting on the table crying because I was crying, and Prince was howling, jumping up in the air to avoid the nippers, barking and attacking, all at once. I was trying to calm him when another crab latched onto his foot; he recoiled backwards. He was shaking his foot furiously and backed right into the bin of crabs that I had left the lid off. The bin went flying, crabs spilled from the bin and spread slowly out, in an expanding mass, all over the floor.

We now had a floor covered with very active crabs, unlike the poor old ones in death throes falling over the side of the stove. Crabs were now biting me, so both Prince and I were yowling and hopping around. We couldn't put a foot or paw anywhere where it didn't get bitten.

The table was closest, so I helped Prince onto the table with the girls; I stood on a chair. I finally got the crab off Prince's foot, he had dislodged a second one off his nose, thank heavens. After we calmed down I sat on the table and cried some more. The crabs were walking out the door, into the dining and living rooms, all over the ground floor in fact.

I knew I couldn't sit all day, so I made a path through the crabs with the tongs and raced upstairs to put on thick long pants and heavy boots. With the pants tucked tightly in the boots, I armed myself with dustpan and brush and started scooping up the crabs, crying all the time.

In the middle of this, Charlie called. He had driven down with some of the guests early. He was bringing them, he informed me, over for a few quiet drinks. In a very few colourful words I told him if he turned up with guests before six o'clock I would throw a garbage bin of live crabs over them. I went on to tell him to get home to help me with the mess or all his guests would be eating live crabs. All I heard was, 'But darling', before I slammed the receiver down to return to scooping up crabs.

The coward never turned up, but took his guests to Lloyds Landing, to sit on the porch with his mother, and sip tea and chat until it was time to come to cocktails and dinner. I spent the rest of the day crying and putting crabs to death.

By six o'clock I was exhausted, but we, the children and I, had managed to cook most of the crabs, or at least all we could find. So we still had half a bin of uncooked crabs, and I had no idea of what was roaming the rooms of the ground floor.

But I was running out of time, so I decided if the guests wanted more crabs they could cook their own. I went upstairs to quickly shower and change. Charlie arrived with three car-loads of guests, staying in the middle of the guests so I couldn't get him alone to kick him in the shins. I really didn't care by that time if the night was a success or not, I was so upset I just went through the motions of a hostess. The night, as it turned out, was a howling success and was the talk of 'the Shore' and Washington for weeks. People started cooking their own crabs when all the cooked ones were eaten, and a very serious cooking competition was in full swing in the kitchen, with judges in force. I served Australian pavlova for dessert, which was consumed at an alarming rate and raved about for the rest of the night; they had never heard of pavlova. But by far the highlight of the evening was when one of the escapee crabs came out from under the lounge and nipped one woman's foot.

By now the cooking gourmets had cooked all the crabs in the last bin, but there still were willing cooks to demonstrate their secret recipe, so when they heard crabs were loose wandering around the ground floor, there was a crab hunt. They all had a wonderful time finding the stray crabs. When they found one the cooking was a very serious process and judges received just a morsel each. They all left in the early hours of the morning, saying it was the best dinner they had ever been to, all swapping crab seasoning recipes, all wanting the Aussie dessert recipe.

Charlie complimented me on a job well done; I didn't speak to him for days. When he suggested another crab party a month or so later I gave him such a look, he mumbled, 'Perhaps not.'

I told him the only place I would even look at a crab again was in a restaurant where it was served to me on a platter, ready to eat.

6

LEAVING PRINIE
AND DIFFICULT

The 1960s in America were wild and swinging years: skinny-dipping, wife-swapping, progressive dinner parties. Charlie engaged in the first two without me, though I suppose number two would have to be called wife-borrowing, but the third just involved eating each different course at a different house, so I was allowed to participate. By the end of the night you had covered a lot of the countryside and eaten a lot of food.

My downfall, on my first progressive dinner party, was that I mixed a lot of drinks. By the fourth house I was very pleased with myself and felt on top of the world; I thought to myself, Now I can understand why people drink a lot; if being drunk feels better than this it would be a very pleasant state.

I was far from drunk; I could still walk a straight line and wasn't slurring my words, as many of my co-travellers were. I was also hostess at the last stop, for midnight supper, so I kept this thought foremost in my mind.

Most of the guests (some had collapsed along the way at various houses) arrived and welcomed the coffee, but after a while they lapsed back to hard liquor. Eventually, in the early hours of the morning, the last few left and I was faced with the mess. Charlie had gone to bed the moment we arrived

home so I had entertained a house full of guests while he
snored upstairs.

I put the food in the fridge, left the rest for the morning
and climbed the stairs. I didn't feel tired, in fact I was wide
awake, feeling on top of the world. I took a hot shower,
walked to the bed feeling very pleased with myself, laid my
head on the pillow, then let out a scream as all hell broke
loose. The room swirled, the walls pounded down on me one
at a time; when I closed my eyes it was worse, I could still
see the walls falling on me, but I was also tumbling in a
sickening circle, while swirling. Bile surged up my throat but
I couldn't lift myself up, couldn't speak. One arm hit Charlie
repeatedly to help me, but he snored on. I rolled out of bed
and crashed to the floor flat on my face. I managed to
swallow the vomit that was in the back of my throat and let
out a scream followed by a dying moan. Charlie finally
rallied; when he saw my condition he roared with laughter.

I crawled to the bathroom slowly, not daring to move my
head, so I could not look at Charlie as I hurled a torrent of
abuse. My painful progress across the room continued, eyes
glued to the image of the toilet through the open door, as I
still continued to send a barrage of insults to Charlie. I spent
the rest of the night throwing up, my chin hooked over the
rim of the toilet seat, hour after hour after hour.

I finally stopped dry-retching, crawled into the bath to lie
under the hot shower for the next hour, then crawled to bed
without drying. I do not remember anything until late afternoon, when I forced one eye open to the repeated requests
from my worried children asking me to please say something.
Just the opening of one eye started it all again, only this time
I could run to the toilet to start dry-retching again. It was
well into the next day before I felt like anything resembling
a normal human being, and strong enough to tell Charlie
what I thought of his actions. He told me it was my fault I

got drunk and I had to suffer the consequences. The fact that I didn't know about mixing drinks didn't make him sympathetic, he just kept laughing, saying it was my fault. My only reply was, 'Don't get sick, Charlie, and expect me to look after you.' That sobered him; he offered to cook dinner, which sent me rushing to the bathroom again with his laughter ringing in my ears. Charlie really suffered the next time he was confined to bed with a cold!

I was thirty-two when I got drunk for the first time in my life, and I can still remember vividly every heave... the only thing worse than being drunk is delivering a baby. At least at the end of *that* experience you have something to show for all the pain. Not so with drinking; why any person inflicts that kind of punishment on themselves, willingly, is beyond my comprehension. It was another twenty years before I felt sad enough to descend into that complete oblivion again, in 1986 when Charlie was desperately ill in hospital.

America for me was an alien land. They were so far ahead of Australia in the 1960s it was unbelievable. Freeways, four lanes each way, when we only had roads. You were booked if you went under forty miles per hour on a freeway; in Australia you got booked if you went *over* thirty-five miles an hour. The first time I drove on the New Jersey Turnpike, five lanes each way, I got booked for going too slow in the truck lane. The advice was, 'Geet up to fifty, ma'am, or geet orph!'

Having only known the corner store and the local shops in the main street, I got lost in supermarkets, sometimes for half a day, after wandering down endless rows of products.

America had instant tea way back in the '60s: there was an entire aisle of instant tea and I didn't even think they drank tea! I started walking, fascinated that there could be so many different ways to present tea. I never did find a packet of just plain tea-leaves. But I did find instant tea, plain with artificial sweetener, with artificial milk and artificial sweetener, with real sugar and real milk, with artificial lemon flavouring only, with artificial lemon flavouring and artificial sweetener, or with both real lemon and real sugar; then they started crossing, one artificial this, one real that, then the other way around. So it went all the way down the aisle. Shelves as high as you could reach and stretching a whole city block, offering you endless choices, endless brands.

I think to be raised in such an environment of unlimited selection from an early age would be inclined to make a person stressed out just deciding what tea to drink. It expanded the importance of everyday, trivial, routine decisions, making a simple task into a massive, time-consuming problem. Supermarkets had a terrible effect on me. I became disoriented and irate at being forced to plough through hundreds of product variations, and endless brands, for a simple packet of natural tea-leaves. I constantly had to repeat to myself what I wanted to buy, otherwise by the time I finally found the right aisle, I had forgotten what I wanted. When I finally finished the shopping, I could never manage to find the door I came in by.

Once in Washington I drove into a car park, and after going in circles floor after floor for an interminable time, I found a parking space, then went shopping. The plan was to meet Charlie, a few hours later, on the corner near his office. When I got into the lift at the car park ready to leave, and saw the expanse of buttons, I knew I was in trouble. I knew the car was parked somewhere in the top twelve floors because I had done a lot of circles before I parked. So I started midway and went from floor to floor. It took many hours to find the car. But I learned that lesson well. I now also understand why there are colours for each floor, and a number painted in each parking square. From then on I always wrote down the floor and square number.

Well, let's face it, in the 1960s most parking lots in Australia were outside and on the ground and about the size of a few tennis courts; you could stand and take in the whole parking lot without moving your head. I had had no experience whatsoever in tackling a fifteen-storey car park.

But I didn't fare too well with 'on the ground' parking lots in America either. I would have started to develop an inferiority complex at this stage, only Charlie was there right alongside of me, also confused. We just weren't prepared for the size of the parking lot outside the stadium in New York when Army was playing Navy. Not long after arriving in America we had travelled to New York to meet Charlie's Navy friends and see the game of the year.

Late as usual, we parked, locked the car and hurried towards the nearest entrance, which told us we couldn't enter unless our ticket numbers were between this number and that; if our tickers were higher, go left; if lower, go right. We started briskly in the right direction, as instructed, and twenty minutes later we arrived breathless at the correct gate. This was a big stadium.

Of course, the problem arose when we went to find our car, or should I say, Mrs Henderson's car. It was a long way from a one-acre car park, there were cars as far as the eye could see. We also came out a different gate from the one we went in, so we were well and truly lost.

Charlie could fly off an aircraft carrier in the middle of an ocean, find an enemy ship, sink it and return to a cruising carrier all in the middle of the night. But this miraculous talent did not operate in a car park.

I remembered there was a red tartan travelling rug on the back seat. We knew the car was that year's Buick and dark blue, but unfortunately for us it was the car of the year. And it seemed all the purchasers were Army–Navy football fans: there were more dark blue Buicks in the parking lot than at the Buick assembly plant. We spent hours peering in the back windows looking for a tartan travelling rug. You would be surprised how many Americans with dark blue Buicks have red tartan travelling rugs!

After many cars didn't open when we tried the keys we finally, after a few hours, hit the jackpot. As the key turned the lock and opened the door, a hand came down on Charlie's shoulder, and a policeman asked for identification. It seemed he had been following us, watching our unusual behaviour. Charlie explained we had forgotten where we parked the car and were looking in the windows for the rug on the back seat.

When he asked why we had tried to open so many cars, Charlie told him we didn't know the licence number. Well, apparently in America everyone knew their licence number. Not knowing your licence number was the equivalent of a suspect spy not knowing who won the world series in baseball during the war. The policeman asked for a driver's licence, but Charlie only had an international one; social security number then? . . . nope, hadn't been in the country long enough to apply for one; car registration? . . . didn't seem to have it with us. We ended up at the downtown police station while the police called Mrs Henderson to ask if her son and his wife were driving her car to New York for the Army–Navy game. They then escorted us to our car, waved us goodbye and hoped we had a pleasant stay in New York! When we left our friends at the stadium it had been arranged to all meet for dinner later; by the time we arrived at the restaurant, they were sipping coffee.

In every field I found myself readjusting and learning; some fields were fun and amusing. At the supermarket in the country town where we lived (this was considered a small supermarket, only about four acres inside area) there was a very nice Afro–American man. His job was loading groceries into the cars. Even thirty years ago in America, these shopping centres were open twenty-four hours a day, and always seemed full and busy. So there were many parcel loaders at the kerbside to help keep the traffic moving. He was the parcel-loading assistant I would seek out; he was always cheerful and chatted away. I was fascinated with his Southern way of speaking; he was fascinated with my Australian accent. Each of us would prolong the conversation on weather and so on, just to listen to each other. But we soon got into swapping different words each of us used for the same thing. This game started the first time I managed to get out of the supermarket under four hours, and knew where I had parked the car.

He told me to 'go bring der or-toe-mo-beale to the kerb, an he would load it, yes um'. When I parked the car he asked me where would he put the groceries.

I said, 'In the boot.'

He smiled and asked again where I would like the groceries.

'In the boot.' So he opened the rear door and stacked them all on the back seat.

The next week I opened the boot and said, 'In here.'

'Oh, in the *trunk*!'

So we started comparing things like bonnet and hood,

petrol and gas, automobile and car, footpath and sidewalk, lift and elevator, to mention a few. Each week I would tell him one or two new words, and he would pull out a piece of paper and ask me what we called something. One time he asked me what we called 'pork belly and grits', and I told him 'nothing'.

'Nuthin'? Why's you calls it that?'

'No, we don't call it that, we don't eat pork belly and grits; it's not food we eat in Australia.'

He walked away mumbling to himself, 'No pork belly and grits, strange place.'

When we left to come back to Australia, I said goodbye to him on our last trip to the supermarket. He said he would miss the children and me a lot. His parting words were, 'Darn, and I wers jest gittin' u-stir that "boot", yes um!'

Almost everything about America was new, different or bigger. I had to get used to heated houses, which were rare in Australia. Our house in Sydney, where I grew up, was cold and draughty away from the open fires in the winter. But I had been away from the cold weather for fourteen years, living in the tropics; I had almost forgotten the need for heating. Maryland in the winter was very cold, so I soon became acquainted with the furnace in the basement which provided the heating for the house.

I always kept the temperature in the house low, but most people had their houses so hot you could wear light clothes inside quite comfortably while it was well below freezing outside. I found this out the hard way, early in the piece. We had been invited to dinner and I wore a black angora wool dress, also a woollen spencer, insurance against the chill; unfortunately. The hostess kept the house at 80° Fahrenheit (27° Celsius). After the first hour I was the colour of a ripe tomato and feeling extremely uncomfortable, so I went to the bathroom and removed the spencer, next trip my slip, then stockings. Progressively, as the hours passed, I took off everything down to my briefs and bra, but perspiration was still running down my back. To cool down, I stepped out onto the porch and did a quick freeze at regular intervals for the rest of the evening. I'm amazed I didn't end up with pneumonia as a result. That most unpleasant experience always stayed in my memory, and a light blouse became part of my attire, giving me the option to strip down to it if my hostess maintained hothouse temperatures.

I found American hosts a challenge and very different; being married to Charlie, I shouldn't have been surprised, but I just thought he was the exception to the rule, not the norm. My host at this particular dinner party was a jovial, ruddy-faced, loud-speaking, man. After introductions (I had met his wife only) he asked what I would like to drink; when I replied scotch and dry, he silenced the room with a roar: 'What?'

Everyone waited; I wondered what I had done wrong. He then informed the whole room that there was no way he was going to desecrate good whisky. If people couldn't appreciate good scotch they shouldn't drink it, and he glared at me, eyebrows rippling and bristling. He was an attorney, and I soon learned he always performed, in and out of the courtroom.

So I asked him, 'What about freedom of choice? I thought America upheld this belief.' He was about to deliver a presentation when his wife came over and told him to shut up and just serve my drink. He marched off with a haughty, contemptuous air, and I noticed his wife finally brought me the drink. I made sure it lasted to dinner. So, along with being abused for my choice of drinks, sweating it out inside the house, and cooling down outside in the snow, it was a night to remember.

From the television exposure I had had to America in the 1950s, my impression was that all Americans were cigar-smoking, loud-speaking, floral-shirted, white-panama-hat-wearing tourists, with all the latest technology as part of their everyday life. I soon found out how wrong I was.

During the four years in Talbot County I never met a cigar-smoking, floral-shirted, panama-hatted man. The farmers of the area were quiet-spoken, polite, hardworking people, mostly of German descent. It was a pleasure to see their neat, clean, well-run farms. They were so self-sufficient it was amazing. One farmer in the county was visited by the Internal Revenue because they said they did not believe his family could live on the amount of income he had declared in his tax returns. But the investigator went away amazed that their declaration was indeed true. The family grew their own veg-etables and fruit, raised chickens for eggs and meat, also had pigs and cattle for meat, milk, butter, cream, buttermilk and cheese, fished in the river for fish and crabs, and hunted deer. The wife had a cellar full of preserves of everything you were able to preserve. She knitted pullovers, scarves, socks, beanies, gloves, plaited floor mats out of old clothes, made all her dresses, curtains and covers and all her husband's work clothes. His Sunday best suit was purchased about once every ten years. They bought very little, only coffee, sugar, tea, a few tropical fruits, and anything extra for a special occasion that they couldn't make or grow.

The tax man returned to the big city, and to his computer which had told him the neat, efficient, pleasant home and farm he had just spent the afternoon inspecting with its proud happy owners, could not possibly exist. The computer probably refused his report and continued to spit out reports rejecting the possibility that there were still people like this in America.

Rural areas seem to produce characters no matter what the country, and America was no different. One farmer had never travelled further than the nearest large town of Salisbury, all of three hours drive. He was honest, religious, hardworking, kind and helpful to any living thing, and his theory was, 'Ifn the Lord wan-turd him some-waaar else, he would harv put him thur!'

I met a continuous stream of wonderful people in America, and some really extraordinary characters. One helped me with the children and house cleaning. She was very religious and quite a card. Whenever she stayed with the girls at night she preached them religion every chance she got. The girls were about six and eight and they had asked quite a lot of questions. One question Marlee had was about the statement, 'When the big fire came it would go around and leave unharmed all of her faith'. Marlee wanted to know how the fire knew who to go around.

It was against this woman's 'ligon' as she called it, to give gifts at Christmas, but it didn't seem to have any definite ruling on receiving gifts, so every Christmas she would leave with a carload of gifts for herself and ten children, with a smile and a thank you. There was a very funny incident one night when we were out to dinner and she was staying with the children. On the stove was simmering a pot full of all the leftovers, boiling down to a nice stew for Prince. She went to serve the dog's stew to the children for dinner. Instead of saying it was leftover dog stew, the girls said, 'We can't eat that; Mummy is cooking it for Prince!'

So the talk went around that I fed the dog only the best of food and the children weren't allowed to have any. When my maid told her friend who was Mrs Such-and-Such's maid, and she told her friend who was Mrs Henderson's maid, Mrs Henderson had a serious talk with me about growing children's need for the very best of good food. She had believed this silly tale! The next morning I had a serious chat with my daily help and she went home that night satisfied that the dog's stew was indeed leftovers of a meal my children had had a go at first. I managed to convince her the children always had first choice, then the dog. She then told her friend who worked for Mrs Such-and-Such, and so on down the complicated chain of the gossip network, until it reached the maid who worked for Mrs Henderson, and everything was straightened out. But to avoid more gossip spreading every time I had a dog stew of leftovers on the stove, I put a little sign in front of the pot before I left: LEFT-OVERS STEW—FOR PRINCE.

Of course, the children loved Prince and considered him so much a part of the family, they would have shared their food with him straight off their dinner plates if I didn't stop them. He was indeed considered human, and the one thing he did eat with us regularly was icecream. On the way home from school we passed a wonderful small drive-in place; I think it was called Wendy's. They had good fast food, something very new to me, and the very best icecream. We would stop on the way home from school. Oh boy! did Prince love his icecream. The girls could have taken out a world record as icecream eaters, but Prinie-Boy could even beat them.

He always sat on the front seat next to me. The moment we drove into Wendy's, he would get a very concentrated look on his face, one side of his top lip would get caught on the fang, but he would be so intent on watching the icecream approach, the lip would stay there, giving him a very quizzical expression. He rested his paws on the door-ledge with his head out of the car. I held the icecream while he politely licked around and around it, stopping the drips, just as the children did. The people at Wendy's got to know him and he became quite an attraction; people stood and watched this dog eating icecream in a very civilised manner, hanging out of a car and quietly licking it, with two little girls hanging out the other window doing the same. The owner liked Prince so much he would often give him an extra icecream, on the house.

When Prince was two he started his duck-retrieving lessons. The trainer was very taken with Prince, and put a lot of effort into training him. He also believed Prince could win shows purely on his looks, which made me smile when I remembered my arguments with Charles and the breeders about Prinie being 'a freak'. So on a few occasions I allowed the trainer to show Prince. He came home with the first prize every time; he sometimes also took 'Best of Breed' and 'Best of Show'. Charlie boasted about Prince to all who would listen, completely forgetting his statement when Prince was a puppy, that he didn't even look like a Chesapeake.

Prince's training continued, along with his success at the shows. I finally had to put a stop to the show circuit: Prince won all the shows in Maryland, so his trainer wanted to start showing him interstate. The two afternoons a week for retrieving lessons had now stretched to his staying over on the Thursday night after the second lesson, then travelling to shows interstate on Friday, Saturday and Sunday. Suddenly I was seeing my dog Tuesday, Wednesday and two mornings a week. We all missed him and I felt Prince was getting more reluctant to leave. He really liked Glen, his trainer, and at the beginning would bound out and get in the car to go to lessons, but when show-time was added, although he went quite freely to the car, the bounce was gone. I told Glen, No more shows, just the duck-training, and our family was a lot happier, including Prince.

The big day arrived when Prince was ready to show off all his acquired retrieving skills. Glen sang his praises to the sky. He was what is called a triple retriever; this in the bird-retrieving world was very good, I was told. Charlie was suitably impressed. The big show was held at Lloyds Landing, down the sloping lawn on the river. It was a beautiful day; we walked down the lawn, along the avenue of box bush. At the bottom of the lawn was a tiny sand beach and off to the left was a long wharf reaching across the shallow water and out to the deep channel of the river. We walked along the beach and stopped near the wharf. Glen's wife went out onto the river in a boat to throw the ducks into the water. The ducks were veterans at training dogs; they had special little covers over their wings so they couldn't fly away, but could swim and paddle around in the water. They had been retrieved so many times that being brought back to shore in a dog's mouth didn't seem to faze them, because after Prince deposited them on the shore they stood up and calmly shook their ruffled feathers, as best they could with their wing-jackets still in place. Glen had Prince on the beach ready to command him once the ducks hit the water. Charles had invited his mother down to watch the trials, and Glen had a few friends along also. Anyone from 'the Shore' was an expert on the performance of a bird dog, except maybe the children and me.

Glen explained the signals to me, and everyone waited patiently. Prince, he told me, was going to retrieve a triple; this made him a very smart dog. The three ducks hit the water in different places, Prince would watch their movements then go downstream of the ducks, swim out and intercept. He had to retrieve the duck furthest downstream first, and if every-thing went according to plan, the other ducks just floated to

'The little black car'. Ford Anglia and my sister Sue, with one of her dogs.

'Who's a pretty boy?' Mum and Cocko, early 1950s.

One of the Irish setters as a puppy (Lucky), with the next-door cat
(Timmy) who raised her.

Charlie and myself in a Manila nightclub, circa 1964.

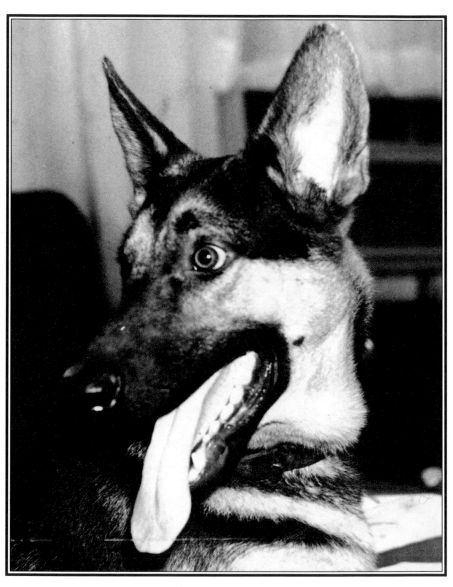

Dasher, in Manila.

Lloyds Landing in Maryland, USA.

Setting out on an adventure in the cornfields. Bonnie and Marlee with Prince (Prinie) and red wagon.

Bonnie and Marlee (aged four and six) on the lawn of Lloyds Landing, USA, 1967.

'The icecream look.' Prince London of Lloyds Landing.

Mrs Henderson and Prinie at Lloyds Landing.

Uncle Dick with a
beer in his hand.

Stumpy (the stock
camp cook), Uncle Dick
and Danielle,
Christmas 1986.

Charlie in an army helicopter on Bullo.

Charlie.

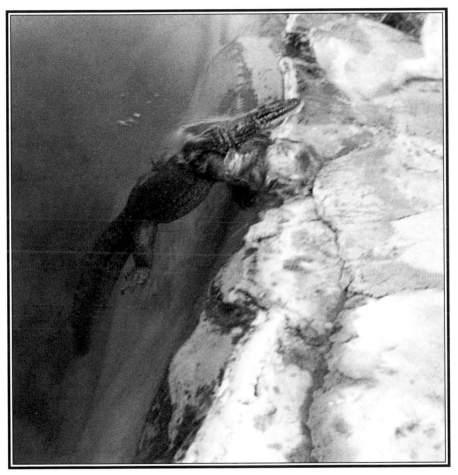

Rosa the goanna climbing out of the swimming pool, after a few laps.

Danielle with a poddy calf.

Pye-wacket the marmalade cat with Shad (Marlee's labrador).

Dogs galore! Hottentot, Honey, Panda, Frisky and Bud.

Hottentot dressed up as Charlie! He is sitting in Charlie's chair at the dining table with Charlie's glass in front of him.

Hottentot posing.

Hottentot sitting in the
helicopter.

Marlee on the
dreaded Sundowner!

Marlee put a western
saddle on Buckshot.
This was not a
successful project!

him as he swam towards them. Sounded like a pretty tall order for a dog to me, but everyone else present nodded profoundly, a sage expression blanketing the group. So I kept quiet and waited.

Prince certainly had retrieving in his blood. I could see he was alert and full of anticipation, a slight tremor passing through him, the same effect that driving into the icecream parlour produced. The boat was in position, Glen gave a shout and the first duck was thrown out of the boat; it arced in the air then hit the water with a plop.

Glen, with arm alongside Prince's head, and finger pointing to the duck, said one word as the duck hit the water, 'Mark!' This was repeated quickly for the next two ducks.

Then he said loudly, 'Back!' On the word 'Back', Prince was supposed to plunge into the icy waters, swim quickly to the duck furthest downstream and then retrieve the other two and come back to us.

The command had been given, all eyes were on Prince, everyone awaited action. Prince surveyed the scene, saw the ducks floating down the river towards us, and instead of swimming out to intercept, he ran up to the wharf, ran the full length of it, did a beautiful swallow dive off the end, then paddled slowly out to wait for the first duck. A few more strokes and the second and third ducks floated to him. He swam back to shore and put the ducks at the trainer's feet.

'Oh what a clever dog!' squealed the children and I.

All the experts were silent.

'He was not supposed to use the wharf', was Glen's solemn statement. I couldn't believe they were disappointed with the performance, but they were. He would be disqualified in a trial, they all said. Not done in trial circles, they said. Well, I told them I thought Prince was extra-smart to work out he could save a lot of swimming by using the wharf, and if a judge would disqualify that type of smart thinking, then

Prince would not be going in any trials. And despite the trainer's many requests for me to let him compete, with statements like 'it would be safe as there are no wharfs at this particular place', he didn't change my mind. I never did relent: Prince was our family dog and we wanted him home with us, not travelling around the country on the show and trial circuit. So we turned his back on fame, kept him at home to play with the children, pull the little red wagon, to guard us when Charlie was not there, and when he was, and to eat icecream on the way home from school.

Prince seemed very happy with this decision, but his trainer was devastated. He told me many times he was convinced Prince could win American Supreme Champion if I would only let him go on one circuit of America, the circuit that was the lead-up to the biggest dog show of all, in New York. When I discovered Prince would be away from home for months, I said no. He already was champion to us and we didn't need a cup to prove it. I didn't like duck hunting either, it was too cruel for me, and the discomfort of sitting in a cold, watery duck blind, at dawn and for hours on end, certainly wasn't my idea of fun. It was enough to see the look on Prince's face when Charlie said, 'Come on, old boy; let's go duck hunting.' The expression said it all.

I told Charlie if he wanted to eat the ducks, he could swim for them himself, or shoot them over dry land, but Prince didn't have to worry about facing this misery all winter. This was Charlie's first duck shooting since he was a young boy; he remembered his experiences of childhood hunting as misty and exciting. Fortunately, forty full years later, the cold stark boring reality hit home with force. So even though the duck hunting group invited Charlie many times, he always had some excuse why he couldn't make it after that first time.

They all returned home that first day with tales of the great feats, when one look at Prince showed who had done all the work. The poor dog was exhausted; I found out he was the only dog, and was retrieving for five men. Prince's fame spread and everyone invited Charlie to join them, and 'bring your dog' was the very specific request.

When Charlie declined with an invented excuse, I knew it was because of his personal comfort; then the other hunters asked could they borrow his dog, and he said yes! We had very heated arguments about these other men expecting to take Prince whenever they pleased, and I told him to call back and say they could not have my dog, ever. He said he couldn't go back on his word. That didn't bother me in the least; I voluntereed to go back on his word! I called the leader of the pack and told him that they could not have Prince on loan for hunting. In an extremely imperialistic tone he informed me he had already discussed this matter with my husband, and he went on to say he would pick up the dog at the arranged time. In an equally imperialistic tone, I replied, 'Oh no you won't; the dog is mine and I am telling you clearly you are not taking my dog hunting. Don't bother dropping by because the dog won't be here!' and slammed the phone down. Prince didn't go hunting that Sunday, or any other day.

Didn't that spread around the country like wildfire! I was given another talking-to regarding my behaviour as a wife. I cut the session short, saying I wasn't about to conform with the county's idea of how I should perform. Putting up with Charlie was about as far as I was prepared to go. And so widened the gap with my mother-in-law as her disapproval of me mounted.

But I was forming a nice group of friends, and apart from the regulation Sunday church, family lunch afterwards, and a few afternoon teas per week, we didn't see much of each other. During these meetings we would maintain a nice level of civil exchange of pleasantries. Although we didn't really get along, the times I enjoyed enormously were when she told stories of the past. Mrs Henderson was the great historian of the family, and devoted a good part of her time to patiently telling everyone the family history so it could be passed on. She was so passionate about this, she was even willing to tell *me*, and I was very interested. I do regret not having spent a lot more time with her to listen to the history, because now I have lost Charlie, there are thousands of questions that will never be answered.

Some of the stories about Charlie's grandmother he told me. Mrs Henderson was strictly only interested in the serious facts, nothing but the facts. But my favourite story was one Charlie loved to tell about his grandma's driver, Sam.

When he drove her to town, in those days in a horse-drawn carriage, they always chatted along the way. 'Sam, I hear you're steppin' out with the kitchen maid, Mary Lou.'

'No um.'

'Now, Sam, I hear you fixin' to get married.'

'No um, I bin married twice and single once, and there ain't no comparison!'

Sam must have been quite a character and Charlie's very, very favourite story could never be told in his mother's presence. Charlie must have told it thousands of times. Sam was returning from fishing at the end of the day with one of the other pretty maids, when one of the men called out, 'Get any?'

Sam replied, 'Yes sir-ree indeedy, an' fish too!'

Accents change drastically from state to state in America; I was just getting to the stage where I could understand the eastern 'Shore' accent when we moved to New York to live for six months. I had to start all over again, listening carefully so as to understand, and speaking slowly so I could be understood. Whenever I needed to buy something, and asked anyone where I should go, the answer was always the same, Macey's. I have never seen such a massive store. It was so big it had people standing throughout the store wearing badges, saying, 'information'. I headed for one of these women and asked what floor for bath mats (pronounced with the English *ar* sound).

The woman looked at me and said, 'Warrrt der you waant?' in a very drawn-out nasal Bronx accent.

I tried to enunciate 'bath' as clearly as possible, it sounded normal to me, but a blank expression just stayed on the ebony face.

'Nar-r-r, ma'am, we don't hav 'em.' And to emphasise this point, she pursed her lips, shook her head while uttering, 'Uh hum' repeatedly.

I wasn't giving up that easily, so I tried again: 'Shower.'

Immediate recognition registered on her face. 'Yes um.'

I repeated and added more: 'Shower-floor-mat, bath-mat.'

The comprehension complete, her face lit up. 'Oh, you wan' a ba-a-a-a-th mat!' The word came out like a sheep stuck on 'baa'.

'Right, I want a ba-a-a-th mat,' copying as best as I could.

'Basement, thank you,' she said in clipped Bronx, and then turned efficiently to the next lost shopper. I walked away, hoping the shopper could speak American.

Time passed quickly in New York and I found living there very educational. I had no desire to live there on a permanent basis, but I did enjoy our short stay. Of course, Prince came along; we all lived in a four-storey brownstone, with an attic with a skylight and, much to the children's delight, a trampoline in the attic. Apart from worrying they would bound right through the skylight and end up on the street below, the trampoline made life easy for me.

There was nowhere outside for them to play; the courtyard was so small you couldn't swing a cat. Running around it a few thousand times a day didn't even wind the girls, and the weather didn't add to the courtyard's attractiveness. So the girls spent most of their time in the attic. The six months stay in New York had us all decidedly fitter from walking up and down stairs all day. The children were amazing: they could go from the kitchen on the lower ground floor to the trampoline in the attic without a rest, and not be out of breath.

They got their sun in the early morning, lying on the trampoline and sunbaking as the sun passed over the skylight. Many a time I would find the two girls with Prince between them on his back and all legs in the air, all of them sound asleep. Other times they'd be just chatting with him, and listening as if he was about to give his opinion.

So we went back to the farm considerably healthier than when we left. Prince was very pleased to be out in the fields again, he was tiring of getting his exercise on the flights of stairs, about the only place in New York where he could extend himself. He spent the whole day rushing between me on the ground floor or the lower ground in the kitchen, and the children in the attic, with messages tucked in his collar.

But the fact was, we were all happier back in Maryland.

We were only home a few weeks when I received a phone call from a friend who was working as a receptionist for our vet. She wanted me to take home a dog that had been sent in to be put down. He was a short-haired English Pointer, had a pedigree a mile long and was, she said, a wonderful dog. The owners were putting the dog down because his bottom teeth were crooked! Apparently they showed dogs.

'It just isn't fair, he's a beautiful dog, and you have all that space out there, please take him,' she pleaded.

Charlie wasn't too pleased, but now we had two dogs. Prince didn't seem to mind; he took one look at the simpering dog, decided he wasn't any threat to his standing and accepted him on the spot. I called him 'Difficult' because he was just that. The dog had spent its life in a cage or in the show ring. He wouldn't walk properly, he did the 'show spring' as we called it, bounding along in a carefree manner, looking in the direction of the centre of the ring to impress the judges. As a result, in the house he continually ran into walls and furniture because he was always looking sideways. The poor thing was a nervous wreck; if you said 'no' to him or anything above a whisper, he wet himself on the spot. When you gave him food he growled the whole time as he devoured the contents of the bowl. It was worse than training a puppy because I had to untrain all his bad habits before I could start teaching him the basics. And there were plenty of bad habits!

Prince wasn't any help in the training. At first, if Difficult stepped out of line, Prince growled a warning; this would cause Difficult to immediately wet on the floor, and then collapse in a heap into the puddle. He had lots of baths the first few months. I gradually taught him to walk slowly, and when he realised he got a good amount of food daily the growling over his bowl stopped; he watched and copied Prince's dignified eating habits. After he settled down and knew he was on a good wicket, every time he was in doubt he just watched Prince. So before long he started to act more like a normal dog. He was a long way from perfect, but we had the eating and the wetting under control, and as winter was approaching both Difficult and I were pleased about that. He still couldn't run without falling over his feet and ending up in a heap. If he got too excited he couldn't control himself and would knock the children over, so he still had a long way to go.

When the children went exploring in the little red wagon, Difficult tagged along and regularly got lost. A search party wouldn't take long to find him. If you stood still you could hear this terrible mournful howl; by following the howl you would find Difficult under a tree rolled in a tight ball, terrified and shivering.

I am sure animals know if they don't fit in with certain people. We took care of Difficult and gave him food and shelter, but he wasn't our kind of dog. This became very clear to me when the new Shore farmer arrived at the front door, introduced himself, and said he would be ploughing the fields on Rigby's Marsh that year, so we would be seeing him from time to time during the season. I invited him in and we were sitting talking and drinking a cup of tea, when the children, Prince and Difficult exploded in the kitchen door. The farmer's eyes landed on Difficult picking himself up off the floor where he had landed in a heap after colliding with Alan's chair.

One look at Difficult finally standing in all his glory and it was love at first sight, 'What a beautiful dog!'

Prince, used to compliments, drew himself to his full height waiting to be patted, and all our eyes were on Prince, including Difficult's, confirming this statement, when Alan's hand went out and patted Difficult. Difficult got such a fright, he yelped, jumped backwards, almost knocking himself out on the fridge and once again ended up in a heap on the floor. Painfully he rose to his feet as Alan helped him, Difficult all the time looking up with a quizzical expression. He liked Difficult! I couldn't believe my eyes, and watched delightedly as he spoke soothing words and the heap on the floor materialised into a dog again.

'Would you like him?' I asked anxiously.

Alan said he would love to have him, but a dog like Difficult was worth a thousand dollars and he couldn't afford money like that. He ran his hand lovingly over Difficult again, and this time the dog seemed to transform under Alan's touch.

'I would venture to say, this dog would have some of the best breeding blood in the country. He would have to be one of the best short-haired English Pointers I have seen. I love this type of dog, have studied them for years.' Difficult could obviously feel the love coming through the hand gently stroking him, because he was looking lovingly into Alan's eyes.

'He's yours,' I said triumphantly, happy I had stumbled on the perfect match of man and dog. 'We didn't pay for him, only saved him from being put down. If you look after him and give him a good home, he's yours.'

The change in that dog over the next few months was miraculous. He gained confidence, became the very best in the county at bird hunting, on land, that is—the mind boggles to think of Difficult in the water. Alan and Difficult wandered the woods, blissfully happy; it was a partnership made in heaven. Alan asked me rather nervously a few months later if I'd mind very much if he changed the dog's name. He had trouble explaining it at his gun club, where Difficult was becoming the talk of all the members. I told him of course he could name him; Difficult now belonged to him and I would put it in writing if he wished. He went away a very happy man with an extra-happy newly named hound at his side. So

Difficult was renamed, but he was always Difficult to me, although I never called him by that name again.

The girls settled back into the local school. Marlee stomped in the door one day and told me she wanted to punch out a boy. I said to just calm down and tell me why. This boy sat behind her in the school bus and yanked at her plaits; she had asked him to stop but he just kept doing it.

'Can I punch him out, please, Mum?' I told her to warn him to stop and say if he didn't he would be in trouble. She bounded off to school the next day, hoping to get her plaits pulled.

She burst through the door in the afternoon. 'He did it again, Mum, he did it; can I punch him out?'

I told her to give him one more warning.

'One more! Can't I punch him out tomorrow?'

I told her no, if he pulled her plaits again that was the very last time.

'*Then* can I punch him out?'

'Yes.'

'Oh, boy!' She came home next day actually glad he had pulled her plaits.

The following day she came into the house with a look of sheer bliss on her face. It was very obvious she had punched him out! I asked her could she truthfully say she didn't provoke this plait-pulling. 'No way,' was her reply. He started pulling Bonnie's plaits and so Marlee stepped in to protect her little sister and he started pulling her plaits. So I felt satisfied the boy deserved getting 'punched out', but I didn't realise just how hard my little eight-year-old could punch.

I received a phone call not long after Marlee arrived home from school. One very irate mother was screaming down the phone line about what my son Murray had done to her son. What a vicious unprovoked attack my son had made on her son. Her son had done nothing to my son and my son had punched her son in the teeth and his two front teeth were loose and bleeding. She was going to sue me, she was going to send me the orthodontist's bill. What wasn't she going to do! She didn't draw breath for at least five minutes. When she finally finished, she asked me what I had to say about all that.

I replied, 'Well I suppose the first thing I would have to say is my son is a girl.'

'What?' was screamed at me.

I was about to continue, to say her son had been pulling my daughter's plaits for weeks and had been warned he would be punched if he didn't stop, but she slammed the phone down in my ear.

I could almost feel the boy on the other end of the phone, shrinking away as she screamed, 'A girl!' and smashed the phone into its holder. I almost felt sorry for him.

Many problems were surfacing, in our lives in America and were becoming more and more difficult to handle. So when a letter arrived from Australia telling Charlie there was a cattle recession in the north of Australia and not to expect any more money from cattle sales, because there wasn't even enough money to run the station, we had to make a few decisions. Charlie's affairs which had brought our marriage close to break-up, along with other problems, were the reasons why we packed up and went back to the Outback. As much as I dreaded going back to the station, I wanted to leave America, and yet I didn't. I wanted to leave, I think, because Charlie had too much opportunity to meet too many women with too much time on their hands. But I would have liked to stay for my lifestyle. However, I really didn't have to make a decision between America and the station. With no more money coming from the station, and Charlie doing a lot in Washington, or so he said, but for no wages, we had no choice but to go back.

The really sad part of the whole complicated mess was, we had to leave Prince. I wrestled with this for a long time. It required one year's quarantine time, via England, to bring an animal into Australia. I couldn't bear to put Prince through that. I had to convince myself of this. I dearly wanted to take him to Australia, but after his life as so much a part of the family, I knew twelve months locked up away from us would break his heart. There had been several cases of robbery in the district, and Mrs Henderson, in her late seventies, lived alone in that big house with a cook the same age. So we gave Prince to her as a guard dog.

I had Charlie take him over to Lloyds Landing, after we said our goodbyes at Rigby's Marsh. When I gave him his final hug, and told him to be a good boy and do a good job guarding Mrs Henderson, there were tears in his eyes. He sat on the front seat of the car next to Charlie and watched us as long as he could. At the bottom of the lawn, the road turned left and I saw Prince make that familiar movement I loved so much, for that last time. Whenever you drove around a corner too fast, he would lift up his left paw, brace himself by putting it on the door just behind the window handle, and hold it there until the car was around the corner; then he would put his foot back on the seat and give you a glancing look that clearly said, 'Too fast!'

He put his foot back on the seat and the head turned towards us again. We could see him watching until the car went out of sight.

I did worry that because Mrs Henderson didn't like me she might not treat Prince kindly, but I should not have wasted a moment's thought. Prince won her heart completely. Over the years he had regularly visited Lloyds Landing with us. When the children stayed with their grandmother, so did Prince. So he knew the run of things and the house rules. When staying for the weekend he would be greeted with, 'Don't you think you can come into this house, young man; a dog's place is outside' by Mrs Henderson or her cook, Nora. Prince would dutifully curl up on a rug out on the closed-in porch in the winter, or on the open porch in the summer. So he was not going somewhere strange; he knew the fields and the woods, the outside of the house and the people. But he sooned charmed Mrs Henderson and Nora. It was no time at all before his rug came inside the kitchen door in the winter, because it was a bit cold. Then it also stayed there in the summer. Then he started watching TV with Mrs Henderson at night in front of the log fire in the winter, then in the summer he watched TV in the air-conditioning.

His trainer, Glen, wrote to me and asked if he could take him on the circuit for the lead-up to the 'big daddy of them all', the National Dog Show in New York. I told him Prince was Mrs Henderson's dog now, so he would have to talk to her. Charlie called her and said Prince was there to guard her and that was the most important thing to consider, and she agreed he did a fine job. But Glen was a great persuader, and Prince took to the road on the show and trial circuit for that season, and ended up Supreme Champion of the National Dog Show in New York, 'Best Breed', 'Best Dog of the Country'! Glen sent me the citation and the ribbon, and Prince London of Lloyds was engraved on the massive cup which he could keep for a year. Of course we always knew he was the best, but now it was engraved on a cup. Prince then stayed home and carried out his job of guarding the treasures of Lloyds Landing and did a superb job.

He died around the age of fourteen, only six months before I took Bonnie back to Maryland for a visit in 1979. I was so looking forward to seeing him again, but it was not to be. The last photo Mrs Henderson sent me was of Prince having his afternoon nap in the air-conditioned TV room, on a sheet on the antique couch! Not bad from the beginning of, 'And don't think you can come in this house, young man; a dog's place is outside.'

7

UNCLE DICK'S LOVE LIFE

 It was not long after our return to Australia that Dick entered our lives, when Charlie hired him as a mechanic. Because the children were so young they called him Uncle Dick, the name stayed and it was not long before everyone called him Uncle Dick.

I have already written about some of Dick's outrageous behaviour, but regularly I keep remembering more stories. Uncle Dick continued his regular shenanigans and landed in some sort of strife regularly because of his drinking. He had again escaped to town and was on a bender. This time he escaped on the fuel truck. As soon as he saw a new driver, he knew he could get to town. All the regular fuel truck drivers knew not to bring in alcohol for Dick, or give him a ride off the station. It was an exceptionally busy day for me, so the fuel truck driver drove straight past the house unnoticed, and down to the workshop. Dick told the new driver *he* would sign all the documents, and then said he was off to town so he would hitch a ride back with him. He got into the cabin and away they drove together.

Charlie and the girls were out mustering cattle; I was cooking or running back and forth to the office, so no-one even knew Dick had gone until Charlie, returning from the paddock, rode up to the workshop to talk to him. He found the fuel dockets in the middle of the workbench held securely in place by a hefty bearing. Charlie just knew, without looking futher, that Dick was gone again. We tracked him down in Kununurra, only to find he'd left on the morning bus for Darwin. It was hard enough to find him in Kununurra, but Darwin was at least a week's long search. So we just had to wait until he could no longer cadge loans. Friends would eventually call and ask us to come and take him home, once he had well and truly outworn his welcome.

He had been gone a few weeks when I received a call. A woman was desperately trying to speak with a plum in her mouth—that's how it sounded, as if she actually had a real plum in her mouth, or she was drunk, but it was six o'clock in the morning.

The story unfolded. She had met Dick in the bar of one of the very seedy hotels in Darwin. He offered to buy her a drink; she told me she thought he was quite a gentleman (maybe she *was* drunk at six o'clock); they had more than one drink (now why didn't that surprise me?). Thank heavens I was spared the details of the rest of the night after they finished four hours of drinking, taking more drink back to a motel room, hers. Oh, she was quite willing to continue in detail, but I told her no need, she could leave it up to my imagination. She had taken twenty minutes telling about the drinks in the bar, the first night, and we still had a few weeks to go. I interrupted to ask why she had called me. It was another ten minutes before I was asked to guarantee Dick's reliability. Dick's reliability in Darwin with a pub nearly every mile! I said politely, No, not while he was off the station, and again maybe she should tell me why she was actually calling. Dick was involved: there had to be a story. He had been in town a few weeks: there had to be *lots* of stories. She took a deep breath and started again. I got into a comfortable position, knowing full well it would be long and complicated as all Dick's stories were.

It seems somewhere during the first night of drinking, Dick had offered to drive her car to Katherine because she had a broken ankle, in plaster, and couldn't drive. The plan was he would take the car the next day. She was to leave the following day, by bus. Before I asked the inevitable question, why didn't she go in the car with him, she said she had to stay in Darwin to see the doctor.

'Just a minute,' I interrupted. 'You gave your car to a complete stranger you were having a few drinks with in a pub?'

Then the big bombshell was dropped. She informed me quite indignantly that it was only after he proposed that she agreed to let him have the car.

I wasn't capable of words by this stage, not that it mattered, or she noticed; she was well and truly wound up by this time and on she ploughed. She was calling because Dick had taken the car and that was weeks ago. He never turned up in Katherine and she was tired of waiting for the car, and to get married. Apparently that was to happen in Katherine after she arrived in the bus. She told me she was now going to call the police and report the car stolen and give the police Dick's name as the thief and also file charges against him for jilting her. I felt I was in a time warp, and had landed in the 1930s. I could see our mechanic in jail for the next ten years on theft at least! I wasn't too sure what term of incarceration was current for jilting a fiancée after a proposal in a bar four hours after meeting!

I talked her out of calling the police and said I was sure Dick would turn up soon. Even though he was unreliable when drinking, he definitely would not steal her car... I hoped.

'Give me a few days to find him.'

'And the wedding?' came the tense question.

I told her I would find the car, and Dick. She could ask him that question, not me; I only employed him. I finally ended the conversation and sat staring at the phone, wondering what to do.

The next day I called every possible person in Darwin; it seemed Dick had disappeared off the face of the earth. Charlie said he thought he might be dead. My opinion was that Dick woke up the next morning, found himself in bed with a strange woman, remembered he had proposed, and did a bunk. Charlie didn't reply to this idea, but his head was nodding in agreement. Two days later, near the end of the week, I still wasn't any closer to finding Dick. I had spent hours persuading the prospective bride not to lay charges against her prospective groom at least until the following Monday. I assured her something would materialise over the weekend, hopefully Dick.

I answered the phone on Saturday morning and there he was croaking on the other end of the line. He sounded dreadful, on his last legs. He opened with, 'I've got a few problems, Mother.'

I told him I already knew them. But little did I know. His story left out the four hours drinking and the night that followed and the proposal. He was just driving the car to Katherine for a 'damsel in distress' said Sir Galahad. He just happened to take a few mates with him and was dropping them off at one of the stations a few hundred miles down the track. The 'bomb', as he described his fiancée's car, had literally blown up and so he and his mates repaired it at the station. Dick stayed on to do some repair work (and drink endless cartons of beer, and anything else he could get his hands on). He then started out again for Katherine, with a few more newly acquired mates; along the highway he was stopped by a police car. They were very obviously under the weather, and still drinking from a carton in the car...So

Dick was booked for driving under the influence. The next problem arose when he was asked for his licence; he hadn't had a licence for fifteen years... so Dick was booked for driving without a licence. He then told the officer he had to deliver the car because the woman was waiting for it in Katherine and he was a bit late!

The officer said, No way, Dick punched him... so Dick was booked for assaulting an officer. Dick told him what he thought of him... so Dick was booked for abusive language. When the officer told Dick he had to go with him back to Darwin, Dick told him to 'piss off' and walked away... so Dick was booked for resisting arrest!

He was calling me from jail. He needed help; his fines totalled nearly a grand and he was a bit short! Like a grand! There was also the possibility of a jail term.

I told him there was also the possibility of car theft and charges for jilting his fiancée. All I heard was a croak.

I wrote a letter to the judge, telling him we really needed our mechanic, and that it was better to send him back out to the station where we could keep him out of trouble, than to have him in jail at taxpayers' cost. I would pay the fines, and take the money out of his wages, weekly. The judge agreed. When Charlie picked Dick up the next day, the police wanted to know if we ever got any work out of him, and more importantly, why would we even put up with such a person and take him back willingly.

The car was sent down to Katherine by truck at Dick's expense, and when he was sufficiently recovered from his hangover, I put him on the phone to talk to his fiancée. Somehow he talked her out of marriage, without her charging him. After a few more shaky days, he settled back into station routine and started working... until the next time. By the time all the borrowings, charges and expenses were finally tallied, Uncle Dick's trip to town had put him back a few thousand dollars, and he didn't have a thing to show for it except a sore head and the big debt.

Dick kept 'breaking out', despite the judge's order to stay on the property for six months, not to go to town. Dick went to town; he just made sure he didn't end up drunk in Darwin. He 'broke out' on a regular basis every year until his holidays were due.

Dick was very grandiose when it came to his holidays; they were always planned on an ambitious and magnificent scale. That year he was planning to travel right around Australia, no less. The yearly plan (it usually took a year to perfect it) was what kept him going. I was privy to the master plan because months ahead of departure I had to arrange with the bank to have a certain amount of money transferred to a branch in each town he planned to visit. This was the only way Dick could be assured of having a holiday, at least one that closely resembled his wishes when sober.

Once he started drinking he would either lose or give away all his money in the first drinking hotel. That usually was the closest pub once he got off the station. Many a time he only made it one hundred kilometres down the road to Timber Creek; then after he had been slumped over drunk, in the corner of the bar, leaning up against the wall for a week, the owner would ring the station and ask us to come and get him. Or if the police were driving our way, they would just bring him back.

At the beginning of each year he would give me a travel plan, which usually had him flying everywhere. But the debts he accumulated on his regular 'break-outs' gradually eliminated air travel. So I would start on the elaborate schedule, and cut out about half the towns, knowing it was an unrealistic schedule even for a sober person. Then the plan would be reduced to a few major cities where he wanted to visit family and a few old mates in towns close by. Many a year, after I'd spent weeks arranging the bookings, transferring funds to banks around the country, he would only get as far as Kununurra, one hundred and thirty kilometres west, and never move out of the pub. The next year it would be Timber Creek, one hundred kilometres to the east, for variety. A few years ago he did make it south, but only to one capital, and at the very best, a few towns.

I must hold the record for talking long-distance to bank managers. A bank on Dick's itinerary would have instructions to give him funds of three hundred dollars, but Dick would tell them to change it to three thousand. I would receive a phone call for authorisation to increase the amount. When that failed, *he* would call. When drunk, Dick assumed he could charm the leg off an iron pot, and nothing could convince him he was wrong. So he would charm away for ten minutes (he was very repetitious), then he'd usually end with, 'So what do you think, Mother?' Quite confident I had swallowed the ridiculous yarn he was spinning.

He would receive a simple 'No.'

Dick's other gem was, 'Time is of the essence.'

This was always a dead giveaway. He would try so hard to disguise his voice so he didn't sound drunk, and sometimes he'd almost succeed, and I would think he was sober, then in would creep that phrase.

But one particular year he was determined to follow his schedule. He had had a relatively good year with only a few escapes to town, so he had enough money to fly south. This at least ensured, if the flight was direct, that he would reach his first destination. The trouble he had with travelling by bus was that after the fourth stop he was so drunk he couldn't walk, let alone find the bus. If he was lucky and stumbled upon it, the driver refused to take him because of his condition. Dick has been known to take four and a half weeks to make a three-day bus trip.

But this particular year we put him on a direct flight to Perth and he made it. What happened after that, no-one really knows, not even Dick. I had many phone calls from assorted types of people, from bank managers to desperate men out of work with starving families, to whom Dick was lending money to buy food for their starving kids. Other guys needing money for an operation for their wife, mother, kid. A few times he even talked a woman into calling: the money was for *her* desperate operation. He would bombard me for days with these stories, the same each year, all by reverse charge, until even in his drunken stupor he realised he was not going to get extra money. Then he'd stop calling; we would have no idea where he was for, sometimes weeks, sometimes months. Normally it would only be weeks before we'd get a strange or desperate call, reverse charge.

'Dick, speak up, I can't hear you!' It was three o'clock in the morning on this occasion.

'I can't, they'll hear me,' he whispered.

'Who will?'

'The mafia!'

'The mafia?' I screeched.

'Shush, they'll hear you,' he whispered in a screeching, strained voice.

'Dick, where are you?'

'I don't know.'

'Well, ask someone!'

'I can't leave my room. They are waiting for me outside the door,' he whispered desperately.

'Dick, if the mafia wanted to get you, a wooden door wouldn't stop them.'

I could hear the fear in his voice, he was terrified, and there was no way he was going to leave the room. I told him to give me the number of the hotel, to look on the telephone; then I would call the police in whatever town he was in and they would come and take the mafia away from his door.

No, there was an easier way, he said. He only had to pay them eight hundred dollars and they would go away! He must have met some real sharpies, this was definitely new material.

I went along with the plot: 'But how can I send you money if you don't know where you are?'

The name of the hotel, the manager's name, and the town were given to me in a flash; I hung up.

Two minutes later the phone rang again; I took the receiver off the hook and went back to bed.

The next morning I called the manager of the hotel in Broome. Yes, Dick had been in the bar daily; no, he did not have a room, he couldn't afford to pay the bond required (some hotel!). The manager continued, saying Dick was drinking at the bar with anyone who would buy him a drink, and a lot of unsavoury characters who were trying to out-cadge Dick.

When I said Dick had called me from his room, the manager laughed. 'The rooms in this hotel don't have phones, they're lucky to have beds.' He promised to call me back when Dick arrived for his day of drinking.

I called the local police and explained the situation. Told them I would arrange a plane ticket and could they put him in the cooler that night and put him on the plane the next day. This was the only way we could get him sober enough for the airlines to accept him. The police were very helpful and agreed; it meant one less drunk in town for them. We picked him up in Kununurra and he was safely home again

. . . until the next time. It took him almost a week to get over that drinking spree. He had the shakes so badly that I had to feed him because he couldn't hold a fork without doing damage to his face, and a cup of coffee would spill all over the table before it reached his mouth.

Only a few months later, Dick was out again, this time in Darwin. Charlie finally found him. It had been a quiet visit, just the regular stack of charges and a list of loans from 'friends'; when the borrowing ran out, he lost himself in an Aboriginal camp for a few weeks. I was in town with Charlie and the children, so we all had to come home in the plane together.

Charlie had told Dick to wash and clean himself up. He arrived at the plane in clean clothes, wrinkled but clean, and he had washed. But washing couldn't eliminate the smell of whatever he had been drinking, anything from metho to after-shave to cheap plonk, to homemade whatever. This was seeping out his pores as perspiration; the smell was amazing and sickening. He couldn't shave for fear of cutting his throat, so he had a very untidy beard and he had lost his false teeth, again. All in all he was his usual shocking self, looking the same as he always did after a bender. I couldn't stand Dick drunk, or in this sobering-up condition, and he knew it, so he kept his distance until he finally climbed into the plane with us. Charlie had told him to help load the stores into the back of the plane, our Beaver de Havilland, Bertha.

We were also taking with us a quiet young boy who was considering going into the priesthood. One of the Brothers in the Darwin office of the Catholic missions had asked

Charlie could he bring him to Bullo for a few weeks. He had his reservations about whether the boy was ready for priesthood but, like everyone else, thought that if he could survive a few weeks on Bullo under Charlie's command, he would be able to handle anything. He was sitting next to me; Charlie had Dick next to him in the front, the children were in the back with the stores. Before we got into the plane, I caught a whiff of Dick and smelt rum very strongly. Charlie said No way. I insisted I could smell rum; then Charlie's face fell, and he walked to the cargo door to look for the carton of his favourite rum that he had just purchased. He found one bottle almost empty; Dick had consumed it in the few minutes while loading the plane. We both looked at him. He looked harmless enough, but was definitely swaying in the wind. Charlie said it would be all right, he would probably sleep all the way home, but he would make sure Dick was strapped in tightly or he might open the door in flight and fall out.

So with everyone in position, Charlie taxied out for takeoff. He received clearance from the tower and was doing the run-up check, when Dick announced he was not going to Bullo, he wanted to go back to the pub for another drink. Charlie told him to shut up. Our poor guest by this time was wide-eyed, listening to Dick and Charlie abuse each other. I explained to him Dick was drunk, but was a much nicer person when sober... he'd see in a few days time.

Charlie started down the runway; the plane's engine roared as she lifted gracefully despite the full load. Charlie was fully occupied flying the plane during the crucial period when it was only about twenty-five feet off the ground. Suddenly, right out of a sleepy stupor, Dick latched onto Charlie's throat with both hands and started choking him. Charlie had his hands full, keeping the plane straight and level while he pushed Dick away with his elbow. I heard an urgent command uttered in a strange, constricted, rough, husky whisper, 'Get the idiot off me, we'll crash!'

The plane dipped one wing violently every time Charlie tried to fend Dick off with his elbow. We were no longer over the tarmac, but veering wildly sideways as Charlie struggled desperately with the controls in an effort to keep the plane level. Trying to get as much space as he could between the plane and the ground, and still keep climbing without stalling the engine, Charlie took quick swipes at Dick whenever he could, but then had to grab the controls again as the plane lurched in another direction. Dick was swinging his arms and grabbing for Charlie's throat with the ferocity of a windmill out of control in a high wind.

I was transfixed, watching the scene played out in front of me, eyes darting from the unbelievable happening in the plane, to the trees, houses, roadways and telegraph poles that kept rushing up at us every now and then, too close for comfort. Landing was now out of the question because we were still veering and dipping sideways and had long since run out of landing strip.

All these events happened within seconds, but seemed like an eternity. Charlie fought Dick and the controls, gasped for air whenever he got the chance, and resisted blacking out. The next gasping request had such urgency, it jolted me into action. 'Sara, quickly!'

I undid my seat belt, lurched forward and put an arm around Dick's neck. I was fully committed now; I had no seat belt, so if we crashed, I was history. I was also in quite a state of panic by this stage, my heart pounded and my pulse was racing. The adrenalin release must have been 'all floodgates open'; heaven knows how much pressure I was exerting on poor old Dick's neck, but it must have been superhuman because his eyes nearly shot out of his head. He let go of Charlie's neck instantly, and his hands, in a frantic fumble, shot to his neck and my arm.

It seemed forever; my back was aching, my arm was cramping, but I still held Dick immobilised in an arm lock. My eyes were on Charlie, watching as he gained control of his breathing and Bertha settled down to a calm climbing pattern.

'Darwin Control, to Echo-Papa-X-ray,' shouted the radio.

But Charlie ignored Darwin Control as he coaxed the plane slowly higher, moving and changing controls until he was satisfied the plane was performing at maximum. After a deep breath of air, he glanced sidewards at Dick and said, 'Sara, you had better release your grip and give him some air, he's turning blue.'

My arm around poor old Dick's neck was still in a death-lock. I had quite forgotten Dick, so intent was I on Charlie's fight to bring the plane back under control. I looked at Dick and true, he was a terrible colour and his pleas for air were very feeble indeed. I let go and sprang back in horror.

But Charlie yelled, 'Don't let him go, for Christ's sake!'

I was shaking and near tears. Poor old Dick slumped into a heap up against the door, looking not even capable of blowing out a candle. I told Charlie I could not sit for two hours with my arm around Dick's neck, and besides he looked harmless now.

The words had barely left my lips when Dick came to life and grabbed, not Charlie's neck, but the controls!

Again we started swooping and weaving all over the sky as Charlie alternated between pushing Dick away and correcting the plane's crazy lurching. The control tower kept calling, 'Echo-Papa-X-ray report, Echo-Papa-X-ray report!' over and over without let-up. The cabin drowned in their repeated call as we careered all over the sky, with Charlie yelling above it for me to put an armlock on Dick again.

As the plane once more lurched in a downward, sideways

motion, I leapt forward and wrapped my arm around Dick's neck again. This time my strength was a result of pure anger: his stupid behaviour could kill everyone. As my forearm tightened over his Adam's apple, his hands left the controls. Charlie's next orders, still shouted over the control tower's unrelenting calls, were for me to get Dick out of the front seat. We argued at high volume over how I was supposed to achieve this; Charlie said he didn't care how, just get him away from the controls or the next time we might not be so lucky. He again had the plane flying normally and, ignoring my questions, answered the still-persistent Darwin Control. He told them everything was now in order, just had a minor problem for a few minutes. Minor!

He then smoothly launched into report procedure, altitude such and such, tracking Bullo River, etc, etc, and finished by saying he would phone in an Incident Report on the malfunction when he arrived at Bullo River, and would come into the briefing office tomorrow, then give his ETA Bullo. They weren't happy, but knew they wouldn't get any more out of Charlie on why his takeoff had not been by the book. He certainly couldn't blame the brakes, as he had for a lot of the unusual landings over the years. Never in a million years could they guess the reason for the takeoff they had just witnessed. I could just see it typed neatly in an incident report: 'Strangled by drunk on takeoff!'

Charlie had dealt with air control; we were climbing past eight hundred feeet, but we still had Dick sitting with vital controls only inches from his fingertips, not to mention Charlie's throat. Our poor young guest had himself jammed in the corner as far away from the action as posssible. When I asked him to help me drag Dick over the seat into the second row where we were sitting, I thought he was going to jump out the door. Somehow, with Charlie holding Dick's feet so he didn't kick any of the instruments or controls, and my firm hold still on his neck and with little help from our terrified guest, I dragged and shoved Dick, kicking and thrashing, away from the controls. I told the young boy to climb over into the front seat. I had to endure the smell of sour alcohol that was seeping out of Dick's every pore, right next to me, for the remaining hours of the flight, so I wanted as much space between us on the seat as possible.

By now my anger was bristling; if Dick even as much as moved a finger I screeched at him like a banshee. He slumped in the corner of the seat, as far from me as possible, very hesitant to move, as I bombarded him about his disgusting behaviour. I didn't draw breath until we landed at Bullo, by which time Dick was holding his head with his hands over his ears, and thankfully stumbled out of the plane, out of earshot.

The children took it all in their stride; to them it seemed an adventure. The entire journey they played games or did drawings except when there was action, and then three little faces up to nose-level, and six sets of fingers, would appear over the back of the seat, watching with interest. I often worried what effect this type of travel had on their young minds. But the moment the propeller had turned its last three hundred and sixty degree rotation, they were out of the plane, off at high speed for the horse paddock, and the next adventure.

Their mother, drained of all energy, headed for the kitchen and the next meal. Charlie was walking silently beside me, no doubt deep in thought, inventing the reason for his out-standingly unusual takeoff, when the sounds of Bertha's engine, spluttering and stailing, filled the air. We spun around and there was Dick trying to start the plane. Charlie sprinted back, threw the door open, dragged Dick out, and propelled him, arm up his back, to the house, where he locked him in one of the rooms to sleep off his drunken stupor.

When he woke the next morning, Dick said he didn't remember any of it; he was completely mystified as to how he got to Bullo, so he said. Knowing Dick, I suspect this was a convenient way to get out of apologising for his really disgraceful and unacceptable behaviour.

The young boy survived the flight, and his stay with us. When he returned to Darwin he told the Brothers he did not think he knew enough about life; he still wanted to enter the priesthood, but to make him a better priest he should first see a bit more of life. Bullo had made him realise that in order to help people deal with life, he needed to know what they are talking about.

The Brother asked Charlie what on earth had happened in the two weeks to bring about such a change. Charlie's only reply was, 'Where can I possibly begin?'

As you have probably gathered by now, Dick was one continuous story; events like these happened almost every week, whether on the station or away. I could probably write a whole book just on Dick's trips to town; on or off the station, he was a one-man disaster area.

The next Uncle Dick problem was on the station; the mustering camp was at Bull Creek, a good twenty-five miles or forty kilometres away, by a very treacherous and slow road through miles of sand. The children and I were in Darwin for two days. Dick was supposed to be sober and running the generators and the workshop. Charlie flew straight back to the station after dropping us in Darwin, to load meat for a delivery to Port Keats Mission. He arrived to find Dick had used bolt cutters to cut through the padlock on the liquor store room. He and a good percentage of the meatworks staff had consumed wine, beer, rum, vodka, scotch, tequila, right across the board. They had cleaned out the whole store room. What they hadn't consumed, Dick had hidden, for later. A complete and utter mess greeted Charlie when he arrived. Charlie had meat to deliver urgently, but he couldn't leave Dick at the homestead alone, even for the half day to fly me back. The best solution he could come up with was to take Dick out to the stock camp so they could take care of him.

All the four wheel drive vehicles were out at the camp and you could not get over that road in any of the vehicles left at the house, so the only other way was by horse. Charlie saddled up his horse and one for Dick, and tried to get him into the saddle. Dick kept getting on back to front and would end up facing the wrong way, or fall off. So Charlie tied him on, still back to front, and rode all the way out to Bull Creek with Dick bumping up and down in the saddle, shouting to Charlie to stop, laughing uproariously, and complaining all the way. Somewhere on the trip, while laughing or shouting or coughing, Dick lost his teeth, yet again. Charlie left him in the care of the head stockman at the camp and drove back in one of the Toyotas. He delivered the meat to Port Keats and came on to Darwin to pick me up, cutting short the visit. I had to return to the station to guard the house and liquor while Charlie delivered the rest of the meat orders.

He needn't have bothered; Dick was so saddle-sore he couldn't even sit for days. We didn't see him for three days and still he could only just hobble; even sober, Dick didn't ride.

Unfortunately, my prediction expressed over the last few years, of never seeing Uncle Dick again, came true. He died in the first week of September 1994, while I was in San Francisco speaking at a conference. And so I write these final words about someone who was so much a part of my life, and the developing years (and quite a lot of times the destruction, when he was on a drinking spree) of Bullo. I am sure he will end up in the same place as Charlie. So maybe, somewhere, they are sitting on a cloud, both laughing, and—more likely—arguing, over old times, drinking endless drinks. Even if they aren't in heaven, with an endless supply of drinks at their disposal and no work to do, they would think it was heaven! Wherever it is, how everyone else there will put up with both Charlie and Uncle Dick, I really don't know.

Goodbye, old mate...

8

FRUIT BAT AND CHARLIE

It was early morning, the sun had not yet appeared over the hills; everyone had departed in various directions for the day's work, although the din in the kitchen of a stock camp eating breakfast was still hanging in the air. I made myself a cup of coffee and sat in a cane chair on the front verandah, a favourite spot.

With feet resting on the stone table, I sipped the coffee, savouring my few minutes of peace and solitude, the only possible time I could relax before the bedlam of a normal day at Bullo started. My eyes wandered peacefully across the familiar landscape, while my mind frantically raced through the day's impossible agenda. The sun's first rays shot tiny shafts of red-gold light across the semi-dark valley, darting through the trees and around and over buildings. It was a vista of intangible beauty, witnessed just in those minutes before the sun broke free of the earth's bondage. That ethereal, spirit-like mist of first light revealing a grazing horse, birds in flight, the red mountain range on the far side of the valley, was having a wonderful effect on my mood.

Soon the brilliant flashes of red reminded my racing brain of the heat of the fast-approaching day. Still, the desire to stay put for a few extra minutes was strong.

But gradually I realised something was amiss. My eyes went back slowly over the familiar landscape, looking for that 'something' out of place. A sick animal lying on the ground?... Or an animal limping? The eyes scanned again ...then stopped, lingered and waited for the brain to register. Yuk! A fruit bat hanging by one wing on the barbed wire fence.

I jumped up and thought, Now what? Everyone had gone; I was alone with the dogs until lunchtime, with a thousand and one things to do, and now a bat impaled on a barbed wire fence.

I hate bats, no, I am terrified of bats. Ever since my childhood and Saturday matinées about vampires, I have felt a complete repulsion for bats; I found them more frightening than the vampires. But there I was faced with a very large fruit bat hanging captive on barbed wire. I couldn't leave it there to die in the heat of the day. I put down my coffee and walked across the lawn.

The main joint of one wing was impaled on the prongs of the barb. In an effort to free itself, the bat had tried to fly and had wound its wing around the wire many times, so I couldn't see the barb prongs at all. In its struggle to get free the other wing was also caught, though not nearly as completely. The frightened eyes looked at me. I reached out to free the less tangled wing, to take pressure off the badly impaled one. The bat's head darted forward, teeth bared. I recoiled in horror, as all the vampire matinées flashed again before my eyes. After many, many words reassuring the bat that I was only trying to help, I approached again from the rear to free the wing. It twisted around and almost bit my hand; too close for comfort. Even though it was still early, the sun on my back had started trickles of sweat. I rushed back to the homestead and put on a pair of heavy gardening gloves and a large hat, then gingerly approached once more.

The bat kept biting the gloves as I worked on the wing. I started at the very tip of the wing, as the wide wingspan was caught in several places on the barbs. As I got closer to the body the bat attacked my glove repeatedly. I had to control a feeling of sheer panic as its teeth repeatedly dug into the thick suede material of the gloves, and I could feel the pressure on my fingers.

At last the wing was free, allowing the bat more freedom of movement. It immediately swung around and wrapped its feet around my arm. I let out a piercing scream and fell backwards over the dogs in my attempt to get away from those clammy miniature hands. When I had regained my composure I sat up and looked at the bat. It was hanging by one wing, attacking my glove viciously to counteract the pain it was feeling in the still-impaled wing. Now I only had one glove; attempts to retrieve the other almost had little teeth biting my fingers. And I had another major problem. To get it free I would have to unwind the bat around the fence wire. That meant holding the bat's body.

It was now quite hot, and sweat was dripping freely from my nose and elbows. If I didn't find a solution quickly, the bat wouldn't need rescuing. I remembered reading that if you wanted to handle a frightened or wild animal you should cover its eyes. Back to the house I raced, dogs at my heels, for a few large towels. We certainly used this method successfully with horses, so I was hoping for the same results with the bat.

I returned with the towels, lots of safety pins and a pair of pliers. It would be easier to free the wing if I cut the spikes off the barb, if I could find them. I wrapped the towel around the bat's body and a double layer around its head, and pinned everything securely in place. Then I quickly took the weight in my hand, as everything was now hanging on the injured wing joint.

Covering the eyes had a miraculous effect. The bat stayed completely still as I went about my task. Without the distractions of the pain-filled eyes and predatory teeth, I was able to study the wing closely for the first time. The joint seemed okay, certainly stretched to its limit, but not broken. I carefully rotated my towel-clad bundle around the wire. Even one rotation helped immensely. The joint now had some slack, the towel stopped wriggling and squeaking, and I could see the end of one of the barbs.

Carefully and gently pushing the tangled wing down the barb as far as I could, I snipped off the point. This allowed another rotation, and I moved my bundle once again around the fence wire. Sweat was running into my eyes at such a rate I had to blink rapidly to keep my vision clear—I had no free hands. My shirt was saturated, and sweat was running down my legs so fast that it was hard to move without slipping in my thongs. I worked as fast as possible, worried I might be suffocating the poor thing in the towels. I still could not see the ends of the other barbs. I marvelled at how many times the wing was wrapped around the wire, yet not broken. My back was aching as I stooped over the wire, left hand supporting the bundled bat while the right hand tried to free the wing.

Finally I decided there was only one thing left to do. The bat was caught on the wire a few feet from a picket with the longest expanse of wire, about eight feet to the next picket, on the right. Crouching low and still supporting my bundle, I cut the fence wire a few inches to the right of the wing. The taut wire made a loud twang and catapulted into a twisted heap near the far picket. I quickly snapped the wire on the other side of the wing and the short piece of wire just fell against the picket.

Carefully cradling the injured wing, I carried the very still bundle of towel and bat back to the welcome cool of the homestead. Took the extra towel from around the head, giving the poor creature some air, but left one towel in place; I still had to untangle and clean the wound, so I couldn't let the teeth free yet. With only a few inches of wire to contend with, I had the wing free in no time at all. I quickly washed the wound with antiseptic and the job was done.

What to do now? The poor thing would need rest; it could have been hanging there all night. I found a box with a lid, put in a dish of water and some cut-up apple, then lowered in the bundle of towels, undid the pins and peeled back the towel carefully. It did not look well: its little hands were tightly clenched, its eyes were closed and there was no movement. I closed the lid and left it in peace; I had done all I could. I put the box in a cool spot and went into the bathroom, stripped off all my sweat-dripping clothes and took a cold shower.

With clean clothes and washed hair I felt refreshed, so I again sat down to drink that quiet, first of the morning, cup of coffee. Only now it was mid-morning and I had done nothing except save a bat from dying, impaled on barbed wire. It still might die in the box, but even though that was my entire morning's effort, I felt the satisfaction of having accomplished something. Sitting with my feet up on the table, sipping coffee, I felt good inside and all my frantic worries had gone. By the time I organised myself and got through the basics, lunch would have to be cold meat and salad.

I checked the bat regularly; by the afternoon most of the apple was gone, so I dropped more in through the little peep-hole. I thought it best to put the bat back into its natural environment, so the next morning just before sunrise I opened the box and again carefully covered the bat with a towel, lifted it out of the box and carried it out to the nearest tree. I opened the towel and lifted the bundle up to a low branch, hoping the little feet would close over it. They did! Gradually

I moved my hands and the towel away, letting the bat take its own weight. It hung there upside down, eyes on me, no sign of teeth, and slowly adjusting its wings and flexing the injured joint carefully. It seemed to be doing very well. Then it decided the branch was too low and it started to crawl along to the tree trunk to climb higher. I held up the towel to catch it if it slipped.

The bat paused, looked at me again with eyes calm and free of pain, and then before I realised what was happening, one of the little black hand-like feet came out of the voluminous folds of wings, and with the gentleness of a flutter of silk, it was laid on my hand. It was the strangest moment. I didn't recoil in horror, but immediately realised I wasn't frightened; transfixed would be more like it. I had a clear sensation that something wonderful was happening.

The hand stayed there and I didn't move a muscle. Those amazingly soulful eyes looked into mine and I know they said 'thank you'. The little hand moved back and I could clearly see the claws extend, which were not visible seconds before, to grip the bark. I watched mesmerised as the bat climbed slowly up the trunk, favouring the injured wing. It reached a branch halfway up the tree, moved along to a position of its liking, and spread its amazing wings of skin. I still watched. The sun flooded the valley for a new day, and illuminated the fine network of blood vessels coursing through the wing. I could clearly see the congestion, an inflammation in the joint of the injured wing. As the sun's rays increased in warmth, the bat moved to a position in the shade cast by the trunk. It folded, moved and positioned its wing until it resembled a cocoon, the eyes touched mine once more, then the head disappeared into the cocoon.

I checked during the day as it moved to different positions in the tree, avoiding the direct sun. The next morning it was gone. When I close my eyes I can still see that soft little hand resting on mine, and those big soulful eyes saying 'thank you'.

Charlie resumed his terrorising of the Department of Civil Aviation on our return to Australia in January 1970. His reputation had certainly become established in the previous eighteen months we had been on the station, but on our return he proceeded to enhance it. Many of his escapades were recorded as '225', the flying world's absolute no-no's, but there was one particularly outrageous adventure that did not appear on the official record.

Charlie and Gus had bought Montejinni Station and Charlie flew back and forth regularly in the Super-cub. Unfortunately the direction was south-east from Bullo and he would always encounter a headwind on the way there and most of the time coming home, making the two-hour trip anything up to three and a half hours. So to pass the time, Charlie would read or work on business papers, his briefcase a virtual travelling, portable office.

On this particular trip he had flown from Bullo to Darwin to Montejinni, and was on the last leg home to Bullo. The Super-cub is only a two-seater, with the second seat in tandem, behind the pilot's. Charlie had supplies on the back seat of the plane, piled high, and on top were his requirements for a long trip: cold beer, a block of cheese, packets of crackers, a paperback book, reading glasses, notebook and briefcase. The little plane was slogging it out with a strong headwind, and was barely winning. Charlie was flying into the western sunset, the sky was a golden red glow and the sun was close to the horizon; he admitted to himself it would be a 'last light' landing... way after last light if he had to be truthful. He glanced down at the position of a landmark he had picked out five minutes before and gauged the headwind was even stronger than he had originally thought. He sighed deeply and reached back for yet another liquid refreshment. He had been in the air so long, even the beer was losing its chill. As his hand emerged from the beer carton behind his back with another can, the can hit the door handle. The Super-cub's door opens half up and half down; the halves meet and are locked together in the middle by turning the handle. When the beer can hooked the handle, the two halves of the door flew open. Cheese, crackers, beer and briefcase, one by one, slipped silently off the top of the pile and cascaded, tumbling over and over through the sky towards earth.

Charlie snapped into action and was in hot pursuit, kamikaze-diving after his belongings. But it was a futile gesture; by the time he had recovered from the shock and snapped into action, quick as he was, the lost articles had almost reached the ground, helped along by their landing on a high, flat plateau of around one thousand feet. Charlie circled the spot, and swooped low to pinpoint his briefcase, now burst open, the contents strewn over the plateau; in the last rays of the setting sun he could see money fluttering everywhere, the four thousand dollars in payroll wages he had drawn out of the bank that day.

He called on the radio to see if there were any helicopters in the vicinity. A guy he knew answered; he was on his way to Kununurra, a little to the south-west. Charlie asked him to detour to the plateau, land, and pick up the four thousand dollars. The pilot declined this suggestion and Charlie's offer of a small reward for the deed; he explained he was low on fuel, had just enough to make Kununurra on the straight course he was on. It was now dark and he didn't relish landing on some plateau in the dark even if Charlie gave him the whole four thousand, which he knew he wouldn't. Any way he looked at it, if he could see to land safely he would have to spend the night there or somewhere along the track home, as he would run out of fuel. Charlie's requests would certainly not make his boss happy or comply with insurance criteria, he explained, declining the offer. Charlie was still furious when he landed at Bullo in the pitch dark, aided by the lights of several torches and two Toyotas.

To this day, as far as I know, the cheese, crackers, beer, briefcase and money are still on top of the plateau... unless the helicopter pilot went back the next day with plenty of fuel and time to collect the four thousand—and the beer. If he didn't, most of it would not have survived to this day, but somewhere out there, on the track from Montejinni to Bullo, the remains of the beer cans and briefcase, and maybe some money, are still sitting on a thousand-foot plateau, waiting for some bushwalker or cliff-climber to stumble over it.

The part of the story that was repeated around Darwin for many moons was when Charlie went into the bank the next day and told the bank manager that the four thousand dollars he had given him was very definitely out of circulation, and it was all right for him to record the money as lost and give Charlie another four thousand to replace it! Charlie thought the manager was decidedly narrow-minded when he laughed at Charlie's suggestion and failed to see his reasoning.

The stock camp was twenty-two miles from the homestead. Musters, in the days before helicopters, were done on horseback. On some musters the stockmen could be away for weeks at a time. Charlie communicated with them in regular radio sessions, but this wasn't good enough for Charlie; he had to be there to 'command his troops', but always in maximum comfort. To get out to the camp by road took a good hour each way, too much of his precious time, so he'd have the men clear an area near the camp for a bush landing strip; then he could fly out in fifteen minutes. That suited Charlie ideally as he could pop out to the camp to give new orders (definitely his favourite pastime) many times a day. But it didn't suit the stock camp at all; the poor head stockman could not get through a day without three or four visits from Charlie with revised plans. Luckily for the men, not all the camp sites were situated to allow for a bush strip to be cleared, which meant Charlie could only fly over the camp and drop messages. Which was okay from the head stockman's point of view, but not satisfactory for Charlie because he couldn't get any update or progress reports. He would fly around in circles dropping notes with instructions and then a follow-up note asking a question and telling the head stockman to stand out in a clearing and nod 'yes' or shake his head for 'no'.

The mode of message dropping was uniquely, distinctively Charlie! He would stuff the written note inside a full roll of toilet paper and throw it out of the plane. The toilet paper would unravel as the roll plummeted to earth, leaving a long streamer of white paper to mark where it fell, making it easy for a stockman to lope across the paddock and retrieve the message. By the end of the season, most of the station trees looked like Chinese New Year, all festooned with paper decorations. The yearly toilet paper purchases were staggering, and people constantly asked Charlie why he carried a carton of toilet paper in the aircraft. Of course anyone remotely connected with the station in the early 1970s would be well acquainted with Charlie's communication system. Transport drivers would be bombarded with toilet roll messages all the way along our road. New drivers sometimes had problems; one chap finally made it to the station, marched into the kitchen and wanted to know who the crazy weirdo was that flew up and down our road pelting trucks with toilet rolls (he didn't look for any messsage). Charlie was standing there, arms folded, eyes glaring and foot tapping. By the time that driver departed, he was fully *au fait* with Bullo River, Charlie, and the communication system, and would dutifully leap out of his truck and reply with the obligatory nod or shake of the head to pertinent questions like, 'How's it going?' or the thumbs-up message that warned him about a bad 'jump-up' (a steep ascent or descent) ahead. Most drivers would head for the front gate at all possible speed hoping to escape to the sane world outside, away from Charlie and the bombarding toilet rolls.

I put my foot down when Charlie wanted the children to fill paper bags with flour so he could drop those to gauge his accuracy. I knew he just wanted to play games; and he knew I knew. I just said the budget couldn't extend to flour, toilet paper was expensive enough. Charlie immediately went out and dropped a note on the stock camp to instruct them to retrieve the toilet paper and roll it up again to be used for its original purpose. But when he got some recycled paper that had landed in a prickle patch he wasn't so keen on that idea, and it was re-used only to drop messages.

He finally modified the system to a rock in an empty orange onion bag with long red ribbons, this was recyclable and didn't have stockmen spending hours rolling toilet paper. Of course there had to be quite a few bags, because they had to be brought back to the homestead by Toyota only a few times a week. So there were times when the stock camp would be dropped a note saying 'out of bags, drive them in to the homestead', which of course completely defeated the time-saving purpose of the messsage-dropping system. If the head stockman didn't get in to the homestead in a few hours, Charlie would be up in the sky again dropping toilet rolls, requesting an ETA on bags.

Charlie had never really got enough of the war, so he loved all these extra excuses to drop anything from the plane, reliving his bombing days. And he tried to drop almost anything. It got to the point where we almost had a full-time 'air-drop' packing department. Of course that consisted of the children and me! Every morning he would issue instructions on what he wanted packed that day for the dropping zone. Eventually I had to put my foot down and refuse or we would have spent the whole day in Charlie's 'drop zone' packaging department. When we went on strike, he would roam around and find something he could drop that didn't require much preparation.

Charlie found out, the hard way, that you cannot drop beer just by the carton; or perhaps I should say the poor old stockmen, eagerly awaiting their evening beer, found out. The whole carton of beer cans split open on impact before their eyes. But Charlie wouldn't give up; when it was reported back to him, he said he would drop the cans one at a time, and they could catch them. This practice was one of Charlie's favourites as it really did test the accuracy of his spot bombing. However, it must have slipped since the war because the practice had to be stopped when stockmen ran into trees, or the backs of cattle, or barbed wire fences, or fell into the river, trying to catch the precious cargo. He found meat dropped well, but since the camp could mostly kill their own on site, requests for meat were few and far between. So he was constantly on the prowl looking for any excuse to bombard someone or something with the dreaded toilet roll or rock missile.

One of his most famous drops was on a very new employee. The chap was driving out along the road; Charlie was prowling the skies for action, when he saw the cloud of dust rising from the road. On closer inspection he decided the driver was going too fast. He quickly wrote a note, stuffed it in the onion bag with the rock, banked the plane and started a strafing run. The poor driver was scared out of his wits as the truck came up over a rise, to see a plane in a kamikaze dive-run, coming straight at the truck. Charlie bombed him with the message bag and swooped into the sky, thoroughly pleased with his efforts. The poor driver, on the other hand, had unprintable opinions. With shaking hands he opened the bag to read a note telling him he was driving too fast and would damage the truck, to reduce speed immediately. Charlie's message bag and rock had gone right through the windscreen, almost knocking him out; it had caused him to swerve off the road, and the truck had ended up hopelessly bogged in a rainwater ditch.

Of course one day the unthinkable happened: he ran out of message bags after the first drop. The toilet paper box had been stolen out of the plane, put to better use, so Charlie's communication system was 'up the creek'. His only drop was off the mark, so he put his head out the window to shout his instructions as he swooped low over the camp, and his glasses blew off. Not to be defeated, he dropped a message tied to a set of the plane's wheel-chocks, telling the men to find his glasses, dropped longitude such and such, latitude such and such, and not to forget to bring back the wheel-chocks! It is not hard to understand why we had a regular almost one hundred percent turnover of staff.

Another driver, in one of the ancient trucks that Uncle Dick somehow kept running, held together with nothing but baling wire, was again on the arduous trek out along our road, when the vehicle went over one too many large rocks, came down with a sickening clunk and ended up with a broken axle. When the truck was overdue, Charlie was up in the air on a search and rescue... well, maybe just the 'search'. He swooped low over the truck and soon ascertained it was a breakdown, dropped yet another famous message, telling the driver to stay put, then he flew back to the homestead to dispatch Uncle Dick out there. Dick returned and said the truck had a broken axle, but he had a spare so he would take it out and repair the truck. Dick made the unfortunate remark that the 'bloody young pup was probably driving too fast'. This made Charlie see red. He jumped into the plane, flew out to the stranded truck and dropped the driver a note which simply read, 'You're fired!'

Around Charlie, pandemonium reigned in the air and on the ground. There were continual problems, breakdowns, staff leaving, arrangements delayed or just completely forgotten. To this day, I am not sure if it was bad luck, lack of funds, bad equipment, untrained staff, or having a cattle station run—oops—commanded by a frustrated, would-be fighter pilot... maybe it was all of these things. Whatever, the result was devastation, a constant seemingly hopeless situation, that bumbled and stumbled from one fiasco to the next.

It was not out of the norm for the cattle trucks to arrive at the yards and find no cattle to load. On many occasions, the stock camp would 'down tools' and walk out because of one of Charlie's outrageous demands. The muster would be delayed until more unsuspecting stockmen arrived and picked up the pieces. But Charlie would regularly forget to notify the trucking company of the delay. Trucks would arrive at the appointed time and find the yards empty. Often the drivers would find themselves on a horse, whether they could ride or not, out in a paddock, with the girls (out of school again), the cook-cum-teacher-cum-nurse-cum-typist, namely me, on horses, racing around the paddock rounding up cattle, while Charlie swooped around the sky shouting orders at us out the window.

As one stockman put it, 'Missus, I don't mind the rough conditions, I don't mind riding a half-broken mad horse. I don't mind working for a bloke that doesn't know what he's doing most of the time; I don't even mind all his crazy ideas. But I don't much like the idea of getting my head chopped off by a propellor blade while riding a horse, mustering cattle. Wild cattle ain't the danger out here!'

But sometimes, not often, there were unexpected bonuses in working for Charlie. Peter Per, Uncle Dick's assistant hooch-maker, drinking mate and deputy mechanic, left the station for the umpteenth time after Charlie made him mad. He applied for a job in Darwin at one of the big hotels. The job was fairly cushy after Bullo, taking care of the swimming pool filtering machinery, plus various garden-tending duties. There were hundreds of applicants. The manager was interviewing the long line of men. He asked their name, where they had worked last, and a few other questions, took a phone contact and told the man he would be in touch. This was done without lifting his head or looking at the man. He knew the reason most of the men were applying for the job was to be near the grog, and that was their only qualification. Per was no different in this respect, but he was also a mechanic.

Peter Per finally reached the desk. He was asked his name, age and occupation in rapid fire, then where he worked last. When he replied Bullo River the manager stopped writing and looked up for the first time. 'How long did you work for Charlie Henderson?'

When Peter told him six months, he was hired on the spot.

Charlie stayed at the hotel when in Darwin, and the manager knew him well. He said to Peter, 'Anyone who can stay in Charlie Henderson's employ for six months is the man for me!' Such was Charlie's 'impossible to please' reputation.

9

DENNIS THE PODDY CALF AND ROSA THE GOANNA

Charlie was not the only character in the Outback, there were many, many characters, and some of them had tails. One of the first animal characters I came across was a poddy calf (an orphan calf hand-fed on powdered milk from an early age). They are called poddies because they develop a large tummy or 'pod' in the first year due to not getting their mother's milk.

This calf, when I met him, was close to six months old and was quite large; he had been taken care of by the cook who was on the station the year before we arrived back from America. The poddy only liked women, it seemed; he charged many of the stockmen, so he had spent a very neglected and unhappy period between the cook's departure and my arrival. But when the children and I arrived and started paying him attention, he very quickly became our pet. He took a very particular liking to me, and followed me everywhere—and I mean everywhere. This was not difficult to achieve; the shed still had no outside walls, so he could wander almost any-where inside. I was safe in the toilet as that door had a bolt, but he could head-butt the bathroom door open, and did so many times, trying to join me in the shower. He was called Dennis the Menace for very obvious reasons.

One of his favourite pastimes was licking any sleeping stockman he could find. Most of the men slept on their swags rolled out on wire bed-frames with folding legs. Many a time in the dark of the night a muffled, disgusted, complaining voice would shout, 'Get the f... out, Dennis!', usually followed by the crash of a folding bed collapsing on the cement floor. Dennis, having licked a face, would then put his big head down and give the bed a gentle nudge, sending it and occupant flying. The stockman would set up the legs of the bed again, after finding something large and heavy to throw at Dennis. But Dennis would wait until the man was comfortable and then nudge the bed again. If a gun had been handy, Dennis would have had a very short life.

When he tipped the scales at eight hundred pounds (over three hundred and sixty kilograms) it was becoming a bit hard to keep him in the house garden. The stockmen complained about not getting any sleep, and I had lost many a meal when Dennis had walked through the kitchen and helped himself to food set out on the table for the stockmen. But one of the final deciders was his dislike for the plane. If anyone left the gate onto the airstrip open, he would be out there in a flash to attack the plane. Often I just managed to call him off when there were only a few yards between his horns and the fabric side of the plane. Luckily he was instantly obedient and would swerve away from a full charge to come loping back to me in long bouncing strides just like a dog. But I wasn't always there at the last moment and one day he managed to score a hit. The little plane ended up with two perfect horn-holes mid-centre of the fuselage.

This was one major reason for Dennis to be banished to a distant paddock. But the final cause of his being sent away was his obvious dislike of Charlie. I think why he always tried to charge the plane was because he knew it was connected with Charlie. When Charlie was around he was always shooing Dennis out of the house, so Dennis didn't like Charlie or anything to do with him. His very favourite occupation in the evening was to wait for Charlie to leave the bedroom for the long trek to the bathroom. Dennis would then take up position in front of the bedroom door, protecting me inside. When Charlie returned, Dennis wouldn't budge and Charlie would have to chase him away with a lump of wood, or ask me to call him away. As Dennis grew bigger, it was mostly me calling him away, as it was very dicey for Charlie to bluff Dennis with the piece of wood: Dennis would lower his head with every intention of charging. When this practice extended to the early hours of the morning, every time Charlie went to the toilet, that was the last straw. I would be awoken from a deep sleep by Charlie shouting to me and abusing Dennis. I'd stagger sleepily to the door to find a Mexican standoff—Dennis with head lowered and pawing the floor, emitting a low rumbling moan, and Charlie, usually stark naked, with a lump of wood in hand, trying to get Dennis away from the door. One of them had to go, Charlie or Dennis.

Charlie was content just to get him out of the garden and away from the plane, so it was agreed Dennis could be put in the river paddock on the other side of the airstrip, across from the house; I could go and visit each day and talk to him. The first few weeks were terrible; he stood at the fence looking across at the house and bellowing all day. If I walked into the garden, the noise increased. He wouldn't leave the fence to graze, so he became thinner and thinner. The advice was, 'Don't go over and talk to him, and he will start behaving like a normal bull.' I stayed away, and out of sight as much as possible. Gradually he left the fence and started eating; after a few months he was behaving normally. I could even visit him each afternoon with special titbits, and he would not bellow his head off after I left.

However, he disgraced himself when I was away in Darwin

for a few days. He slipped through the gate onto the airstrip and once more damaged the plane; also badly roughed up one of the stockmen trying to protect the plane. The writing was on the wall for Dennis. Charlie knew how much I loved this crazy bull and he waited until I returned to tell me he had to be banished to a distant paddock. This was not all plain sailing, however. Dennis still would not go anywhere near the other cattle; he was totally convinced he was human and flatly refused to even let them near him. So I pleaded with Charlie to let Dennis stay close to home long enough to find new friends before being banished. Charlie solved this problem very quickly by putting a load of cows in his paddock and before long Dennis discovered what being a bull was all about. He wandered off down the flat with a bunch of cows, heading for a distant paddock, and was so engrossed in his new role he didn't even give me a farewell bellow when I called his name.

Poddy calves became a part of my life; every year we found orphans; when it was a bad season, or the rains were late, we always had many more poddies. The girls came rushing into the kitchen one day and told me there was a new poddy tied to the coconut tree. They had found it all alone, no cows in sight, in the paddock they were mustering. They asked me to give it a drink of milk and said they would take care of it later when they had finished the muster; then they were gone out the door at breakneck speed.

I sighed, stopped peeling the stack of potatoes for thirty people for lunch, mixed powdered milk in a bucket, and headed out to the coconut tree near the back gate. There, standing under the tree, was this small, angelic picture of beauty and innocence, long satin ears, large liquid chocolate brown eyes, and a cute black button nose. There it stood, tied to the tree, head hung low, swaying on its long gangly legs. My heart melted looking at this forlorn lost animal. I approached, quietly crooning soft words to it as I held out the bucket so it could get the smell of the milk.

Its head jerked up as it sensed me approaching; it took one look at the offered bucket, let out a blood curdling *b-l-a-r-r-r-r* and charged me. The long rope whipped out at an alarming rate as this tiny frail-looking creature hit the bucket and me with surprising force. With plenty of slack in the long rope and its full weight in forward flight, I went over backwards, completely unprepared for such a vicious attack. The bucket of milk upended all over me.

It had been a bad day, and my temper had not been far from the surface; this certainly saw it burst out into the open. I staggered to my feet, spluttering milk and wiping it from my eyes. The calf, its tongue hanging out, was standing panting, where the rope had stopped short its maniacal wild charge. Ignoring it, I was about to head for the bathroom to wash the milk out of my eyes: milk baths might be good for the skin, but my eyes were starting to sting. As soon as I moved, however, the crazed animal darted in the opposite direction. The rope was now wound around my legs; I grabbed it and pulled the calf towards me, so I could get some slack to free my legs. Again it did its bloodcurdling *b-l-a-r-r-r*, charged and knocked me off my feet, trampling right over the top of me in its insane dash in another direction. The rope cut into my legs as the calf came to a shuddering halt again.

My temper really took over at that point, I am ashamed to say. I gave the rope a tremendous yank, which pulled the calf right off its feet, and I was able to get my legs free. We both got to our feet at the same time. It charged again, but I was ready: I pulled in the rope, picked up the calf and threw it over the barbed wire fence next to the tree. After it gained its feet, we both stood there for a few minutes, panting heavily. When I was sure I hadn't hurt the poor thing I headed once more for the shower, tears streaming down my face from my smarting eyes and from sheer frustration. I told the calf it could wait until the girls came home for its drink; I wasn't going anywhere near it until it learned a few manners.

When the girls did come home, they asked what the calf was doing on the other side of the fence. I told them they didn't want to know; by then I was thoroughly ashamed of my actions. But the calf didn't seem to have suffered from its short flight, and a week later I again had to feed it while the girls were out mustering. It walked up meek as can be and started sipping the milk out of the bucket, but I didn't relax my guard for a moment. In the next few weeks, though, I had to admit the girls had trained it well and it became one of the quietest and best behaved poddies in the group, but never a favourite of mine.

Luckily my temper didn't do any harm that time. But on one other occasion when it got the better of me the results were a little more drastic. The piggery was growing in numbers and the expanding fencing just couldn't keep up with the demand. On many occasions the pigs would break through the temporary fencing and be free to roam until the girls rounded them up, locking them back into their run. One afternoon they broke through the fence while the girls and I were in the schoolroom working hard, and headed straight for my vegetable garden. The garden had the normal barbed wire fence around it, which kept cattle and horses out, but was useless against roaming pigs. The girls finished school and exploded outside to adventure. I had plodded laboriously into the kitchen to start dinner, when the children exploded back in the door to tell me the pigs were in the garden.

I grabbed the straw broom and raced out the door. This was a regular confrontation and when the pigs saw me approaching, waving the broom, they were off around the other side of the house. I cut back and waited at the far corner, knowing they would come past me to get back to the pig pen, the safest place for them, at that moment. As the mob rushed by I wound up and let the broom fly with a mighty swing. It whistled and whooshed through the air and hit one pig with such a force that it broke its leg. The startled pig began screeching and going around in circles, one leg hanging uselessly from the knee joint. The rest of the pigs headed for the piggery at the speed of light.

The children looked with amazement and wanted to know how I did that. I was so upset I burst into tears; I had only wanted to scare it, not break its leg. The pig wouldn't stop screeching and wouldn't go away, which didn't help matters. The girls led me to my bedroom, assuring me the pig knew I didn't mean to hurt it; they would go and get one of the stockmen to help. I had a good cry and after washing my face decided to go and set the leg, or do something for the poor animal. But when I arrived back at the spot with the first-aid kit, the pig was gone. The stockman had shot it and taken it down to the abattoir to be processed. This set me off crying all over again.

The pigs caused me to lose my temper regularly. One less comrade didn't stop the raiding parties or slow them up in the least. Until the day we closed the piggery, much to my delight, they performed regular raids day and night on any part of my garden. If the vegie garden was out of season, they would just uproot the lawn. A ploughed field would greet me in the morning, where the night before a lawn had been. But the most devastating raid of all time happened one night when the entire populace of the pig pen, down to the smallest piglet, staged an all-out commando raid on my entire garden.

Along the bedroom side of the house I had planted thirty banana trees; a friend had brought the young plants out from Kununurra. A lot of work went into digging holes, fertilising and watering, to get them to glorious, ten-foot-high, green, healthy specimens. Every morning when I woke up I sat on the side of the bed and looked at my lovely growing banana trees, while I stretched, and generally talked myself into starting the day.

One morning I looked out the window and stopped stretching; I looked, blinked and looked again. There were no banana trees; thirty-three-metre tall banana trees were gone! I checked to see if I was lying on the right side of the bed; maybe I was looking out of the wrong window... I oriented myself and confirmed I was looking out of the right window. Where were my banana trees? I quickly dressed and rushed out to where last night had stood an orchard of healthy trees. All that was left were thirty holes where the pigs had dug down and even devoured the roots after they had eaten the trees to ground level.

There wasn't one scrap of evidence of a leaf, limb or trunk; it was as if a giant vacuum cleaner had just sucked up each tree, roots and all, leaving only the hole. If you didn't know an orchard of trees had stood there ten hours ago, I don't think you could be convinced of the fact. I was so amazed I didn't even lose my temper. Although I had to admit a few hundred pigs make a good imitation of a vacuum cleaner.

That was the last time I ever planted a garden. I gave Charlie a list of requirements for an animal-proof garden and said I would not plant another thing until a fence was built and all the pigs were gone. Well, the pigs were gone four years later, but the enclosed garden area was never built so I refused to waste my time planting vegetables for the cattle, horses, goannas and birds. I waited fifteen years but never got my garden.

I had to smile when Marlee this year asked her husband Franz to build her an animal- and bird-proof garden; history repeating itself, I thought. He built her a beautiful screened, steel-framed cool house. But it was so well screened even the bees couldn't get in to pollinate the flowers; we had beautiful tomato plants, but no tomatoes. Franz made some holes for the bees to get in and do their job. We had lovely herbs and other vegies growing... and Marlee is ready for a bumper tomato crop next year as soon as the bees know they are allowed in!

Of course, when I refused to plant vegetables any more Charlie hired Fred, our Italian gardener. Apart from making moonshine in the weed patch, Fred was a very good gardener, and had a large garden growing in no time at all. His caravan was parked right in the middle of the garden, and I can only assume he stayed awake all night because the pigs never carried out one successful raid on his garden. You would hear shocking noises that could indicate some pig had been caught in the act, but they never wrought havoc as they did in my garden. Finally the pigs became too great in number, and the piggery had to be moved to another site. It was with great delight when I watched them being carted away, disappearing down the road to the other side of the cattle yard.

Fred only had the birds to contend with then, but he built such elaborate scarecrows that they even frightened people. So he was a little mystified when his 'beaut-a-ful' plants were being eaten. He decided to stand guard all night and 'catch-a this-a thief'.

'I know-a who tak-a the plants, is-a big-a lizard!' he told me triumphantly the next morning. 'I will kill this-a big-a lizard,' he went on in a determined manner.

The children were immediately up in arms. The lizard was a goanna; it lived next to the pool in the big hole; the girls fed it meat and bread, it was becoming quite friendly. So we had to find some other way to stop it having its salad over in Fred's garden. The girls gave it more to eat, hoping the variety would satisfy the goanna and keep it out of Fred's garden. But it ate all the children's offerings and still visited the garden. So I told Fred to put some greens on the same plate the girls used to feed the goanna daily, and this seemed to do the trick. Each night Fred would set out a variety of leaves and trimmings on the plate near a large log, the lizard's favourite sitting spot, and each morning most of the food would be gone. The garden seemed to be undamaged.

During the day, the girls fed the goanna back at its hole, next to the partly finished swimming pool. Life settled down to a happy situation with the goanna growing and Fred's garden growing, and everyone friendly. Fred's tomatoes were a bumper crop, and just starting to ripen, so he didn't get much sleep because of the fruit bat raids. He asked Charlie could he keep a shotgun in the garden to scare off the bats. Charlie gave him the gun but soon realised it was a bad move to put a gun into the hands of an untrained person. At all hours of the night everyone would be jolted awake by shotgun fire, and hear Fred swearing in Italian, running around the garden naked except for a towel, waving a clenched fist at the retreating, terrified fruit bats. After a few nights of this, the staff started to complain; the tomatoes just weren't worth the sleepless nights, they would gladly go without! The final straw was when Fred's towel fell off while he was rushing around the garden and he tripped and fell, and the shotgun went off and sprayed the side of the house. Fred was finally given a large slingshot and rock-salt instead of the shotgun and everyone got some sleep. Fred sat on his log and guarded with the slingshot.

Fred was having a busy night; the smell of ripe tomatoes and fruit, thick on the night air, had the bats coming in fast and regularly. He was resting on his log, having repelled repeated attacks, when he noticed movement out of the corner of his eye. He slowly turned his head, and there, peeping over the top of the log, were two black eyes. Fred remained very still and the 'big-a lizard' slowly climbed onto the log and starting eating its nightly meal from the tin plate. Fred had placed the food there at sunset, but with the unrelenting fruit bat attacks he had forgotten the goanna. They sat together on the log, eyeing each other curiously. While Fred would rush off to sling rock-salt at the bats, the goanna sat eating, watching this crazy man running around doing strange things.

As the sun started to rise, Fred was pleased he had once again saved his beloved garden from the ravaging hordes, and when Fred was happy, he sang... Italian opera. Slowly the first rays of sunlight bathed the valley and washed over Fred, singing opera, with his friendly goanna sitting on the log beside him listening. The months passed and the goanna spent most of the day in someone's company. With the children out watching the progress of the swimming pool, in the kitchen begging me for food or in the garden with Fred. But Fred soon became the favourite. The big lizard seemed to enjoy his rather unusual style of singing.

Fred said the 'big-a lizard' had to have a name, 'can't keep-a calling it big-a lizard', and so he proudly announced that he had decided to call her Rosa. He had also decided the lizard was a girl, 'Because she was-a too pretty to be-a boy!'

Rosa grew and grew, happy with all the love and attention she received. Most of the time you would find her in the garden with Fred, following him around as he tended the garden. He would talk and sing to her all day. If he wasn't in full voice singing opera, you would hear conversations like, 'Hey, Rosa! watch-a where you put-a the foot', as she tried to follow him through the plant beds on the narrow path.

When the sun became too hot, she would sit in the shade and watch, and Fred would shout to her, 'Hey, Rosa, come help me pull-a the weeds! Wha's the madder with you?' She would just blink those strange eyes or stretch her neck, put her head on the side and look at him with one eye, but continue to sit in the shade and observe.

Fred grew to know Rosa's every favourite plant and it was not long before he was growing a special garden bed, just for Rosa. He would show it to her, telling her she could go and nibble whenever she wanted, but he still put a selection on her plate on the log for her. She had grown so big that if she did wander onto a garden bed she wiped out most of the plants with her feet or tail. So Fred would hand-pick her favourite food daily. Rosa just kept growing, eating and sitting on the log with Fred listening to Italian opera. She still visited the kitchen occasionally and did tricks to receive her cubes of roast beef from the children, but she was Fred's goanna.

When it was time for his holidays we were all a bit concerned how she would react when he was gone. She watched him carry his suitcase out to Bertha, our Beaver aircraft, and saw Fred wave out the window as Charlie flew him to Darwin.

The girls and I watered the vegie garden and she sat on the log watching us. She spent more time in the kitchen and playing by the pool, but although she missed Fred, and often wandered over to the caravan or the log looking for him, she stayed in good spirits and was eating well. It was a relief to see her handling his absence so well. But sometimes you would see her sitting on their log, a silhouette against the setting sun, just waiting.

The stockmen arrived from town to start the season's mustering. About a week later one of them spotted Rosa strolling across the lawn and thought what a great meal she would make. No-one had remembered to tell them Rosa was a pet. He found a big rock and was creeping up behind an unsuspecting Rosa, sunning herself beside the pool. One of the girls saw him and let out a high-pitched scream; Rosa woke with such a start that the rock only gave her a glancing blow. Still, we had a very dazed Rosa on our hands. The stockman was so upset when he was told the goanna was the children's pet, he carefully helped them carry Rosa into the medical room where the children bathed her cut and tried, without luck, to keep a bandage on her head. When Fred arrived back the next week, the children did manage to have a very impressive bandage in place for the few minutes after he landed. She was still quite shaken by the blow, so she continued her recovery period sitting out on their log, contentedly listening to Fred singing. As she regained her strength, she was again happily going from the log to the kitchen, to supervise the building of the swimming pool.

The pool was a long and slow project as work was only done on it during lulls in mustering or spare time, and there was never much of that. However, its eventual progress caused a major problem. Rosa's hole would have to be covered with cement and sandstone. Fred discussed this problem with the children and me and a decision was made that Rosa would have a new home near the log, so Fred busied himself with this project. Rosa sat on the log and watched with interest.

A few days before her house was to be officially finished, and Fred was arranging a big celebration, Rosa disappeared. The children and Fred searched and called her daily, even the Aboriginals went on tracking missions. They reported her tracks led off into the bush and to the nearby billabong in Nutwood Paddock, but they lost them in amongst the cattle and bird prints at the billabong.

Weeks passed and we had to accept she was gone. Fred missed her terribly. He would sit on their log and look sadly at the little sign that he had painted her name on and decorated with roughly drawn flowers. This was nailed to the log, just over the entrance to the hole he had started for her, hoping she would continue and make it her new home. The mustering was in full swing, so everyone was instructed to speak to any goanna they came across out in the bush to see if it was friendly and was maybe Rosa, lost.

The months went by and the pool was finally completed, and the children couldn't wait for it to fill so they could jump in. Of course it leaked and it took days for the ground around to soak up its share of water before the pool filled. But soon it was brimming and everyone was jumping in any time of the day and night to cool down.

Along with being a swimming pool, it also became a favourite watering hole for any animal that could get into the garden. The horses much preferred the pool to their drinking trough not far away. The cattle would also try to get into the garden and sample the water. As it turned out, it was not only for drinking; they were used to the billabong where they could walk into the shallows and take a drink. They regularly tried to step into the pool, and would go head over turkey into the water. Rescuing cattle and even horses out of the pool got to be such a regular event that, during the winter, the pool was pumped out and the steps were enlarged so the animals could get in and out of the pool without our help. Guests were sometimes shocked when they looked out and saw a horse emerging from the swimming pool, looking for all the world as if it had just finished a few laps.

Hundreds of little birds drank at the pool. The surrounds were uneven sandstone, giving the pool the look of a natural rock pool, and the birds could get down to the water level without too much trouble. The pool was always a hive of activity, everyone was there at some time of the day, except Rosa. Oh, how we missed her.

Then one morning Fred came bounding into the kitchen so excited he could hardly speak. We finally understood—he was trying to tell us Rosa was back! We rushed out to find Rosa standing next to where her hole near the swimming pool had been, but was no longer. And if a goanna could fold its arms and assume the expression of 'Well, explain this!', Rosa achieved it without the folded arms.

Fred led her over to her new home under the log, but she wasn't too impressed and kept returning to where her home used to be, to sit with a dissatisfied expression on her face. This was in between her cooling-off swims, up and down the pool; Rosa was certainly impressed with the pool.

Fred put a plate of her special greens in front of her new home every night and would sit there each day and explain all its advantages to Rosa. Privacy, coolness, protection, he would elaborate for hours, but Rosa sat on top of the log and would not go anywhere near it.

Fred wasn't sure where she was going to sleep, but he knew it wasn't in her new home. She disappeared regularly but he was content just to have her back, even if she didn't like his carefully planned residence. Then, when we had all forgotten about the new house, Rosa decided to move in. Fred walked into the garden early one morning and there she was busy excavating further the hole Fred had started for her. Soon Rosa was firmly entrenched in her new home, and enjoying herself immensely in the pool.

Sometimes we would forget to tell guests about our big lizard, and she would scare them half to death by surfacing just in front of them. You would see someone swimming at breakneck speed for the steps and would have to rush out and tell them not to be frightened, she was friendly. Even though you assured them of this, not too many went back in, not while Rosa was there anyway. I often found her in the kitchen scaring the cat half to death as she ate its food. She spent quite a lot of her time in the house, but if Fred whistled she would be off in a dash, even leaving food.

They spent most of the day together. Fred would take the wheelbarrow out onto the airstrip and collect horse manure for his garden. You could see Rosa walking along beside him. When the grass was too long you couldn't see her, but there was Fred in animated conversation, waving his arms around, pointing out different objects of interest, seemingly to no-one. It was not until he reached the mowed lawn of the garden that Rosa came into view, looking at him as if she understood every word.

When he set off to get the cows to milk, Rosa had to stay quite a distance away. The cows were wild bush cows that the girls had broken in for milking, but they were still very touchy, and even though they would follow the bucket of feed anything strange upset them. So Rosa would hide in the grass until Fred had the cows well and truly tethered in the bail, then she would slowly walk out and sit on a nearby post to watch the milking. She really was quite a help at this point because the cows would keep their eyes fixed on Rosa and stand still, making Fred's job a lot easier.

Rosa started acting strangely, she wouldn't swim, she disappeared for days on end, she wouldn't eat. I told Fred he had to face the fact that she would probably go back to the wild and he had to be ready to expect this. She was fully grown, or at least looked it, and the time would come when she would want to be with other goannas. Or at least I thought this would be the case; I wasn't very versed on goannas or their habits, and didn't have any books on them. Fred was quite sure Rosa would never leave, so the subject was dropped.

Fred once more rushed into the kitchen one day, too excited for anyone to understand what he was saying, so we followed him out to the garden. Rosa had returned after an absence of many weeks, and there with her was a baby goanna! This certainly explained her strange behaviour of late. Fred was over the moon with excitement, and wanted to enlarge her hole immediately. I said I was sure Rosa would handle this, and he controlled himself and didn't interfere. He worried constantly that she would leave and was always thinking of ways to make her life and Rosetta's so comfortable that they would not go.

I fully expected it would be Rosa who would go back to the wild, but it was actually Fred who left Rosa. His father became ill and Fred had to leave to go home to Perth, telling Rosa first, then us, that he would be back soon. But he never returned.

We couldn't get another gardener as good as Fred, and Rosa certainly didn't like any of them. It wasn't long before she moved out of the log house and back into the bush. The vegie garden soon developed that uncared-for look as the growing season came to an end and all the plants went to seed. I found her a few times wandering down the paths in between the beds, still being careful as if she could hear Fred's voice, loud and clear, saying, 'Watch-a where you put-a the foot, Rosa!'

The neat garden plot soon became natural paddock again and it seemed to be a signal to Rosa that Fred, this time, would never return. She visited the pool for a swim now and again, but when the girls and I went to Sydney to visit my sister and Mum for a holiday she left for good.

10

PYE-WACKET THE MARMALADE CAT

 Not all our unusual animals were creatures from the wild who returned to the wild. We raised just as many domesticated animals who were truly remarkable and in some cases almost human. One of these was a marmalade cat that I called Pye-wacket after the magical cat in the book *Bell, Book and Candle*. Of course, being orange and white, he was not the right colour for a magical cat, but just the same he possessed definite powers.

Pye-wacket was found in a gutter in Darwin as a small kitten, starved and almost at death's door. The little girl who took the miserable creature home promptly poured a whole bottle of liquid baby vitamins down his throat to help him along. Her parents were not as sympathetic. Horrified that their daughter would even touch such a thing, they tried to get the dying animal away from her. But she was bent on saving this kitten, and threw a screaming tantrum every time they came near it.

The children and I were in Darwin on one of our rare visits; Marlee just happened to be playing with friends next door, and was shown the kitten. When she saw how distressed the little girl was and the lack of concern of the parents, she offered to take the kitten back to Bullo where, she assured its worried guardian, it would live in a 'kitten paradise'. She proudly presented me with a frail, skeleton-like creature lying in the bottom of a small basket.

The first thing that struck me were the amazing large yellow eyes that consumed the entire face of the very sick kitten. I held the basket, staring at the poor creature, feeling it was only minutes from death, but not having the heart to tell this to two sets of pleading eyes that were asking silently for a miracle and watching my every expression for confirmation. The little girl was so upset and worried, I had no choice but to cheerfully tell her that after a few weeks at Bullo her kitten would be restored. This calmed her considerably. She told Marlee she had heard her father say he would dispose of 'it' when she went to school the next day, so she was happy when the kitten safely took off in the Beaver aircraft with us, heading for safety and Bullo.

Somehow it lived through the flight, never moving the entire time. The only evidence of life was a slight movement of the rib cage, and the occasional opening of one eye in response to very gentle one-finger stroking by the ever-attentive girls, who spent the whole trip staring at it. When we arrived at Bullo, the kitten had top priority. Charlie had to unload the plane himself, as Mum and girls set up living quarters for this tiny creature. Charlie understood these priorities, and unloaded the plane without a word while the grand project proceeded. A cardboard box was set up on its side in a quiet spot, safe from all the dogs, who were allowed one sniff apiece, and told in very stern voices, not to touch. They all quietly sat down and watched the installation of the new animal into the menagerie.

The children searched for soft bedding, and after I reclaimed the only decent linen I possessed, the box was lined with clean soft dusting rags. Then everyone, dogs included, held their breath as I carefully transferred the lifeless piece of tatty fur into its new home.

Food was the urgent priority. I made up a formula of milk, baby porridge and a few drops of baby vitamins—not the bottle-at-a-time dose the little kitten had somehow miraculously survived. This was administered by eye-dropper for long hours and days. I would have to say the kitten owed its life to the children's ever-constant vigil. Even school was temporarily suspended for feeding times, which seemed to come every ten minutes on the children's schedule. After the first week, kitten and box were moved into the schoolroom to cut down the never-ending requests to go and check the patient.

How the kitten survived the first week is still a mystery to me. But at week's end it was still breathing, was slightly less of a skeleton, the movement of its rib cage was a little more evident and it could breathe without the terrible rattling sound. The kitten looked more comfortable and was sleeping in a curled-up position with its tiny head resting on its paws. It obviously moved about the box as it would be in a different position when we checked it each morning, but as yet we had not seen it standing. I really don't think it had the strength to stand; it moved, I'm sure, by dragging itself the small distance it moved daily.

It was halfway through the second week that big changes started to happen. We were working quietly in school when the girls let out an almighty yell and pointed at the box. The kitten was standing, shakily, very unsure, and swaying dangerously. So much effort was going into this first manoeuvre: the head was down, the eyes staring at the ground, legs spread at the most extreme angles; it looked like a shed without support struts in a high wind. Eventually, despite the encouragement of the girls' combined squeals, over it went with a thump. The rest of the school day was suspended as willing hands repeatedly helped the scrawny little kitten to stand.

From then on it never looked back; the change was miraculous. At the end of the second week the kitten was declared out of danger and given a good chance of surviving, and was named Pye-wacket.

Maybe it was the whole bottle of vitamins and the constant twenty-four-hour feeding regime of the first weeks. Whatever, the kitten grew into the biggest cat I had ever seen. After he had all his shots at the vet's and was desexed, he grew even bigger, and was more than half the size of the Labradors, Shad and Honey. Pye-wacket grew up believing he was a dog. He had never seen another cat, and was surrounded by four dogs, so he assumed he was one of those, and spent his entire life trying to be like them.

When anyone approached the homestead gate, the dogs rushed out and stood in a row on the lawn and barked. Pye-wacket tried for many years to achieve this; he was up to the running and would join in when the dogs assumed their lines of defence, but try as he might, he couldn't bark. On a few occasions he did manage a terrible-sounding yowl, which caused all the dogs to stop barking and stare at him in disgust, so he never tried again. He would run out, take up his position in the barking line, and swish his tail madly.

You could find him lying in the sun with all the dogs every morning, getting his dose of vitamin D. And at feeding time he lined up with them all for his plate to be put in front of him. There was no doubt in Pye-wacket's mind, he was a dog.

He was a very playful kitten, and remained a very playful fully grown cat. Danielle was just a toddler at the time; Pye-wacket would hide behind the door, and when she passed, he would jump out and sink his teeth into the back of her nappy and latch his claws into the sides. Danielle would come squealing into the kitchen with Pye-wacket being dragged behind her, enjoying the ride immensely. There was a problem getting Danielle out of nappies because of this strange habit. It was a morning thing; it seemed to be his way of saying good morning to Danielle, and once the initial morning greeting was over, it was safe to let her wear lighter playsuits. But I was worrying needlessly; when the nappy stage was finished, Pye-wacket just jumped in front of her in a crazy spread-eagled fashion to greet her at the beginning of the day and then they both raced into the kitchen to have breakfast.

Every now and then when he felt particularly playful, he would somehow manage to get his teeth and claws into the thin material of a playsuit without scratching Danielle, and she would tow him into the kitchen once more, squealing with delight, but it never could equal the nappy period. Later, when she wore a dress, they would spend hours playing hide and seek, with Pye-wacket hiding, and lunging out to embed teeth and claws into the back of Danielle's dress, then being towed around the house. They both had a wonderful childhood. As Pye-wacket grew, his personality expanded. He was afraid of nothing and no-one; he would hunt and kill snakes, and Uncle Dick came back from checking the windmill on Number Two Bore one day to report that he'd seen 'that cat' swimming across the river on his way home.

Charles was not fond of cats; he liked dogs, but he only just tolerated cats. If they came near him he would push them away. But his attitude towards Pye-wacket was different; he treated him like a dog.

Pye-wacket had singled me out as his person, and when he returned from his hunting trips, I would be the first person he would look for to greet, and often to get a good meal. But whatever time of day it was, he would seek me out. The cutest game he played with Charles was if he returned home at night and Charles and I were sitting in bed reading; he would come to the door and yowl to be let in. Charles would begrudgingly open the door and Pye-wacket would march past him in an imperious manner. He would then jump up on the foot of the bed, walk up my legs and body, and finally sit on my chest, look down into my face and yowl the closest sound to 'Hullo' that you could hear. If he was hungry he would jump down from the bed and wait at the door; if he did not want to be fed, he would curl up next to me and sleep for a few hours before he went out to check on the girls and the rest of his territory.

But he never went to sleep or left without going through another of his funny little rituals with Charles. He would start at Charlie's feet and balancing on his ankles, then slowly walk up his legs and body, as he did with me. But with Charles it was super-slow, and he wouldn't start until Charles first acknowledged his presence. If Charles was deep in his book, Pye-wacket would dig in his claws very slightly, until Charles protested and paid attention to him. Then he would walk slowly up his legs and body with Charles calling to me to 'remove that cat' and 'look at that cat', and many other remarks about 'that cat'. So they played this marvellous game that both thoroughly enjoyed, although Charles voiced disapproval the entire time and would never admit he enjoyed the whole ritual. He seemed pleased that Pye-wacket singled him out for this funny little performance. Sometimes Charles would overact and declare Pye-wacket had dug his claws in too deeply and I should remove him at once. Pye-wacket would pause and give Charles such a look as to convey his opinion quite clearly, then look at me as if to say, 'He is exaggerating; I hardly touched him!'

So the little game would continue. When Pye-wacket

reached Charlie's chest he paused, waiting for the same remark Charlie always made: 'Sara, remove that cat!'

Pye-wacket, taking his time, would stare at Charlie for a few seconds, then turn around and swish his tail right under Charlie's nose; after a few rapid flicks back and forth, he would leap gracefully to the floor and walk regally out the door, or withdraw to my side of the bed, curl up and go to sleep. He never missed this routine when he returned home after an absence.

Pye-wacket was so strong, he could beg standing his full height on his hind legs, and could walk right across the kitchen on his hind legs. He would stand on two legs and gently take a piece of meat out of your hand with his paws, without as much as a waver: a long way from that first time when it took every ounce of his strength and concentration just to stand on all fours for a few seconds.

Pye-wacket was an impressive-looking cat, with whiter than-white chest, stomach and paws and a white tip on the end of his tail for balance. The rest of him was a vivid orange-and-white marmalade pattern; he was extremely striking, and knew it.

He didn't live to old age, though; he went out in the prime of his life, still a top athlete. His ability as a hunter was his downfall in the wild Outback, when he took on one snake too many and it got the better of him.

He had been gone for well over two weeks, which was not normal for him, and I was beginning to worry about him, but hoping all the time he would come cheerfully bounding in to annoy Charles, in bed reading once more. But this was not to be. The girls found him on the airstrip only a hundred yards from home. We buried him under the bottle tree, just outside my bedroom window.

Pye-wacket was a wonderful animal, who probably had many more than the reputed nine lives a cat is supposed to have. His biggest victory was surely those first weeks of life, when he must have used up most of the nine. But once he got over that hurdle, he lived life to the full, enjoying every moment, and he gave so much fun and entertainment to his whole human family. Even Charlie shed a tear at his passing and many a time at night if he heard a sound at the door, would sleepily ask if it was 'that cat' wanting to come in. He is remembered to this day as 'the best cat', and will always have a place in my heart; and maybe, somewhere up there, he's again flicking his tail under Charlie's nose.

11

HOTTENTOT

We acquired Pye-wacket by accident as we seemed to with all the cats we have ever had. Our dogs were a mixture: some were very definite and deliberate purchases, but others were unplanned acquisitions for various reasons, usually because they were about to be put down, were found injured or lost, or just didn't have a home or someone to care for them. But it was not only dogs this applied to, it extended to all dimensions of the animal and bird world.

My first dog when we returned to Bullo from America, in 1970, was a Rhodesian Ridgeback. The people on the farm next to us in Maryland had had one; she would romp through the fields with Prince and was a truly beautiful dog.

Not long after we arrived back at the station, Charles flew into Kununurra, and while he was picking up the grocery order found out that the shop owner was a breeder of Rhodesian Ridgebacks. Charles knew the children and I missed Prince terribly; he also knew there were no Chesapeake Retrievers in Australia. So he arrived home one day with the groceries and an eight-week-old Rhodesian Ridgeback puppy for me, and not long after that, with one black and one golden Labrador puppy for each of the two older girls. Marlee called her black Lab Shad, and Bonnie's golden

Lab was Honey. I read up on Rhodesian Ridgebacks in the dog encyclopedia and found out that one of their ancestors was the native dog of the Hottentot tribe, so that was what I called my puppy, Hottentot. And he was every bit as unusual as his name. The three puppies grew up together and were constant friends. Hottentot and Honey fussed over Shad after her nearly fatal episode with a crocodile, and all three watched out for each other at all times. They were the regular three musketeers.

Although they were always together, they all developed very distinct personalities. Shad was a brilliant hunter, she could track anything; she was a smart dog and would learn tricks very fast. Honey was very beautiful and so completely and hopelessly dumb that it was hard to imagine; she was very skilled at shaking hands, only with one paw though, and that was the extreme extent of her ability. Hottentot . . . well, Hottentot was Hottentot.

He knew he was King of the Castle; the two Labs fussed around him all day, and his human family told him regularly he was wonderful; he even had Charlie under his spell. So Hottentot didn't see any necessity to extend himself in any way. It was enough that he was there.

He grew to a very big, beautiful dog and it didn't take him long to realise that Charlie was King of the Castle in human terms, so Hottentot started to mimic Charlie whenever or however possible. This pleased Charlie no end, but sometimes when it got a bit too close to home he would good-heartedly complain. This usually was when we went walking. Hottentot would happily bound along beside us with a sprightly spring to his step. Periodically, though, Charles would become winded and have to stop and lean up against a tree. His breath would come in an asthmatic wheezing, whistling sound until it returned to normal. It didn't take Hottentot long to imitate this regular occurrence. On one outing,

Charlie stopped to regain his breath; he had his back to the tree, leaning his full weight on the conveniently leaning trunk, his eyes closed, hands on hips, breathing deeply with a wheezing inhale and a whistling exhale. When Hottentot assumed a sitting position next to him, even Charlie had to stop and laugh as the big dog started a very good imitation of Charlie wheezing. Reminiscent of the Pye-wacket remarks, now it was, 'Tell that dog to stop!'

Hottentot knew he was 'that dog', and he would look at me when the phrase was uttered, awaiting instructions; I would shake my head with a suitably stern expression, trying desperately not to smile, and Hottentot would jump up and walk ahead with a confident swagger.

So our walks would be peppered with statements like, 'That dog is doing it again, Sara', or 'Sara, tell that dog he can't come with us if he keeps doing that!' But I think Charles was flattered that yet again one of my pets had singled out his character to imitate, because there was always a chuckle in his voice when he said, 'Sara, tell that dog . . . '

Another amusing habit that Hottentot acquired without prompting or training was that whenever Charles left the dinner table, after dinner, to go to bed to read, Hottentot would climb into his chair and sit with us for the rest of the meal. One night he just climbed into the chair to everyone's amazement, and of course when he was showered with praise for being such a smart dog, he continued to sit in Charlie's chair whenever possible.

Sometimes Charles would leave the table to answer the phone. When he returned to find Hottentot holding court in his place, he would say, 'Sara, tell that dog to get out of my chair!' Hottentot would look at me, waiting for my response. Of course, we all knew what that would be, but Charles and Hottentot seemed to enjoy the exchange tremendously.

Hottentot would reluctantly vacate the position of power

and curl up on the floor on the other side of my chair waiting for Charlie to leave once more. Sometimes this would be repeated three times a night. Some nights Charles would not be in a good mood and Hottentot could sense this immediately by the expression on Charlie's face as he crossed the room. On these occasions, Hottentot was out of the chair long before Charles even reached the table. When he did miss the warning signs, just a touch of my hand on his side was enough and he would be out of the chair in a flash.

But on nights when Charles went to bed early, he was in his element and would sit in the chair for long periods, even managing to achieve Charlie's superior expression of bored arrogance, a look he often assumed when presiding over dinner.

Hottentot was a major hero twice in his life... well, Charles would usually only sanction once. The trouble with the second time was that Hottentot saved the day by protecting the girls and me, and indeed Charlie, against danger, and of course in Charlie's eyes this was his job, so he didn't look too kindly on a dog taking it over. So he wouldn't readily give Hottentot credit, except when the children and I were around and forced him to admit to Tot's bravery.

The time when in Charlie's eyes Hottentot was a major hero was when he upstaged Gus Trippe's super-trained ribbon-winning obedience dog.

Gus and Charlie had a long business/friend relationship that began when they were around eight years old and started their own lawn-mowing business. Gus was visiting with his wife and dog, and relating the dog's latest ribbon winnings, much to Charlie's chagrin. This determined competitiveness between them even extended to their pets.

The German Shepherd dog, feeling a little lost in a strange place, had wandered into the office looking for a familiar face. Charlie seized the opportunity, being thoroughly sick of hearing of the dog's conquests, and promptly said that dogs were not allowed in the homestead. Which of course was not so at all. Gus, not to tarnish the dog's reputation, immediately ordered it outside. Horror upon horrors, it ignored him! Charles made cutting remarks about ribbon-winning obedience dogs which resulted in Gus shouting louder; still no response from the dog, and more remarks from Charlie. The competition became serious and was getting tenser by the moment.

Gus handed over the controls to his wife who apparently had done the obedience course with the dog, and knew all the magic instructions. On cue, she jumped out of her chair, and in a 'sergeant major on parade' voice, index finger rigidly pointing in the direction of the door, boomed, 'Colt... out!' The command was a smidgin short of breaking the sound-barrier, but didn't move the dog. After a few more sound-barrier attempts with the same result, all peppered by Charlie's continual sarcastic remarks, the dog was forcibly dragged from the room under instructions from Gus.

Silence was the only acceptable way to respond, after such a verbal build-up of the dog's accomplishments, and such a miserable performance. The poor dog had probably only wanted to stay close to his owner, where he thought he would be safe, rather than outside, where the odds were three dogs to one against him. Unfortunately, he wasn't aware of all the laurels that had been heaped on his outstanding obedience qualities. He stayed pressed up against the outside door where he had been dragged, longing to get back inside, which didn't add in any way to the brave, strong, obedient image that had been built of him.

Into this silent vacuum wandered Hottentot, with the care-free expression of 'Hi, guys; what's new?', supreme in the knowledge that he had full run of the house.

Gus didn't miss the opportunity, picked it up in a split fraction of a second. 'Charlie, your dog is in the house.'

Charlie, equally quick and not wanting to lose the position of power by letting the dog have the chance to ignore him, merely said, 'Sara.'

Hottentot had immediately sensed the tension in the air as the first words were uttered, and was now following every movement carefully.

When hearing my name uttered by Charlie in that special 'this is extremely important' tone, he turned his head and looked at me. My eyes moved to the door and back to his, and just for good measure and a safety margin, I casually pointed to the door by just moving my index finger in my lap. Hottentot came through with flying colours. He quietly turned and walked out of the room with a 'didn't want to stay anyway' swagger.

Charlie roared with laughter at his victory, and couldn't resist a final triumphant remark along the lines of, our dog wasn't smart enough to follow verbal commands, so we had to do it all with signals! Hottentot was elevated to top position in Charlie's estimation, right next to Prince. And Charles dined out on that story for many months to come, and with especial satisfaction if poor Gus was present.

The other truly heroic act by Hottentot was when he saved Charlie's life. Charles was in bed with pneumonia, running a raging temperature and quite delirious.

The stock-camp cook came racing up the flat in the middle of the night to say the stockmen had bashed him up, taken the key and taken all the beer out of the store room. And all the men were blind drunk, and the bully of the mob was even at that moment staggering his way up the flat, shouting in his drunken state that he was going to kill Charlie.

I rushed in to tell Charlie, fully expecting him to rise from his sick bed, strap on his revolver, and stride out to defend his family and home.

To my amazement, he mumbled something incoherent, rolled over and went on sleeping. Blind panic hit me with physical force. I had three young children, a sick and delirious husband, I was in the middle of nowhere, nearest help over one hundred and fifty kilometres away, and apparently the entire stock camp, all drunk, were approaching the house to carry out... whatever, or settle some of their grievances against Charlie. The cook then conveniently disappeared.

Suddenly I was protector of life and home! I was shaking so violently with fright that my teeth were chattering. There was no way I could lock the children and Charles in a room for safety as most of the outside walls of our bedroom were flyscreen and our windows were glass louvres; you could simply pull out the panes of glass and step in, or just break them.

Thousands of thoughts raced through my mind. If I could just hide the children, was foremost. How much time did I have? I raced to the back of the living room, a wide expanse of flyscreen, and looked down at the flat.

My panic subsided slightly as I could only make out one figure swaggering and weaving up the flat, but then alarm surged through me as I could see more shapes just emerging from the trees on the far side of the flat.

'A weapon, I need a weapon!' I said out loud. I had reached the stage of talking to, and answering, myself. 'But what?'

I raced through the house grabbing and rejecting objects: frying pans, hammers, pieces of wood, brooms. In the store room, my eyes locked onto the de-horners, an enormous over-size pair of bolt cutters used to cut the horns off cattle. They were so heavy I could just lift them, but the wooden handles, the length and size of a baseball bat, screwed out of the steel blades and one of these made a more manageable weapon.

I raced to the flyscreen again; I could hear the man now, shouting Charlie's name and a lot of unintelligible and unre-peatable words regularly mixed around the repetitive 'Charlie'. I didn't like the tone or the implication.

I was still talking to myself, still shaking, and by the time I was in position and waiting, I was sick to the stomach and fighting to keep vomit down in my throat.

I had retreated to behind the door in the office, our bedroom door behind me, on the far wall. This was the only wall there was to hide behind, the rest were flyscreens. I had decided surprise was my best plan of attack. I had left more beer and rum on the kitchen table, and left on the light, hoping the fellow would go to the kitchen, take the grog and wander off. All the other lights I had turned off, and I was watching through the crack of the open door... waiting, sweat making it difficult to hold the weapon and making my vision blurred. I couldn't stop my teeth chattering. Charles lay in the next room, delirious and ill, and the three children were sleeping in the adjoining rooms. It was the early hours of the morning, and I was crouched behind a door in the middle of the Outback, waiting to crack a drunk over the head with a handle of a de-horner! The inevitable 'why me?' went through my mind. He was opening the back gate. I heard the clang of the bolt echo through the night; he left it open.

'Why must I face this alone?' I blubbered to myself and the darkness. Then, in this quietness of waiting, for the first time

I realised I was not alone. All through my blind panic of rushing around the house, Hottentot had been at my side. Indeed, a few times I had nearly fallen over him when I had changed direction suddenly in one of my wild dashes to somewhere.

He was still at my side, sensing my out-of-control blind panic, and was really very alert and concerned as he had never seen me like this before. He kept putting his nose in my hand, waiting for a reassuring pat. I kept pushing him away with a mumbled 'Not now', which only increased his agitation.

We were both behind the door, waiting, wound tight as coiled springs. Like Hottentot, I had no idea what was ahead.

The dark outline of a man appeared at the screen door at the back of the large living area. He had not gone to the lighted kitchen and the grog on the table. He opened the screen door into the living room and started across the room towards my door. He was forty feet away; my panic increased. He was quite out of his mind, ranting and raving and shouting Charlie's name. Thirty feet... the children's door opened and sleepy heads poked out. I screeched at them in a whisper to close the door and lock it. Such was the urgency in my voice, the door slammed shut in a flash.

Twenty feet... the shape loomed larger! I had no idea what I was going to do. I was weak with fright. I was sure my arms would fail, I was convinced I would just collapse in a heap when he staggered into the room. I knew I was not capable of what I was trying to achieve. Hottentot jumped up on me, worried by the state of frenzy he could clearly sense I was in.

The dark shape had paused in the middle of the living room, still mumbling incoherently, and drinking from a bottle. I could hear the children crying my name. I was crouched behind the door and also crying, knowing I couldn't, yet had to, face this drunk. Hottentot was licking my tears as they streamed down my face.

A crashing bottle brought me to my feet and without realising what I was doing, I rushed out the door, Hottentot at my side, and shouted as loud as I could, 'Get him, Hottentot!' I stood amazed and shaking as my very spoilt, gentle giant of a dog transformed before my eyes into a raging, ferocious, snarling, charging beast. He charged in the direction of my shaking pointed finger.

Even in the dark, I saw the whites of the man's eyes, as realisation penetrated the drink-fogged brain, that a large, savage beast was bearing down on him at an alarming rate. He turned, and without bothering to open the door, dived straight through the panel of flyscreen next to it, out the open gate and down the flat, screaming, with a snarling Hottentot right on his heels.

He made it to a large tree and clambered up to safety. Hottentot, carried away with his new-found character, chased away all the other dark shapes staggering around the flat. When they all disappeared back to the camp, he took up position at the foot of the tree to guard his captive, who spent the rest of the night up there. Every time he attempted to climb down, he brought on a new wave of snarling and snapping, so loud it could be heard clearly in the homestead. So the man decided to stay put.

I finally calmed down and assured the crying children Hottentot had saved the day. I found more weapons, just in case, and had time to find Charlie's revolver and load it. I told the girls to run to the pantry in the kitchen and lock themselves in if I called them to do so, or if anything else happened.

And I spent the rest of the night sitting facing the door with a revolver in my hand. My nerves stayed at high pitch until daybreak.

The cook came up the flat, making a wide detour around

Hottentot and approaching the house from the opposite direction. The offending stockman, he said, was now sober, was suffering from a horrendous hangover, and was very stiff from sitting in a tree all night. He would like to come down and apologise. And could I please call Hottentot off.

Apologise! I was so mad, sick, nervous and angry that I was capable of shooting him on sight! I told the cook he could stay up the tree for a while longer.

Charlie was awake and, although still very ill, his fever was down and he could now carry on a normal conversation; but he was too weak to get out of bed. He had to admit Hottentot was the hero of the day. But then he went on to give me instructions and a plan of action.

My first thought was to feed and water Hottentot. So with the gun in a holster strapped to my side, I walked down the flat and took him a big bowl of meat and some water. Told him he was a brave dog and to stay for a while longer. Ignoring the pathetic pleas from up the tree, I went back to the house.

The stockman was eventually let down out of the tree and Hottentot, the conquering hero, came back to the house to bask in the glory. The stock camp did not see one drop of alcohol for the rest of the muster, and had to be content with tea. I kept the gun handy and Hottentot constantly at my side, and periodically gave him the attack command if any of the men were close to the garden. He would launch himself into a ferocious display of fangs and growls, to send everyone scurrying away at top speed.

When the muster was over and Charles had recovered sufficiently to take the men to town, he said they made it in record time into the nearest pub for that long-awaited drink. They didn't have one ounce of my sympathy. If I had had my way they would not have seen any alcohol for the rest of their lives. That would have been fitting justice for the terror their drinking had put the little girls and me through. After days of endless, senseless drinking in town, the story of the savage lion-dog of Bullo River, called Hottentot, grew out of all recognition.

Back at the station poor Charlie had to listen to the true story again, and again, and again, while Hottentot sat there looking sagely at him. I blackmailed Charlie into many situations just with the threat that I would tell Gus how Hottentot had saved his life...

Charlie, good-heartedly, put up with the girls and me constantly singing Hottentot's praises. The girls would also tease their father whenever the opportunity presented itself. Once they dressed Hottentot in Charlie's red velvet smoking jacket, sat him in Charlie's bed, leaning back surrounded by pillows, with Charlie's glasses perched on his nose, and a *Newsweek* magazine on a pillow between his paws.

Charlie walked into the room, saw all the girls crouched at the foot of the bed giggling, and me sitting in bed beside Hottentot, also reading. Hottentot never moved a hair, only his eyes looked at Charlie over the glasses. Charlie played the game and thundered and roared protests, the girls squealed with delight, and Hottentot, as usual, enjoyed being the centre of attention.

Another time, when the Army were carrying out exercises on Bullo River, they dressed Hot up in the gear of one of the Army helicopter pilots, and sat him in the helicopter. The pilot opened the door and was shocked to find a dog in his seat, wearing headphones and flying cap.

Hottentot just calmly looked at him with a 'why not?'

expression and finally had to be persuaded to vacate the seat.

When I moved to Adelaide for a few months, so the girls could finish the last term of at least one uninterrupted school year, Hottentot came along as protector. Charles stayed on the station. Along with allowing the children to finish the school year, it was also one of Charles's and my many, many trial separations, to decide if we would stay apart or try again.

So Hottentot was the 'man' of the house in Adelaide. He stepped into the position without a moment's hesitation, and enjoyed not having to compete with Charlie for the number one position.

Having been used to roaming free in the wild, wide Outback, a small suburban yard was way too small. He had no trouble with the fences and could get out at will. He was lost so many times in the first weeks, I finally typed a long story on a large luggage tag and put it on the big 'Brutus' type collar, complete with studs, I had bought him.

The story was along the lines of 'Please excuse me, but I am from a cattle station in the Northern Territory; if I look lost, have done anything wrong or damaged anything, please call my owner and she will fix everything.' It finished with large letters: 'P.S. I'm friendly!'

Hottentot became a celebrity overnight. I found out he had a large territory, stretching from swimming in a private swimming pool about half a block away, to the shopping centre miles away. Each morning he would jump the fence, and swim a few laps of the pool, lie in the sun for a while on their porch, then disappear. He continued on down to the small shopping centre where he would swing by the butcher's for a small snack, and finish up a few shops further down, where he somehow cadged an icecream out of the owner— or anyone close by who happened to have an icecream.

The story on the luggage tag got everyone in; Hottentot would stand still as they read the story and the reader would always finish by saying, 'Oh, he's friendly'. You would see people leaning close enough to read the tag, but still trying to stay far enough away not to get bitten; then when they reached the friendly bit they would relax and immediately start patting him. One day he stopped all the traffic when he decided to sun himself in the middle of the main road through the shopping centre. The only way they got him off the road was with a meaty bone, and an icecream.

I finally went back to Charlie, yet again, at the end of the school year. But during the time we were away, the airlines changed their regulations on carrying pets. When we went from Darwin to Adelaide, Hottentot only cost five dollars, a flat rate for any pet travelling with people. When I called to arrange a cage for transport back to Darwin, they told me it was now calculated by weight, so many dollars per kilo. Hottentot weighed one hundred and thirty pounds, almost sixty kilograms; it was going to cost more than my ticket to get him home.

I spoke to the manager and said they should have told me when we booked down to Adelaide, and I would not have brought him. But now I had to take him home and couldn't afford the new charges, so I would bring my children down to his office and he could break the news to them that we had to leave their dog in Adelaide. He quickly agreed that if Hottentot travelled down for five dollars, he should indeed return home for the same amount. I thanked him.

The funny part of the story was when we took Hottentot to the freight office to check him in for the flight. There was a woman checking in a miniature poodle, and as we walked in with Hottentot, the clerk was telling her it would cost her thirty-five dollars for her dog. After paying the money, she turned and saw Hottentot lumbering in, and a massive cage waiting for him. She didn't leave, but stood and watched us put him in the cage, and all say our goodbyes, and was waiting to see the monstrous cage lifted onto a scale to assess the horrendous amount of money.

She froze in amazement as I handed over five dollars to the clerk, and he wrote me a receipt. The children and I departed, leaving her holding up her thirty-five-dollar receipt for a dog that didn't weigh as much as one of Hottentot's paws. And spluttering, 'But, but, I don't ... !'

Hottentot was part of our family for twelve years, which is a long time for a dog in the Outback. The heat is one of the first things that affects their longevity, along with snakes and crocodiles. Of course, Hottentot lived the life of Riley; the two Labs did all the hunting, while Hottentot reclined somewhere quiet and cool. And if he wanted anything extra to eat, he wasn't past nicking something off the chopping block in the kitchen. This was a great temptation, seeing his nose was level with any tasty morsel. Like the whole gigantic rump roast that was all seasoned, sitting in the baking dish, ready to go in the oven, when Tot happened to wander by and decided he would not put me to the trouble of cooking it.

I just caught a glimpse of him tip-toeing out of the kitchen with a rather large and strange addition to his jawline and I was after him. That was the last time Hottentot stole meat off the chopping block; in fact he only had to look at the chopping block and the memory of his slip from grace was enough.

His life with the two Labs, Honey and Shad, and Pyewacket, and growing up with the children, was sheer enjoyment. His passing was normal; I walked across the living room one morning on my way to the kitchen to start breakfast, and saw him still curled up on his favourite rug, sleeping peacefully. I told him he was late for playtime in the sandpit, the other dogs were already there. When he didn't respond to my voice, I walked over and touched him, and knew he had left us.

12

SUNDOWNER, SCRUFFY AND BUCKSHOT

We were working hard and were kept busy raising poddy calves. Every year we have a fair number, and as we have been raising them since we arrived on the station, there are a lot of cows on Bullo that were hand-fed from their first weeks of life. They all have names, and to this day, if you call to one of them in the paddock, it will usually turn around and moo back to you, responding to the familiar name that triggers old memories. I could fill a book with poddy calf stories alone, but as usual there are a few that will always stand out in my memory.

Sundowner was the absolute menace of the animal world. If it shouldn't be touched, enter Sundowner. The children were small when we raised her with a mob of other poddies, but for no special reason, Sundowner became a pet. After feeding time, she would attach herself to the children and follow them back to the house. Many a time I had to chase her out of the house because she forgot herself. But try as they did, the children couldn't teach her to go to the toilet outside; in fact she seemed to make a point of coming into the house to relieve herself. So my association with Sundowner was always chasing her with a broom. I think she must have suffered brain damage at birth, because you could not teach or train her to do anything.

By the time she grew into a small heifer, the children had singled out the next small calf to raise as their special pet, and Sundowner was drafted out into the herd with the rest of the now bigger poddy calves. But Sundowner had other ideas. I suppose she had spent so much time with humans, she didn't like being sent away with a bunch of cattle. So she would crawl under and through fences until she arrived back at the homestead gate, wait, and squeeze through with the next person who happened along. In record time, Sundowner would be in the house again. If she just stood there or walked around, that would be acceptable, but Sundowner really was a menace.

She wandered into the store room one Saturday night when we were showing a movie, back before the days of videos, way back in the days of movie projectors. All the staff were sitting in the living room, so she had a whole hour or more alone in the store room before someone wandered by and discovered her. By that time, she had split open and consumed half a huge seventy-pound bag of sugar, and a large bag of onions along with spaghetti, flour and a bit of tea for flavour.

For the next few days, out on the airstrip, she made some amazing sounds, both ends, and no-one went anywhere near her because you would need a gas mask to survive. Even the cattle ran away from her!

For years, we had sheets and towels with chewed corners. This was Sundowner's very, very favourite pastime. Whatever is in the saliva or the chewing method, the process seemed to break and wrinkle all the fibres in the material, and you could not wash or iron it out. So for years, sheets, towels, T-shirts, all of Charlie's business shirts had chewed corners or shirt-tails. Most of the offending chewed areas could be tucked under or in, so it wasn't too bad, but it made interesting decoration when the towels were hanging in the bathroom, with those corners you couldn't hide. She ate half of one of the hired movie reels that was left on the projector one night after the movie night. I came into the living room the next morning to find Sundowner standing in a sea of unrolled 35mm film, casually devouring it frame by frame. What she didn't eat and ruin beyond recognition, she stood on, slobbered on, or pooped on; the whole movie was gone for ever.

When I look back, I suppose we were extremely patient with this miserable cow, who really didn't give any pleasure, only trouble! For some reason, the children liked her, but she really was impossible. She ate the music off the piano, she ate the children's schoolwork, she ate our mail, any typed letters she could find, and like Honky-Tonk, our pet donkey, she chased the cooks if they were carrying food. None of which was funny.

But she did give us non-stop laughter when the girls got her drunk. Charles had left his rum and grapefruit juice evening drink on the coffee table to go and get something in the office, and Sundowner happened by, strolling on the lawn; she saw the cheese and crackers unattended and hoed in. Having finished the plate of food in a few seconds flat, she tried the drink. Charles arrived back and caused such an uproar we all came running. He went on and on about the cow drinking his precious rum.

This set idea lights flashing in the children's minds, and it wasn't long before they gave her a mickey-finn of mammoth proportions. They mixed a dash of everything they could find in the liquor cabinet, and finished off with beer for volume.

That cow staggered around the airstrip, bellowing, passing wind, hiccupping, sneezing, groaning and regularly falling flat on her nose. The next day was just as funny, as she worked her way through what must have been a terrible hangover. It seemed all her life's punishments had come at once. Maybe it was fitting repayment for all the destruction she had caused.

When I managed to grow banana trees and protect them from the pigs to the stage that hands of bananas actually developed, it was in vain. Sundowner would eat whole hands of green bananas at a single sitting. When I think back about Sundowner, all I can remember was that she ate anything, she ate a lot, and she passed wind and belched continuously—not what one would call fond memories of an endearing pet.

The children came screaming into the kitchen one day to tell me Sundowner's tongue had stretched and was lying on the ground in front of her. I raced out to find her quietly devouring one of our crêpe bandages. The bandage had been washed and was on the clothes line, which she had apparently just visited. It was a wide beige elastic bandage, and when Sundowner looked up at you, indeed it seemed as if her tongue was hanging down to the ground.

When she saw me running towards her, her chewing accelerated to such a rate that I just managed to grab the last handful of the bandage before it disappeared into the cavernous mouth. With my knuckles up against Sundowner's teeth and her reputation of eating anything, my first reflex was to pull, and so I did. The children howled behind me, 'Is Sundowner going to die?' My silent thoughts wished she *would*, while foot after foot of sloppy, slimy bandage was pulled out from the depths of heaven knows where. Unlike the film, I was able to retrieve the entire bandage.

Sundowner had the most amazing expressions on her face as her eating process went into reverse. She stood and coughed for quite a while when the other end of the bandage finally joined the rest on the ground. The bandage was washed, but it was never quite the same again. On the sections she had chewed, rather than just gulped down, all the elastic had gone, so the bandage had a ruffled, seersucker effect when wrapped around a sprained limb.

178

Although she was quiet enough to enable me to haul a twenty-foot bandage out of her mouth, she had grown to a large heifer. Unfortunately, though, Sundowner still thought she was a small calf, and this caused trouble when she wanted to play or nudge you with a friendly toss of her head. You would suddenly find you had moved several paces from where you had been standing. But action had to be taken when, again in a playful mood, she knocked Bonnie down on the ground, and started rolling her along like a ball.

Sundowner was excommunicated from the garden and had to take up residence in the far paddock of Bullo Creek; and so the association with another unusual animal came to an end.

As mad as Sundowner was, other calves were delightful. The girls arrived home one day carrying a very small, frail, starving, motley, miserable calf. I gave him one chance in a million of surviving, but the girls assured me he had spunk and a will to live, so we tried to help him along. He was such a motheaten creature which I called Scruffy.

Scruffy was that one in a million, that beats the odds. I didn't put him with the other calves, but kept him under the tree just outside the kitchen window so I could keep an eye on him. He was so weak that when he fell over he couldn't stand up again, so I would go out and help him. But he was keen to keep living, and would try to get up even before I appeared. He seemed to know that as long as he was on his feet he would live. The weeks passed, and his bony ribs slowly disappeared as the regular feedings of milk took effect, and to my amazement, he became strong and stopped falling over. His coat still looked as if a few hundred moths had been feeding on it, but a slight shine began to show through on the new coat growing underneath.

He finally joined the other calves in the pen when he was strong enough to fend for himself. I remember Scruff as a gentle soul; he would always come up to me at feeding time and stand waiting for a pat before he romped off with the other calves. I felt this was a 'thank you' to me for bringing him through those touch-and-go first months. For all the times I told him he could make it, when I am sure he was tired of trying, when he was thin and weak and swaying around trying to control his legs.

Like all the others, he grew to the size where he could go out into the big paddocks and live on grass and water, and so the day came when his group left the safety of the poddy pen, and ventured out into the big wide world, a little hesitant group, holding back in doubt, wondering what was in store out there in the unknown. He grew and survived. The next year, Danielle and I were riding through one of the paddocks and she called out, 'Hi, Scruff' to a big, shiny, sleek steer grazing close by. The steer raised its head and bellowed back in reply. I couldn't believe it was my ratty little Scruffy; I walked my horse over for a closer look and also called him by name. He recognised me immediately, and gave me an extra-loud, long bellow. I looked into his face and knew, yes, that's my Scruffy. He certainly had made up for lost time; he was a very handsome-looking steer.

The poddy calf that takes honours as everyone's most favourite of all has to be Buckshot. She is still alive, around fifteen years old. Marlee had saved her from being trampled on in

Prima Donna.

Ready-set-go! Donna diving in to race.

Danielle and Donna (post-race).

Max at the staff quarters.

Marlee with grader. *(David Hancock/Skyscans)*

Marlee and me. *(David Hancock/Skyscans)*

Hunter, the stock market dog.

Tennis outback style. I'm telling Cosmo he can't chase and chew the tennis ball, while Donna (not in the picture) waits, ready to pounce. We didn't stand much of a chance between the two of them!

Did someone say dinner? Cosmo looking hungry.

The homestead at sunset. *(David Hancock/Skyscans)*

Milking cow, Pumpkin, with her adopted calves. *(David Hancock/Skyscans)*

I tempt Pumpkin with some feed, prior to milking. *(David Hancock/Skyscans)*

Marlee and me with Bazza, our French bull. *(David Hancock/Skyscans)*

Beautiful Boots. *(John Curnow)*

Marlee and Franz with Mustang (Muzzie). *(David Hancock/Skyscans)*

Muzzie taking a well-deserved break in the cattle yards.

Sumie in the shadehouse, helping me with the gardening. *(David Hancock/Skyscans)*

Bullo River Gorge. *(David Hancock/Skyscans)*

The house where Franz grew up, no. 1 Obermillstatt. It's over 400 years old.

Gold Deck skiing lodge, overlooking the valley where I wrote the second half of this book.

the yards when all the cattle were crowded in after a muster. Later, when the cattle had been sorted into their different pens and the little calves branded, this calf still had no mother, so Marlee put her in the back of the Toyota and brought her back to the poddy pen.

The petrol fumes of the Toyota was the calf's first remembered smell, and for months the crazy calf thought the Toyota was her mother. If the Toyota was anywhere near, you would find Buckshot running around and around the vehicle trying to find a drink. She never gave up looking for an udder under the Toyota. We had to watch her whenever the vehicle drove away from the house, or there she would be, trotting along behind it. Thankfully she outgrew this strange behaviour, realised that milk was in regular supply in the feeding shed, and became a nice, friendly, normal calf.

She was a late end-of-the-season calf, and there were fewer to feed, so the girls had more time to spend with these calves than during the season, when we were feeding up to thirty or forty.

Marlee called this calf Buckshot, and she grew into a big, beautiful, black and tan Brahman with long, wide, impressive horns. Buckshot, over the years, has presented us with some very beautiful calves. There is quite a Buckshot dynasty, out there, her daughter and grand and great grand daughters being called Spot Shot, Big Shot, Hot Shot and Pot Shot; Marlee gave up naming at this stage.

Marlee can walk up to Buckshot anywhere on the station and she will stand there while Marlee pats her or scratches her chin. She knows the mustering routine so well, she is always the first animal through the yards when we muster in her area. She works her way through all the cattle in the yards to arrive at the gate that will let her into the 'pushing pen'. Unless a cow needs medical attention, she goes straight through the yards and out the 'bush' gate, as nothing needs to be done to her. Buckshot knows this routine, and is first at each gate, until the round yard, where she walks straight to the 'bush' gate and waits to be let out.'

Buckshot is a great help to Marlee if she has a few 'smart-aleck' stockmen in the camp who look like they will cause trouble because they have a female boss. Buckshot is in the area where we have our first muster each year; Marlee always looks out for her and lets her through to the round yard straight-away. So when the men are ready to start, if we have a few troublemakers, Marlee will gather the men around the round yard and give them the rules of the yards. With a straight face and a serious expression, Marlee tells them that the cattle must be moved through the yards at a fast pace. She continues, saying if the animal won't move through the round yard, then you jump down and do this; and she casually jumps into the round yard with Buckshot.

Now Buckshot is a very, very big and impressive animal with horns of a three-foot span, almost a metre. She is by no means a sleepy-looking cow, but very bright, and always watching. Just the horns alone are enough to deter anyone from sharing a small yard with her. So the moment Marlee jumps into the yard, the men are immediately alert and sucking in their breath in admiration for her guts or stupidity. Of course they don't know Buckshot was hand-raised by Marlee; they think she is just another of the few thousand wild cows penned in the last ten minutes.

Buckshot turns to face Marlee, and all the stockmen hold their breath waiting for the wild cow to smash Marlee against the steel rails. Before they can see the obvious love in her eyes for Marlee, Marlee tells them, 'Don't give the animal time to charge you. Rush in and grab it by the horns, twist its head to the side, and push it through the gate!'

The stockmen almost fall off the rails in amazement as Marlee does just that. Unbeknown to them, and out of their sight, she is scratching Buckshsot under the chin with one hand, while pretending to wrest her head and twist it violently around by the horn with the other. The secret is, if you scratch Buckshot under the chin she turns to putty and you can do anything with her. Of course she would also just follow Marlee through the gate, if asked, but then the stockmen would know she was a quiet cow. Marlee's way had far more impact.

After wrestling Buckshot to the gate, she appears to kick her out the 'bush' gate and, slamming it shut, tells the stockmen that's how she wants them to handle the wild cattle. If this didn't convince them that their female boss was as good as, or maybe even a little better at handling cattle than they were, when they saw how fast and efficiently Marlee could castrate the male cattle, they were left in no doubt that she excelled in the art of cattle work, and suddenly were quite willing to take orders from a woman.

Eventually they would learn that Buckshot was as quiet as a lamb, and would take the joke in good humour. Although it nearly backfired one day in the next muster, when one of the stockmen jumped down into the yards with a big black Brahman cow with enormous horns, and shouted to Marlee, 'Will I throw this stubborn cow out of the yards?' It looked as if Buckshot had been mustered again, and the stockman was going to play Marlee's joke, on her this time. Just as he was about to grab the horns of the cow, Marlee said she thought he maybe shouldn't try with that cow, because it wasn't Buckshot. The stockman scaled the rails at lightning speed, with enthusiastic help from the cow.

Buckshot still rules supreme in her paddock, and she visits us now and again at the homestead to show off a new calf or to just say 'hullo' when passing. A few years ago, I came into the living room to find Buckshot quietly chewing away on our Christmas tree; the rains were late that year, and it was the only green feed in sight that was low enough to reach, so she walked in and started eating. She avoided the decorations, but still had made quite a mess of our Christmas tree by the time she was discovered.

13

BEER, CHICKENS AND DONNA

While thinking back over the early days in the North, I would have to say beer was the major problem. If you had beer it was a problem guarding it, if you didn't have any it was also a problem. Especially during the days of the operation of the Bullo River Abattoir. If you ran out of beer, the abattoir staff would down tools: no beer, no work. If the beer wasn't cold at the end of the day, more trouble. Keeping up the supply was a major problem. Charlie used to fly it in by the crate; the Beaver often carried a ton of beer at a time.

The big problem was where to put it when it arrived at the station. Where to put it where it was safe, that is! It had to be under lock and key at all times, or there was havoc. On the few occasions the entire abattoir staff got drunk, the experience defies description. The problem was you could lock it in a secure shed, with extra padlocks. If you went away you'd be sure to hide the bolt cutters or take them with you, and the jemmy, but on your return, the shed would still have been broken into. Uncle Dick was almost always the ringleader. Once when we took with us all the implements that we thought could be used to cut padlocks, or pull the tin sheets off the frame or roof, we arrived back to find Dick had cut an opening in the tin wall with the oxyacetylene torch.

Another time when we both had to leave the station for only half a day, Charlie also took the oxy fittings. But we came back to a massive excavating project—they had dug in under the foundations and broken through the floor. Again the entire population of Bullo was raving drunk; Charles and I were the only sober bodies within a few hundred miles, but we were raving mad.

So the beer not only had to be always under lock and key, but also had to be right under our noses, where it couldn't be got at, especially at night, the favourite raiding time. Though stealing beer was actually a twenty-four-hour project, the thought was never out of their minds.

So in desperation, the beer ended up in our bedroom, under our bed. Charles congratulated me on the brilliant idea. Well, at least we didn't have to sit up and guard it all night or race out and check the store room, every time we heard a noise. But, of course, this didn't solve the problem completely. One night the bedroom door slowly opened, inch by inch; I was lying awake planning the next day, and Charlie was snoring deeply. I heard rustling and then tearing. I turned on the light, and there was Dick, flat on his stomach on the floor on Charlie's side of the bed, trying to pull a case of beer out from under the bed. So our bedroom door had to be locked nightly.

Then daytime raids were made on the beer fortress. While I was in the kitchen cooking, the flyscreen was cut away, and the glass louvres were in the process of being removed, when the sound of my key in the lock caused a hasty retreat down the flat. I opened the door to find the beer still intact, but the louvres had been removed to the stage where, in another few minutes, the beer would have been going out the window at an alarming rate. I recognised some familiar figures scurrying down the flat to the staff quarters.

Our bed was an old wire frame that sagged badly, but when there was a pallet of beer stacked under it, it was very firm, and wouldn't sag. As the cases of beer were taken out, my backaches returned. So I dragged the frame outside, built a bed-base out of beer cartons, then put the mattress on top; no more backaches. But it couldn't eliminate the headaches. New ideas for stealing continued to be thought up daily.

We had to keep two pallets of beer always on hand as the staff consumed fifty cases of beer a week. That was with them on a daily ration. If they had been allowed to drink their fill, the Beaver couldn't keep up the supply. Most of the workers were capable of consuming a couple of cases a day each, given the opportunity. I didn't know if they could do it every day, continuously, but they certainly could do it for a few days when they broke into the beer supply.

When I made a larger bed-base out of beer cartons, I didn't have so many stacks of cartons around the room, which was an improvement; I was tired of a room whose walls were lined with beer. The base of the bed was the reserve beer, and was neatly covered by the bedspread. So I didn't have to check it, only the piles up against the wall, to make sure someone hadn't thought up another beer-stealing ruse.

The beer-under-the-bed scheme had been working successfully for many months, but there was only one reason why it was a successful system; because Charlie or I, at least one of us, was always in the house. It was usually me in residence, but the time came when we both had to be away from the station and our first thought was for the beer. What to do with the beer?

When we had a few planning days in advance, the cases of beer were loaded onto the Toyota, and taken many miles— like twenty or more—into the bush, and hidden. All tracks carefully brushed over with branches, and phoney tracks set up to fool the avid beer trackers who started out on the search the moment the wheels of the plane left the ground. But we needed at least a day to set this up. On one occasion, wc didn't have time, so Charles reverted to a fear campaign, about the only option he had.

He threatened Dick and the beer-stealing group with castration, instant dismissal, large deductions from salary, twenty-mile walks, no beer for weeks, and anything else he could think up. He left, quite confident they would not dare approach the 'off-limits' beer bedroom. I didn't share his confidence; no threat devised by man or the devil would stop that mob. Charles said it was time we stopped being keepers; they were grown men, and it was time they took charge of their lives, faced a little responsibility! My answer to that speech was simply: 'Ha!'

We returned just before sunset, and of course both made a beeline for the bedroom. Charlie opened the door with the key; so far, so good. I had expected the door to be in splinters.

'See,' said Charles. 'I told you I put the fear of God into them,' he continued smugly.

The room was untouched, at first glance, but the bedcovers didn't seem right. I checked all around the sides of the bed-base of beer: not one case missing, not one case opened with a few cans missing; or the other trick was to fill the case with empty cans, the box looking full until you lifted it. No, all the cartons were heavy, all cans full.

I was sure they had stolen beer, but couldn't see any missing. One strong indication to me that something was amiss was that no-one was around. At the end of the day, usually they'd all be in the homestead waiting for dinner. The only time they didn't want food was when they were drunk—or busy getting that way. Today there was not a soul in sight—and no-one appeared to pick up their nightly ration of beer!

Charlie had finished his shower when I presented my suspicions to him, and said he'd better go down to the staff quarters and see what was amiss. He laughed and told me I worried too much; he was going to read his new paperback and not worry, because with no beer missing they couldn't possibly be drunk.

He sat down on the edge of the bed, swung his feet onto the bed, turned to make his pillows comfortable—and disappeared into a hole in the middle of what was supposed to be a solid base of beer. All the cases in the middle had been removed. They had cunningly stood some cartons on their ends, with a carton flat on top to stop the mattress from sagging. I suppose they thought the cartons would stay in place and hold the mattress up. Charles rolled onto the temporary structure at an angle, and it all collapsed.

He emerged from the hole, a look of black, thunderous gloom on his face, strapped on his revolver and headed off down the flat. Shots rang out in the night, but the staff were used to Charlie shooting up the place, and on this occasion they were probably so drunk they were applauding him as a sideshow. Thirty cases of beer were counted as missing, so I was sure the shooting didn't faze them in the least.

I didn't have to cook for quite a few meals. There wasn't much work done for days, and there were a lot of shaky hands around as they worked through hangovers, and lack of 'the hair of the dog' to stop shakes, in the following days.

I soon got sick of my bed going from ten inches high to three feet high, or sloping at different angles, and generally living with, or dragging cases of beer out of my bedroom daily. So another fortress had to be found for the beer. The new fortress was a difficult place for me to get the beer out of, but also difficult for the beer stealers.

In the middle of the slowly developing living room, the former equipment shed, there was a big cement hole, built as a mechanic's pit, to work under machinery. It made a perfect beer fortress—easy to get the beer in, hard to get it out—but I never lacked helping hands to get the cases out daily. At night, with the padlock in place and Hottentot sleeping on the rug, the beer was safe. When we went away, we were back to taking bolt cutters and oxy fittings with us, and also the saw, as the cover was wood, very heavy wood, but still wood. Even so, the beer was stolen if we were away long enough for them to hack through the locks. We never did find a one hundred per cent safe place to store beer; the only time it was safe was if one of us stayed on the station and guarded it.

These days, with no alcoholics on the station, a fortress isn't necessary; it is such a pleasure not having to lock up the alcohol. But after all those years, I still can't completely put the nightmares out of my mind, and many times when walking past the store room in deep thought, I stop and close the door and pull the bolt across without realising I am doing it.

Hottentot was not a conscientious guardian of the beer; I used to have to stuff him with meat, or he could be coaxed away by a tasty side of rump, which the beer stealers would take out of the abattoir without a twinge of guilt. If I fed him to the point of not being bribable he would snore the night through on top of the beer and nothing could budge him; but it took a lot of meat to stuff Hottentot!

Donna, my next dog after Hottentot, was a different matter. True, she would eat any morsel of food offered, but at night she switched to 'guard mode', and the beer stealers, even with meat offerings, couldn't get within a hundred yards of the house before Donna had the entire station wide awake.

Donna took guarding seriously, especially guarding my

office and bedroom, so while I had her in the house it was very hard for anyone to get in unnoticed. Donna would sneak along after them, watching their every move with her head on one side and an intent expression, then she would pounce and scare the daylights out of them.

Many of the dedicated drinkers tried vainly to win Donna over with meat offerings. (I am sure our abattoir would have operated at a profit if it had not been manned by dedicated drinkers.) Donna would take all the offerings, then nearly bite their leg off if they tried to sneak into the house in the middle of the night.

One night prowler came into the kitchen one morning and declared my dog had just bitten him. He showed me the bite on his leg; you could easily see it was not fresh, but many hours old. I told him that was pretty remarkable since she was sitting under the bench behind him, and had been there all morning. He swung around to see Donna's eyes staring intently at him, a low growl escaping her slightly opened, bared teeth. He said she should be destroyed. I told him I knew someone had been prowling around my house at night, and Donna was doing her job, and if Charlie ever caught him prowling at night, maybe *he* should start worrying about being destroyed. Donna continued to chase him and growl at him whenever he appeared, until finally she wouldn't let him in the back gate. The problem was solved when Charles fired him over some other matter, and Donna got a bit more sleep.

During her reign as 'top dog' at Bullo, we had quite a large chicken run. The old chicken pen, housing hundreds of chickens down by the pig pen, was closed down when we closed the abattoir. We ended up with about thirty chickens in a pen behind the aircraft hangar, nearer the house. This kept them safe from dingoes. With four dogs in the garden, the dingoes tended to stay away unless they were very hungry. If the dogs were asleep and the dingoes did get too close, the chickens set up such a racket that someone came running to their aid.

I let the chickens out every day so they could get some green pick, and this hour gradually stretched until they were free all day, and were only locked into their pen up night, to be safe from the dingoes and feral cats.

But their being out all day caused problems. The soft dirt around the plants close to the house was quite desirable for digging and laying eggs, and thirty chickens soon made a mess of my small garden. They also started wandering onto the sand and stone floor, and even into the rooms. When I found one laying an egg on my bed, I knew action had to be taken. Each time I found them near the house I chased them with the broom, and it soon got to the point where if I just appeared at the door with a broom they would take flight back to the chicken pen.

One particularly tiring, hectic day I had collapsed into a chair in the living room for a few minutes rest. I looked out the arches, and there were twenty or so chickens scratching up the lawn, digging holes under the plants, and roaming into the house. My first thought was, Who cares, I'm too tired. But there was ever-diligent Donna, poised and looking at me as if to say, 'Come on! the chickens need to be put in their place; that's your job.'

I gave her a 'get stuffed' look and said out loud, '*You* chase the chickens if you want them back in the pens; I'm too tired.'

Her head went on one side with a 'What?' expression clearly in her eyes.

'You heard me. You chase the chickens,' I said, pointing at them. 'Get those chickens.'

Well, what a reaction! She went out at double speed, and soon frantic chickens and Donna were colliding and running around in circles. I had to rush out and save the chickens.

But she looked trainable, so I persevered. Each day, with Donna at my side, I would herd the chickens halfway across the lawn towards the pen, until they realised there was an invisible circle at a certain distance from the house, over which they were not allowed to pass. If they did, they would be chased by the woman with the broom and her dog.

It wasn't long before I could just say, if chickens appeared on the lawn, 'What are those chickens doing on the lawn?' Donna would be out in a flash, and I'd watch in amazement as she patiently mustered all the chickens back across the lawn towards the chicken pen, in exactly the routine she had been following with me. When the chickens realised she wasn't going to eat them, and was following a routine they knew well from the past month, they'd head towards the invisible line halfway across the lawn, running, head and neck stretched out, in that loping fashion hens assume when moving is urgent. Once they reached the point where I always stopped chasing them, they'd stop running, and Donna would stop shepherding them and turn back towards the house. Such a funny sight, like a football match in full swing, and then the full-time whistle blows and everyone just stops what they're doing and walks off the field.

I never had to chase the chickens again. As soon as I said, 'What?' Donna's head would lift, and if she saw the chickens, she was off. She would herd them all across the magic line, then return to sleep at my feet. If a chicken became scared and just squatted down, Donna would put her nose under its tail and flip it over and over until it either reached the line or chose to get up and walk to the line, and it usually did.

193

The chickens soon learnt that Donna would not give up until they crossed the agreed line, so it wasn't long before there was a perfect understanding between the two parties.

They were very smart chickens; they had to be, because each day presented challenges and risks to life. Much as they loved being out in the open, their lives were in danger from chicken-hawks, which can kill a chicken with their claws in one sweeping dive, then carry it away in a second dive. At first the chickens would only graze close to their pen, so they could rush back in at the first sign of a hawk, but they slowly became braver and moved further afield. That was why the lawn in front of the house was a favourite place: if a hawk appeared they could run into the house for shelter.

When Donna's vigilant patrols barred them from the house, they found another shelter. They ventured far afield from the pen, and scrounged and scratched through the grass. But always with a beady eye on the sky, for a chicken-hawk to start its death run. Then a general alarm would go up in the form of a shrill petrified squawk, capable of mobilising any hearing creature. On this signal, all the chickens would run under the nearest cow, or horse, and stand under their stomachs. The diving chicken-hawk would have to abort its death dive, and circle, waiting, but the smart chickens would just stay put, and scratch at leisure, moving with the slow-grazing cattle or horse.

Occasionally, you would hear a terrible squawk and rush out, worried a hawk had taken a chicken, only to find a chicken had been concentrating on looking out from under its protection platform to suss out the chicken-hawk above, and the mobile shelter had moved and stepped on its toes. You would see the poor chicken running back to the pen with a very evident limp. The horse would bolt because of the noise, and again a terrible squawk would pierce the air, as a bundle of feathers and claws got tangled up with pounding hooves. Miraculously, a bundle of dusty feathers would pick itself up, and after a few violent shakes, turn back into a slightly ruffled chicken again. Because of this, they mostly chose the cattle for their protection. But even the horses' hooves were preferable to the swoop of the chicken-hawk out in the open, which was sure death.

Our chickens learnt survival skills at an early age. When they got to the egg-laying stage, they had more problems. The goannas would raid the laying boxes in their pen and eat the eggs. Soon we weren't getting any eggs. We changed the laying-box entrances to the point where it was such an obstacle course even the chickens could only just get in; but still the goannas ate the eggs.

Despite Donna's almost constant vigil, chickens still managed to sneak into the house, and they started laying eggs in the strangest places. Over the wet season, we park the bull-catcher buggy on the verandah, out of the rain. One day, Marlee went to get into it to drive down to the workshop, and found a dozen eggs on the floor around the accelerator pedal. So I put a few boxes lined with hay on the floor of the bull-catcher, more on the seat, and as demand grew, more in the back of the vehicle. I soon had thirty hens laying in the bull-catcher.

Of course, the goannas didn't like the new set-up at all, and soon there were egg-raids on the house. One morning a hen set up a terrible commotion; when I came running around the corner, there was a goanna, claws holding onto the top of the box, its head in the box, fighting the hen for her egg. The hen was standing her ground, pecking vigorously at the goanna. Interestingly, the other hens were also attacking the poor old goanna, and it soon realised it was fighting a losing battle. It was already retreating when I whacked it with the broom. Soon the goannas decided there was easier fare else-where, and left the hens to lay their eggs in peace.

In the first few weeks of our new laying project, the chicken-hawks also tried an inside attack, flying in under the arches of the verandah to grab a chicken while it was sitting on the bar of the bull-catcher waiting for a vacant laying box.

It was a daring manoeuvre; the hawk had to swoop under the arch at high speed, grab the chicken, do a 180-degree steep bank to avoid the ceiling fan, and then swoop down again to get out. Several times, a hawk made it under the arch, missed the chickens, clipped the fan, and in a dazed state tried to find its way out to safety. In the confusion of thirty hens squawking and screaming in alarm, and me swinging a broom, many a hawk finally found itself out in the open again very much the worse for encounters with fan blades and broom.

After a few failed raids, the hawks were content to cruise the skies, waiting for the chickens to make their evening dash to their pen. But Donna and I, and the broom, would escort them across the dangerous stretch, so the hawks mostly gave up.

So the chickens continued with their strange laying routine. They stood patiently in line around the bull-catcher, or perched on the bar over the boxes, all waiting for a box to be vacated. If any hen queue-jumped, she would be pounced on and sent to the end of the line. As a box was vacated, another hen would jump down off the bar to occupy it; the other hens would shuffle along the bar, and one would fly up from the queue on the ground.

They cackled and chattered continuously; it was a very amicable morning gathering. Some hens didn't time their egg-laying too well, and I would hear a plaintive plea at the back of the queue, to which the others would turn a deaf ear, so the hen would just squat where she was in line and lay the egg, then leave with a 'take that' expression. The other hens would just walk around the egg and ignore it, never breaking it. It was a different matter if the hen was sitting on the bar above the laying-boxes. Some of these eggs made a soft landing on a laying hen's back or fell into the hay; others missed the boxes and crashed to the floor. The hen would look at the result with her head on the side, and one beady eye on the smashed egg, then with an 'oh, well' expression she'd be on her way.

One morning when I was summoned by a great commotion, I went armed with the broom, expecting to confront a goanna, or a wayward chicken-hawk. Nothing. I looked into the laying-box where all the complaints were issuing from, and saw the problem. The next hen in line couldn't wait any longer, and instead of dropping the egg from the roosting-bar, she decided to get into the box. For some reason, two at a time in the box was not acceptable, and the hen in residence wouldn't let the other hen sit with her in the hay. Finally the desperate interloper perched on the other hen's back, laid her egg, then hopped onto the side of the box and was gone.

The six boxes were in hot demand by thirty hens, and some began wandering into the house to lay. Nothing was safe—cupboards, any shelf, boxes, even the hand basin in the bathroom! When Charlie sat on an egg on his office chair, a few stockmen were assigned to me for the purpose of building secure laying boxes in the proper places, the chicken pen. So the hens finally got their laying boxes and settled into a routine of laying in the pen, grazing under cattle during the day, and waited for Donna and me, and the broom, to bring their feed in the evening.

On my call, thirty hens would leave the protection of the cow or horse they were grazing under and make a headlong dash for the pen. If a distant hen saw the chicken-hawk in the sky starting a death dive on her, she would squawk for help, and Donna and I would rush to the rescue. Several times a hawk met nothing but a straw broom at the end of its dive, and waggled away with its steering temporarily out of synchronisation.

14

PRIMA DONNA

When Donna no longer got her exercise keeping the chickens in line all day, our daily walks became top priority. To let me know that it was walking time, she would stand in my path and look up at with an expression that indicated there was something important I should be doing; it was always right on walking time.

Even if I was too tired or too busy, I knew Donna was right, it was important for me to get away from it all and walk. And so we would both go and find my sneakers, then off we would go. Sometimes all the other dogs would join us, and Donna would spend the whole walk bossing them around. Some days, when we set off, you could see one of the other dogs look at Donna, and think, no thanks, you look too crabby and bossy today. And they would go back to sleep.

But Donna thoroughly enjoyed herself, whether she was bossing the other dogs or just with me, bounding over the paddocks, chasing anything that moved, and racing back regularly to check that I was safe. I would walk two miles, Donna covered at least five, zig-zag fashion.

Even when she was having her first litter of puppies, she still didn't want to miss walking! Her labour started in the afternoon, and she had her first puppy at four o'clock, walking time. When I went to put on my runners, I told her to stay. But when I reached the back gate, there was Donna coming out the door, with difficulty, but determined not to miss our walk. Her motto was, if you go, I go. She had left the puppy, and by the way she was walking, it wouldn't be long before the next puppy was due. I abandoned the walk and led her back to the little den I had made for her under my desk, to sit and hold her paw during delivery. The next pup came within the hour; it would have been born out on the road somewhere if Donna had gone walking. Or worse, dropped in long grass during one of her dashes after a lizard! It took Donna a few days to realise the puppies were hers; then she was ecstatic, and became a good mother and a fierce protector.

Before she had the puppies, whenever anyone approached my office Donna would bark and challenge them; but when the puppies were in residence no-one except the children could approach without this fiendish animal launching out of her den, hair standing on end, growling menacingly. Even poor Charlie got the treatment. Donna and Charlie had a 'Mexican stand-off' relationship: he said a perfunctory 'Hullo, Donna' when he saw her; she would just close her eyes and open them in a tolerant way to acknowledge the greeting. He never patted her, she never asked him to. They lived their lives around each other, but with me.

Charles's rule of no dogs in the house was observed only by Charles; Donna, like all other dogs, had fun breaking all his rules. At night, when Charles and I were sitting in bed reading, the door would open a few inches, and just the tip of a black nose would appear and pause, sniffing the atmosphere. Some nights, when Charles was in a bad mood, he would shout 'Out!' and the nose would be gone in a flash. Of course, that was not the end of it; the nose would keep on reappearing until there was no 'out' because Charlie was finally asleep. The door would be pushed further open, a pair of eyes would check that he was asleep, then the door would open wide, and the rest of Donna would walk confidently around to my side of the bed to receive a pat, then curl up on the mat with a contented sigh and drift off to sleep.

Some nights when Charlie was in a more cheerful state of mind, the exchange was different. The nose would appear, sniffing. Charlie would ask me, 'Is *that dog* anywhere around?' I would say no. The door would open further, and he would again ask, 'Are you sure *that dog* is not here?' Donna, now in full view, knew the game had started. She would start crawling across the floor past Charles, until she was out of sight at the bottom of the bed. At intervals Charles would ask, 'Can I hear *that dog*?', and Donna would freeze in position; I would say 'No', and she would start crawling again until she reached her mat, where she would sigh deeply and curl up.

Charlie would always finish the game by saying, 'There, I heard *that dog*!' Donna's eyes would lock anxiously onto mine, and I would have to reply, 'No, no dog here.' Charlie would chuckle and put out the light, Donna would heave a softer sigh, and we would all go to sleep. In a very short time, I would have Charlie snoring loudly beside me, and Donna providing a stereo effect and amplifying the noise on the other side, on the floor.

Donna was part of every minute of my day, so when I played squash, she too had to join in. As it was, she was quite an important part of my squash game. I used to just hit up against the wall for half an hour or so, for some quick exercise. Like most things on Bullo, in the Charlie years, the squash court was started on the spur of the moment, when Charlie decided he wanted a squash court for a quick workout. Half was to be underground, for coolness in the hot season, and the other half above ground. But it was not built properly from the word go. An alcoholic mechanic as project manager, directing a heavy drinker who was really just a handyman. They were pouring concrete into moulds, though neither of them knew much about concrete or moulds. I am amazed that the structure is still standing and hasn't collapsed inwards in a heap. Of course, they didn't think of drainage, so the squash court fills with a few feet of water every rainy season. And to this day it's only half finished—it never got past ground level. So I had to play low-level squash: any ball higher than eight feet went scudding across the lawn.

This is where Donna came in; she would race off across the lawn, retrieve the squash ball and place it on top of the wall, then stare at me. Eventually, after many shouts of command and a few threats, she would push the ball over the edge with her nose and would immediately start barking, waiting for the next ball to come over the wall. So ball retrieving came at a price! There was no way to stop the barking— I tried. Whether she was barracking or just saying 'hurry up and hit it out, so I can join the game', she made her presence known. If we didn't hit enough out, she told us, and there would be a pause in play while a ball was deliberately hit out for Donna to retrieve.

Charles couldn't play alone, because when he hit a ball out, Donna wouldn't give it back. She would stand looking down into the squash court, ball still in her mouth, and no matter what threats were issued, she just stared at him. If he went to the extreme measure of walking up the stairs to take the ball from her by force, Donna would just run away. So I would be summoned regularly to tell 'that dog' to give Charlie the ball. Which she would do immediately, when I was standing next to her, with an expression that clearly said 'I was just going to do it, when you arrived—truly!' So I had to be present every time Charlie played, because he didn't like a dog getting the better of him. I suggested I lock Donna up when he played, but then he'd have to retrieve the balls. A few times he had her locked in a room, and the children retrieving the balls, but they soon were noticeably absent whenever Dad played squash. So it would be back to barking Donna retrieving the balls, and me standing next to her to see fair play.

Tennis wore Donna out much quicker. She would race back and forth, following the flight of the ball. Sometimes she'd get cunning and wait near you; then, as you were preparing to swing at the ball, Donna would leap into view and take the ball. Other times, she would crouch below the net and take the ball in flight. Unlike the squash ball, you couldn't wipe a tennis ball dry, so you would be sprayed with her saliva each time you hit the ball. To play tennis in relative peace, we had to have four 'Donna' balls, which would be hit off into distant paddocks, so a rally could be played in peace, with a dry ball, while Donna loped off in pursuit of the soggy one. When she returned, another would be hit. Eventually, exhausted, she would sit quietly under a tree in the shade, and chew the last retrieved ball. She couldn't resist the occasional bark and whine, but when threatened with being locked up, she would settle down to low grumbling, and chewing.

Donna's greatest passion was the swimming pool; she lived in the pool. She wouldn't swim or play in the water alone— this required the girls or me—but at other times you could find her sitting on the step in water up to her neck, with her head resting on the top edge of the pool. From this position she could watch everything that was happening in the house. The occasional beer-seeking employee, trying to sneak into the other end of the house when I was in the kitchen, would be scared out of his wits by a charging wet Donna.

Best of all, Donna loved swimming races. She seemed to know they were competing to win, and would line up with the girls at the edge of the pool while I said 'Ready, set, go!' You could see all her muscles ready to leap on 'go'; she knew the word 'go'!

Danielle was given a start because she was the youngest by seven years, so when she reached a certain point in the pool, Donna would look at me, waiting for the countdown, then dive in with the older girls right on cue. The competitiveness showed in every stroke of her paw. She could really swim, and would plough through the water at a fast clip. If she passed, one of the girls, usually Danielle, would grab Donna's tail and be towed along. But Donna wouldn't give up: pulling Danielle, she would still head for the end of the pool with all the determination of an Olympic swimmer.

Donna and the children weren't the only keen swimmers in the pool. Each year at the same time, a cormorant flew in from some distant land to the north, and took up residence in our swimming pool for a few weeks, or until it realised there were no fish in that particular hole. The pool was very natural, made out of sandstone, so I suppose from the sky it would look like a rocky billabong. This bird was very possessive, and didn't like anything else in its billabong. The children had a wonderful time during these weeks. They would dive in and the cormorant would swim after them and peck them; if it got too close, they would call Donna, who would dive in and chase the cormorant, which would dive underwater or hot-foot it out of the pool until Donna had left the water.

This game would go on all day, much to the children's delight. I am surprised they didn't go on to become endurance swimmers; I was sure they would develop gills, they were in the water so much. Finally it would dawn on the cormorant that this fishing hole was minus fish, and it would fly away to a better location. But it returned each year, always hopeful of finding fish—or maybe it just enjoyed a few weeks of fun, playing tag with the girls and Donna.

Like all the animals with which I have had the privilege to share my life, Donna was exceptional, a delight, and gave me so many happy hours, days and years; so many wonderful memories.

15

MAX

One of the beer-searchers that Donna 'had it in for' was Max. As hard as he tried to win her over with endless offers of meat, Donna would take all the meat, let him into the house after dark, then raise the alarm. All the dogs would bail him up against a wall, and someone would have to rescue him. A few times in the early hours of the morning Charlie ignored the pleas for help, and at five-thirty when I went to the kitchen to start the day, there were all the dogs sitting staring at their captive, motionless against the wall.

Donna seemed to take pleasure in bailing up Max; maybe she disliked the particular ingratiating manner he used with her, trying to convince her he was her friend. The only result would be a minute raising of her lip to show a faint snarl, accompanied by a growl so low you couldn't be sure you had heard it. Max never dared lean closer to check! But for some reason, he kept trying to befriend Donna. Dick would warn him he could lose his head, but Max never took advice from anyone, and besides, if he won Donna over, the potential rewards in terms of extra beer were tremendous.

Max is a character of great magnitude; after Uncle Dick, he would have been not the next-longest resident character, but the longest regular temporary visiting character. He used to arrive on the station every year or so, for about three months. The reason was therapeutic; he needed this time to dry out. In town, his normal consumption was two cases of beer a day, just during working hours, not to mention what was consumed when out at night. He always told me he didn't drink while he was working: two cases of beer represented 'not drinking' to Max.

By the end of the year his system would start to get water-logged, or I should say, grog-logged. The doctor would tell him to stop drinking, but instead he would come to Bullo for a three-month drying-out programme. He always arrived the worse for wear: puffy-faced, with bleary, blood-shot eyes—if you could see them through the puffiness.

Over the months, the puffiness would leave his face, his eyes would clear, and his body would recover, and Max would start to eat regularly. Gradually, a healthy-looking person appeared.

On the station, he was on a restricted daily ration, like everyone else, of six beers a day—plus any other alcohol he could get his hands on.

Max was a good worker, but there were language problems: Max only understood what he wanted to. If he didn't agree with you he simply said, 'I no understand', and that was that. Nothing would get him to change his mind, except maybe—no, definitely—beer. It was very tiring playing these stupid games, but it was the only way I could get my house built.

My realisation that there was a language problem came early in the piece. When I finally had a so-called tradesman at my disposal for a reasonable length of time, the most urgent job was to change the terrible hole described as the bathroom. It was the original all-tin affair, unlined, with a cement floor. A washbasin was suspended on the wall; a raised cement ledge outlined the shower recess and a wooden bench finished the décor. You could scrub the tin and cement for hours and it didn't look any better. Charles complained regularly that it looked dirty; I told him it was dirty-grey to start with, and with twenty-plus people using it every day, it couldn't look clean.

Then he complained once too often, on one of my very worst days. In his exasperating manner he took me into the bathroom to show me the dirt on the wall in the shower recess. Twenty people had just been through, and this was grease washed off men who had been working in the work-shop. Charles was of the opinion that I should stop cooking, rush in and clean the shower from ceiling to floor, just for him. His last words were, 'Don't let me see that wall dirty again.'

My response, to myself, was, 'Okay, Charlie-boy, you won't!'

I took a sledgehammer, and knocked the whole wall out! It was only six feet across, so I didn't do too much serious damage to the overall structure. I pulled the shower curtain across, so when you opened the door it wasn't too evident that the wall was missing. The next night the staff hung a blanket over the hole, and went about their showers without a word; they saw the expression on my face. I removed the blanket before Charles turned up for his shower.

He walked past the kitchen while I was cooking, walked in the bathroom, pulled back the shower curtain, and there was the vast expanse of distant mountains—but no dirty wall. Charlie, being Charlie, stepped into the shower recess, pulled the curtain across and proceeded to have a shower, exposing his all to the landscape, and anyone who just happened to be walking by; our Charlie was quite an exhibitionist. He walked back past me in the kitchen and simply said, 'It's an improvement.'

The wall stayed like that for many months, and having a

shower became the highlight of everyone's day. You could be showering and a horse would put its head under the blanket. The milking cow would pinch the soap; a young poddy calf once ended up right in the recess, and had to be forcibly removed; snakes found it a cool place to rest. You always had to check.

So here was my opportunity to improve this situation. I drew a plan for Max; it seemed very clear to me, and I explained the drawing, showing him walls, door, windows, shower and bath. But most of his previous supervisors had been Yugoslav, and could explain plans in his own language; no such luck on this project. So I asked him if he understood what I wanted, and he replied, 'Oh, y-e-e-e-s-s!' So like a fool, I wandered off and left him to it.

As shown clearly on the plan, the bathroom was to be ten foot by ten foot, and the present bathroom, six foot by six foot, would be the entrance area with washbasin. I came back to find Max had got the ten-by-ten part right; the problem was he made the bath ten-by-ten. All hand-moulded, shaped, and cement-rendered, ready for tiling the next day. He was so proud of the mini swimming pool he had created. 'What about the shower, and where can we walk?' I asked. He got an inkling that maybe he had made a mistake, and immediately switched to the 'I no understand' mode.

Well, space was one thing we weren't short of, so we removed a few more walls to provide the walking space, and shower, and ended up with a very large bathroom. I think the bath has only been full a few times in twenty years. Well, let's face it, if you want to swim, you use the pool: it's already full.

We had friends visiting, and their two children went into the bathroom for a shower, came rushing out to tell their mother that we had an indoor swimming pool!

From then on I had to be an on-site supervisor, or at least

check hourly. Max was a tiler by trade, and working in bathrooms, it was okay for him to indulge his passion for tiling. But I had to watch him carefully on any other job because he was likely to put tiles anywhere. If you let him, he would tile a bedroom!

It was highly stressful having Max working in the house, because of the alcohol problem. For peace of mind I put the liquor under padlock, but this still didn't help.

One day Max was working on a sandstone wall near the kitchen, right under my nose, so I thought all would be okay. The wall was solid sandstone and progress was very slow. He was approaching the top of the wall after four days, and had to erect scaffolding to enable him to finish the top. It was afternoon tea time, and I was about to make the tea. Max had been very chirpy most of the day, which was unusual; usually he had constant complaints about something—the stones were the wrong colour, or too small, or too large, the cement too old, too wet, drying too fast, and so on. But not this day. I asked him if he would like a cup of tea. He said he would—and then walked straight off the end of the scaffolding and landed face-down with a sickening 'splat'!

Silence followed, after I dropped the cup of tea and let out a scream. I stared at the motionless, spread-eagled shape on the cement floor. He had to be dead!

I rushed over and called his name; no response! I felt the pulse in his neck: it was thumping, his wrist was even stronger. So he was still alive; how, I don't know. I carefully turned him over, and this seemed to rouse him. The alcohol fumes overwhelmed me as he muttered, 'Whas-sa-madder?' He was as drunk as a skunk! I reeled back in shock. My eyes went straight to the store room door: the oversized padlock was still in place. I helped Max to sit on a stool, but he kept falling off because he was so intoxicated. I tired of helping him off the floor, so the next time he fell, I let him stay there.

At least he couldn't do himself any more damage.

Soon some of the stockmen arrived and carried him down the flat to his room in the staff quarters, so he could sleep it off. Whatever 'it' was, I still had to discover. I opened the padlock on the store room door, and went to the liquor shelf. The alcohol was kept on the very top shelf at the back, so you had to climb a ladder to reach it. This was because it wasn't past Dick to ask if he could look for a special washer he needed among the miscellaneous parts stored in the store room, and take a few quick nips of any bottle he could lay his hands on. He knew it embarrassed me to have to stand guard all the time he was in the store room, and it was equally embarrassing to keep going in and out pretending I needed something for cooking.

So I climbed the ladder, and above the liquor shelf I found a neat hole cut in the ceiling. One half-gallon flagon of rum was all but empty.

All day, it appears, Max had been crawling across the ceiling and drinking at will from the top shelf. No wonder he didn't hurt himself when he walked off the end of the scaffolding! He wasn't capable of coordinating any muscles, so was completely relaxed when he fell.

A patch was nailed over the hole and the liquor moved down to the next shelf. Not that this move stopped them trying, or solved the problem. The portion of the wall built that day would put the Leaning Tower of Pisa to shame. When sober, Max was most upset that he had built a crooked wall. He was a perfectionist about his work, and wanted to knock down the top half of the wall, and rebuild it.

'No way!' I told him. It stayed. I didn't mind it being slightly out of line; it was a thick, double wall, and only the very top was crooked, so I figured once the ceiling went in it would be hardly noticeable. But every now and again I will see a man sitting in the kitchen trying to decide if he has had a bit too much to drink, or if, indeed, the wall he's looking at is leaning!

We had some funny times with our dedicated drinking mob! Well, maybe they are funnier when you look back; at the time they usually were exasperating, and often a lot of more explicit words could be used to describe my feelings.

We had not seen Max for quite a few years when we decided to go into the tourist trade; it was around 1989. We needed some improvements to our guest rooms if we were thinking of having paying guests. So I started sending out feelers to track Max down. It wasn't hard to find him; he was seldom far from Darwin, or a pub, except when he came to Bullo. It was arranged for a friend drivng to Kununurra to pick Max up at the appointed pub, and bring him to Bullo. Max smoked more than he drank; our friend didn't like cigarette smoke in his car. There was an exchange of hostile words; the friend felt he was doing Max a favour driving him five hundred miles to our very door. And Max's attitude was that the man was his chauffeur—which didn't go down too well with this particular friend. Max went back to smoking and drinking at the bar, and the friend travelled to Kununurra alone.

I arranged a second attempt to get Max to Bullo, and he just didn't show. At this point he seemed to vanish. I couldn't track him to any of his regular haunts, so I left messages everywhere, knowing eventually he would surface. We had five or six months leeway, needed when dealing with Max, so if I didn't find him in the next three months, I would have to make other plans.

About right on the deadline, I received a telephone call asking me if I knew a person called —; I cannot pronounce the name without three or four attempts, and wouldn't even try to spell it. I told the caller, very definitely, no! He went on to say this man had worked for me. I assured him if someone of that name had worked for me, I would remember. We hung up. He called back the next day very determined to convince me that this man had been in my employ. I was tiring of this situation, and asked him who he was, and what was his purpose in establishing this fact.

He was a doctor at the Darwin Hospital, and the second call was to say that this man, whose name with all the letters of the alphabet arranged in the most difficult combinations, was known to me as Max! No wonder he called himself Max! So that was how I found out where Max had been for the last three months, and why he didn't arrive at the second arranged pick-up place.

The night before, he had been drinking in a bar with a mob of mates, and a fight broke out. One man called another in the group a 'son-of-a-bitch', in a relatively friendly manner. Because of the man's customs and beliefs, this remark was considered an insult to his mother! Unfortunately for the man who made the remark, and eventually for Max, the insulted man was the size of a bear; he ripped the leg off a nearby table and thumped the man who had insulted his mum over the head with it. After he thumped him a second time, Max stepped in and said he shouldn't do that, so he thumped Max on the head. Well, this is the story Max eventually told me! Whatever did happen, the result was that Max and the other man both ended up in hospital. His mate had more serious injuries than Max. Max received a steel plate in his head, replacing the shattered bone that was once his cranium.

The doctor had called me because Max really needed to be in a home, to be looked after. His hospitalisation was over;

they could not do any more for him. The problem was, the hospital had to discharge him into a convalescent home, or into someone's care. Max wouldn't go into a home, and suddenly all his friends didn't seem to be around. So he told the doctor to call Bullo and say he would live there. I travelled to Darwin to see Max.

The doctor carefully explained Max's injuries and I was bracing myself to see a vegetable sitting in a room waiting for me. The doctor had said that most of the time Max didn't know who he was or where he was, didn't know things like what day it was or what month, and couldn't do simple tests like putting pegs in the right holes, couldn't read newspapers—the list went on and on. I seriously doubted if Max would be able to come back to Bullo with me.

I asked the doctor if he could feed himself, bath and dress. This wasn't the problem by a long shot. It seemed that Max was quite capable of shinnying down the drainpipe from the second floor each night to go on a drinking bender, and return to the hospital in the morning to sleep off his hangover! This sounded more like the Max I knew. He was starting to be a complete nuisance at the hospital, ordering the nurses around, and generally treating the place as a hotel.

The doctor on the one hand wanted to tell me all about Max's dreadful behaviour, and on the other hand, not divulge too much because he wanted to discharge him into my care. So he was in a quandary. Little did he realise, nothing, absolutely nothing he cared to relate of Max's behaviour would surprise me. I was concerned about his injuries, though, and told the doctor I would sit and talk to Max, and see if I thought we could look after him at Bullo and work out a programme that would keep him busy and occupied, in a reasonably happy state of mind.

I braced myself to meet this new Max. The doctor directed me into the room. There sat Max, thinner than I had ever seen him; his thick unruly mop of silver-white hair had been shaved off for the operation on his skull, so he looked strange with only an inch or so of hair in the old Kramer hairstyle. His usual dark suntan had faded to a pallor which increased his look of being unwell.

His dull, bored eyes brightened as he recognised me. He ushered the doctor out of the room in a fussy intolerant manner, closed the door, and started talking ten to the dozen; he was still going strong an hour later. I got the fight in the bar in vivid detail, many times, along with various stories about ten thousand dollars in cash that he had in his pocket before being thumped, and didn't have when he came back to consciousness. The story was never the same, but somewhere in the variations, there was always a woman who could only be described as a cross between Lucrezia Borgia and the devil. Where she came into the sequence of events even Max couldn't tell you, but she was there in every version, and she, as far as I could comprehend, took the ten grand. Most of that first hour he spent telling me to go and get his money back. No words could convince him that if *he* didn't know who she was, or where, in his long journey from Darwin Hospital to Adelaide for an operation, and back, he had encountered her, that I couldn't be expected to find her. Especially with the description Max gave me! This character would only hang out in the house of horrors.

I finally got him to stop raving about her, and at that stage I agreed with the doctor about his mental condition: he appeared very seriously disturbed. I steered him onto a more peaceful subject, I thought, by asking him about his stay in the hospital. Well, off he went again!

'Idiots, all idiots! You gotta get me outa dis place!' He became very confidential: 'E-e-e-a-a-r-rr, you see dat one I push outa the door, see him?'

I nodded, knowing he meant the doctor.

''E mad! Every day 'e say, "Who me?" The first few days, I say "You doctor". He never remember! Next day 'e ask, "Who me?" I get sick of telling him who 'e is, so I say, "Don't know, go ask someone else!"' He continued, ''E so bad, they pin 'is name to his shirt! Y-e-r-r! You look next time!' He sat for a few minutes staring at the wall, tired from continuous chatter, but pushing himself because he had to tell me all.

'They are all mad here, all ask "Who me?" Most of them have to have their names on their shirt.'

'Dis one,' and he acted out a pushing motion, 'he says "What day?" I tell him. Next time I see him, "What day?" I get tired of silly question, so I say to him "Don't know." Stupid man, has to be told ten times a day, what day it is!'

'If he don' ask the stupid question, he wan me put sticks in holes all day. 'E ask if he can puta the square wood in the round hole. Stupid! I tell him, y-a-r, go ahead. You can do it.'

''E not the only one, they all mad, all play with those sticks. 'E tell me to read papers, but no have the glasses; how to see without glasses!'

All this chatter cleared up the doctor's assessment of Max's severe brain damage. He was the same as he always was, stubborn, intolerant, impatient, and refusing to take orders from someone younger than himself.

I fought to keep a serious expression while listening to Max's tales of woe. I wanted so much to burst into laughter. Here was the same rascal, slightly vaguer than before the accident, but still very much the same Max we had always known.

When the doctor asked me how I found Max, I said, 'Much the same as he always was, before the accident.' The doctor protested and said surely not; how would he fail all the tests? When I told him Max's reasons for giving stupid answers or not answering at all, and said that Max was angry because the doctor expected him to read without glasses, the doctor wanted to know why he didn't ask for glasses. Max's reply when I asked that same question had been, ''E's the smart one; 'e should know!'

The doctor walked away shaking his head, thankful he didn't have too many like Max through the system. And hoping against hope he could discharge him into my care!

We took Max home to Bullo. He soon realised he couldn't play on his illness with pleas like, 'I sick, I need lotsa beer', which were received in stony silence. And threats of, 'I leave' were met with, 'Go ahead, I'll call the hospital and tell them to expect you.' He finally settled down to being his normal impossible self.

We started work; it was then I realised I didn't have the Max of old. He could only do a few hours a day. I told him to take it slowly, and he gradually built up his strength. The vagueness was very evident when working, and I almost had to be his constant supervisor/assistant. He would put a tool down and forget where. In the middle of working, he would walk off and not come back. But we persevered, and he slowly improved. He was keen to get back to his old self; he would even come and ask me what job he was doing, if he had a memory lapse.

One of the funniest situations was when we were ready to tile the new bathrooms. If he was doing the same thing each day, he could stay on track fairly well, but switching jobs was difficult. It took a whole day to get him off the plastering track and onto gluing the tiles on the wall. But eventually we made progress.

I gathered the tiles, tools, various buckets needed for the job. He demanded bags of powdered glue, tile spacers, tile cutters, grouting, all the things he needed to tile the walls. After all the equipment was assembled he checked for the hundredth time, before he was satisfied. I thankfully departed, knowing that to Max tiling was a natural reflex, he didn't have to think. Just put him in front of a wall, give him the tiles and tools, and he would start tiling.

He was at my side in the kitchen within ten minutes. He was most upset; it seemed the glue was no good, and he could not stick the tiles on the wall. He didn't like the glue.

In vain, I told him the glue was new, only bought one week ago; I showed him the invoice and date, but to no avail. 'No good the glue' was all I could get out of him. I finally told him I would get more glue in a few days; in the meantime, go away.

The next lot of glue arrived—with the same result. 'No good the glue!' I finally worked out the problem. The glue was okay; he didn't like the brand. The twenty-kilo bags had a picture on the front; the brand he liked only had printing. He had spent three days objecting to a picture! We had to buy more glue and grouting of the right brand; when he finished a bag of the approved brand, I swapped the glue and grouting from the pictured bags into the other bags. I thought I had solved the problem...

'No good the glue!' What now? I wondered. I followed him into the bathroom he was tiling. I could see us years down the track still tiling the four bathrooms.

The problem this time was that he was trying to stick the tiles on with a mixture of grouting powder, not glue powder. But again, in vain, I tried to get this across to him.

'You no tella *me* how to sticka the tile on da wall!'

'I'm not! I'ma tellin' you, you're usin' the wrong stuff!' Now I was talking like him.

'You don' know nothin'!' he shouted.

'Ditto!' came my reply as I stamped out. I was ready to give up. He was just too hard to work with. It was impossible to get a simple fact across.

Then an idea came to me. I had swapped the bags because he didn't like pictures; why not again? For some reason known only to Max, he suddenly had decided that the grouting powder was the tile glue, even though the word 'grouting' was clearly printed on the bag. Why waste time appealing to logic? I would swap the bags again. I gave Max a beer to keep him occupied, and told him to go and sit in the sun and have a cigarette.

I emptied the twenty kilos of grouting out of its bag onto some paper, emptied the glue powder into the grouting bag, and quickly shovelled the glue into the grouting bag. Put everything as it was, then went and found Max. I told him I had found another bag of good glue this time, to come and try it.

'I've beena thinking.' Oh no! I thought, I don't believe it! I looked at him in horror. Yes, it had finally sunk into that brain.

'You right, I use-a the wrong bag!'

And with that he picked up the glue bag, now filled with grouting powder, and said, 'I now use this bag, tile stick very good.'

My mind went through the horrors of trying to explain to Max what I had done, or better still, find a story to cover what I had done! I took the easy way out. 'Have another beer, Max.'

He readily agreed, and went happily back out to his seat in the sun for a beer and cigarette. I hurriedly emptied the glue out of the grouting bag, etc, just finishing as he returned to work.

This was only one of hundreds of incidents. It finally got to the point where he could not be left alone. Franz found him one day up one of the steel power poles, only inches from the power line, trying to cut through a steel bracket on the pole. He was using the nine-inch cross-cut saw blade on the grinding machine, which was used for grinding rough edges off welding joins. Somehow he had managed to attach the cutting blade to the grinder; he had already burnt out the saw. It was dangerous enough using the grinder in this way, the saw blade could fly off at any minute; but he was up a steel ladder, against a steel pole, working with an open blade, inches from power lines. He constantly complained he was so dizzy after his accident that he had trouble walking, yet here he was fifteen feet up a ladder, in rubber thongs, balancing on a narrow ladder rung, trying to cut through a four-inch steel bracket with an open blade on a grinder!

Franz pulled the power cord out of the power point. Max came down the ladder, foaming at the mouth, telling Franz he was only a boy, and had no right to interfere with what he was doing.

Franz, six foot three inches, picked up Max, five foot two inches, by a handful of his shirt and with Max suspended in mid-air, said in a very quiet voice, 'You will pack and be ready to leave in the morning.' He put him back down on the ground and left, taking the grinder.

I realised that if Max stayed any longer he would be sure to injure himself, or worse, kill himself or someone else. He was taken to town the next day, closing the door, finally, on the last of the group of dedicated drinkers of Bullo.

16

FILLING IN TIME

Not all the characters in my life were alcoholics, thank heavens. One very normal and sober character I am privileged to have had in my life for many, many years is my brother-in-law, Ralph Potts. 'Potts', as he is affectionately known to so many friends and acquaintances, is a person full of life and interested in every living thing. He will not tolerate some, but is kind and considerate to all reasonable humans and animals.

Ralph's sense of humour has always been a large part of his life. When he was courting my sister, way back in the 1950s, he would send letters to our house addressed to my mother and father, and the address on the envelope would read: Honest Ida and Aub (my mum's name was Ida, and Dad's was Aubrey), Draught Manor, Croydon Street.

The postman knew everyone on his run, and he was a very curt and serious man who handed you your mail personally. He would hand these letters to Mum with a distinct curl of disapproval on his lips, saying, 'I do believe this letter is for you, Mrs Barton.'

Ralph called Mum and Dad 'Honest Ida and Aub' because he said they were the last of a breed that no longer existed. He called our house 'Draught Manor', because he said it was the coldest house in existence. We only had open fires, and all windows were kept open (Dad said it was healthy). Poppa had a thing about using too much firewood. Every time he left the fireside, everyone would rush to stack logs on the fire; Poppa would return and say, 'Oh, joves', and take them all off. In the winter, the wind howled and whistled through the house, rattling the sliding doors, almost blowing out Poppa's miserable fire as it roared past up and out through the chimney. Poppa seemed to delight in using the least amount of wood possible in a night. The only time you could feel warm was if you stood inside the fire-grate and put your hands over the flames.

To watch a night of televison, Ralph would arrive with a pile of blankets and an armful of pillows. When he was finally in position and rugged up, all you could see were his eyes. If someone called on the phone to speak to him, you told them he had just gone out. He wouldn't get out of his chair because it took too long to get back into all his blankets. He wasn't the only one to be wrapped up to the eyes. Not as many rugs as Potts, but we all were rugged, even Mum had a rug over her legs. Poppa wouldn't, on principle, but I am sure he, too, was cold. When he was away for the evening it was open season, and we would pile on the wood and have a roaring fire—even setting the chimney alight on one occasion.

Poppa apparently had all the logs numbered, because he would remark, 'Oh, joves, too many logs burned!' and the next night we would really freeze, as Poppa barely used any wood to bring to log supply back into balance.

When Mum and Dad went on holidays, we had a field day, with roaring fires all day and night, but we had to buy extra loads of firewood, and ask our firewood man not to tell Poppa. He would allocate so many logs per night, our quota to be used while he was away. This would be left in a separate pile away from the rest of the firewood.

The first thing dad would do when he returned was check the woodpile to see that we had not exceeded our quota. With the extra wood we bought, we'd have six weeks of roaring fires but stay within the quota. Fortunately for us, they took their holidays in the coldest part of winter, so we only had to freeze for about half the winter.

The many holidays the children and I took in Sydney after we started to live on Bullo were always with my Mum, or with Sue. One year when we were staying with Sue and Ralph, they were living in a lovely house right on the water at Yowie Bay. The house was built down a cliff face, and all glass windows faced the water view. The entrance, or front door, was down through the roof, and the clothes hoist was out in space on a platform reached by a bridging walkway. Of course, holidays were never really holidays when Charlie was around. He would give everyone jobs endlessly. He didn't mind relaxing, but for some reason the girls and I had to keep busy. We fouled up his plans as much as possible, and Sue and Ralph were a great help in making our escapes possible. Sue would stand up and tell Charles what she thought of him, which didn't affect Charles in the least, and Ralph would devise intricate plans to outmanoeuvre Charlie; both seemed to enjoy the game immensely, and of course Potts couldn't resist a joke or a bit of fun now and then.

One scheme to get us all out of Charlie's work-plan failed for the girls; well, I suppose, for me also. I had to go to lunch with Charlie, but it was a business lunch, not what I considered a fun day. The girls were to stay home and man the phone. Charlie had put several ads in the weekend classifieds for a cook (again) and handyman for the house, and workers for the abattoir.

We all told him two children aged fourteen and twelve could not interview people over the phone for jobs. He gave the girls a list of answers to likely questions, quite sure these would be the only questions asked. I worried at first, then thought, what the heck, if anyone was stupid enough to answer an ad for a job two thousand miles away, to be interviewed by a twelve-year-old with answers to only a limited number of questions, they would have to be insane, and they would fit in nicely with Charles!

I left for the lunch telling my two very worried telephone operators just to do the best they could and not get upset. I gave them a pad each, and pencils, and told them to write down, at least, the person's name and telephone number and I would call the people back.

Luckily for the children, in the 1970s not too many people were interested in even going to the Outback, let alone working there. But they did receive a few genuine calls, spaced regularly among quite a few calls that were unusual, to say the least.

Marlee answered the phone, and a very strange voice told her he wanted to 'be cook on cattle station'. When Marlee asked was he a good cook, he said, 'Oh, good cook; I cooka the goanna, I cooka the kookaburra, I cooka the snake. I cooka anything!'

Marlee was signalling to Aunty Sue to come and help her, but she couldn't catch her attention, so she went on speaking with her weird applicant. Tactfully as possible, she told him we only had limited accommodation, and we were looking for a female cook, because she had to share a room with another girl. The reply came back, 'It O.K., I share with girl, no problem; I love-a the girls, is O.K. I come straightaway, I leave now, love-a the girls!'

Poor Marlee put her hand over the mouthpiece and called, 'Come quickly, Aunty Sue, I have a maniac on the phone and he wants to come here now. What will I do?'

Sue took the phone and after a few questions, she said, 'Is that you, Ralph?'

Potts couldn't contain himself any longer, and burst into laughter. He was downstairs on the phone in the billiard room, calling to the phone in the lounge room!

After a few more calls, not from Potts, but verging on the same type of insanity, the girls told the rest of the people who called that the positions were taken, and settled down to watching movies.

The absolute best of Ralph's jokes was about six years later, when Marlee was twenty or thereabouts. She was going to Sydney for a holiday, but developed a swollen eye a day or so before she was due to leave. I didn't like the look of the infection, and told her to go to the doctor in Darwin the moment she arrived. The eye was quite bad, and he put her on antiobiotics straightaway, and told her if it didn't improve in three days, to go to a specialist in Sydney. Marlee told me this on the phone before leaving for Sydney, so I called Sue to make sure Marlee didn't forget after she arrived and got caught up in having fun on holidays.

Sue told me Potts had an appointment with their eye specialist the morning after Marlee arrived and she could go along with him, and split the appointment, or she could take his appointment. When they arrived, the eye doctor said he would see them both.

Ralph went first, and in his usual humorous way he told

his doctor friend that Marlee was his niece, and that she had a slight mental problem, and was under therapy. He went on to tell him that she worked as a topless waitress in a restaurant, but all her life, her passion was horses, and all she ever wanted to do was be a jillaroo on an Outback cattle station. This dream had reached the stage where she now believed it to be true, and was having therapy to correct it. And could the doctor, when recording her history, if she started talking about the Outback, treat it carefully, and try and steer her back to reality . . .

In went Marlee. The doctor greeted her with a smile, and said that indeed, her eye needed attention. He said the tablets were working, the swelling was on the decline, but he would also give her ointment to put in the eye, as it seemed irritated.

Marlee replied that this was probably because she had been working in the dusty yards with cattle just before she left the station.

The doctor carefully inquired, 'Oh, where would that be?'

'In the Outback, in the Northern Territory. I am down in Sydney on holidays, staying with my aunt and uncle.'

'And you live in the Outback?'

'Yes.'

'Oh-that-is-nice,' the doctor said slowly, and continued, 'Wouldn't you like to live in the city? Then you wouldn't get eye irritations.'

'No! Besides, the pollution here would irritate anyone's eyes all the time. I'm not in the yards every day. So it's better living in the Outback.'

'Maybe you don't live in the Outback all the time. Maybe you visit, and live here most of the year?' the doctor asked with an encouraging tone.

'No. I live on a cattle station; it's my home. I only visit the city.' Marlee was starting to wonder if the man had a problem, but she remained patient and smiled, and waited for the next question.

There was a pause, as he seemed to be struggling with a problem. 'Maybe it would be better if you worked in the city, perhaps a restaurant. You could be a waitress,' he said in cheerful tones.

There were lots of things Marlee wanted to say at this point, but she refrained. 'Doctor, you don't seem to understand, I have lived on a cattle station since I was a small child. I don't like the city, wouldn't want to live or work here, and certainly wouldn't be a waitress. I think that would be the worst of jobs I could think of; very boring. I like working in the Outback.' She fell silent hoping this was the end.

But he was a dedicated doctor. 'You should really think about living in the city and working in a restaurant; maybe being a topless waitress would not be too boring?'

'No, thanks! I wouldn't think of it!' Marlee replied with forceful determination. Deciding it was time to terminate the conversation, she stood up, bade the doctor good morning, and walked out of the room. The doctor gave Ralph a hands-up gesture, with a sympathetic shrug of his shoulders behind Marlee's back, as she walked into the waiting room.

'How did you go?' Ralph asked.

'The eye is on the mend; I need to get some ointment. Boy, that doctor is a bit of a weirdo! Does he own a restaurant?'

'Not that I know of. Why?' asked Ralph innocently.

'He was dead-set on me working in some topless restaurant here in Sydney! Wouldn't get off the subject; just went on and on!'

'That's strange,' said Ralph, smiling hugely.

We all had a good laugh over dinner when Marlee recounted the strange conversation—which was extremely funny now she knew what Ralph had told the poor doctor.

17

VILLIE AND
THE FLYING DOCTORS

The drive-yourself, rented Toyota stopped at the back gate. I watched the man unwind himself from behind the wheel and stretch; all movements indicated a long journey without rests. As he walked towards the homestead, I got the distinct impression that he was German. Very tall, big shoulders and hands, fair complexion, the purposeful way he walked, his clothes, all suggested that he was German. Then he spoke, and confirmed my assumption.

His big hand shook my hand heartily, the greeting reverberating right up my arm; by the time I let go, the handshake had reached my toes.

'I-am-Villie; I-come-to-help-from-Germany. You-need-help-ya?' The words came out slowly, and each one was accentuated with the pumping of the hand. My head moved in rhythm. I found myself responding in like fashion.

'Ya—ah—yes—ah—I-not-sure.' The head-and-hand-shaking rhythm continued as 'Villie' told me he had seen a documentary in Germany about Bullo River, and it said we were women alone, working a farm the size of half a million acres. So he had decided we needed help, and so he came to help, all the way from Germany! By the time we got to the end of the speech in halting English, with the hand-shake on

231

each word, my eyes were out of focus. This was what I assumed he said, but I wasn't going to question any of it; I just wanted my hand back!

I was at a loss; it seemed the man only had two weeks holiday and he had travelled all the way from Germany to help us. Well, this was what I gleaned from the little English he could speak. There was a lot of head-nodding and ya-ing going on, and I thought I might have got it completely wrong; maybe the poor fellow was lost, and was asking for directions. Nevertheless Villie stayed and pottered around and helped wherever he could in the role of handyman about the place. He was mostly in the workshop with Dick, cleaning parts, sweeping the floor and doing anything that would generally help.

The documentary must have portrayed us as two women completely alone, because Villie showed surprise when he first saw Dick, then the stockmen, arrive for meals. When the film said 'alone' he assumed no-one else was here.

Everyone wanted to know why he was on the station; they all knew *who* he was, that was about all he was able to say. The stockmen would turn around and there would be Villie saying, 'Hullo. I am Villie; I help.' I told them my information was on par with theirs. Villie was there to help, this much we knew; for how long I had no idea, and there wasn't much chance of finding out.

Then he appeared one morning dressed, not in his work clothes, but in the clothes he had arrived in. He had breakfast, and in another rehearsed speech he told me, 'I-finish-help. Germany-I-go.' He pumped my hand a few dozen times again, got into the four-wheel-drive, and was gone in a cloud of dust. He left a gift, a napkin holder in the shape of a black and white Friesian cow, and a small amount of money that he considered represented board for the period of his stay. I never did find out his last name, or where in Germany was home; he remains in my memory as just 'Villie'.

Another of the documentaries on our life on Bullo reached Canada. I answered the phone, and a man introduced himself as the doctor-surgeon of a hospital in a village somewhere in Canada. On behalf of the entire village, he was calling to congratulate us on our success in the Outback. He went on to say the entire village had watched the programme on Bullo. Maybe the fact that they were in the grip of a blizzard, and the village had two metres of snow that day, might have had something to do with our high ratings! But nevertheless, the captive audience enjoyed seeing the sun and the life of the Outback, and I suppose, sitting in seven feet of snow, even the dust could look attractive!

It was a long and friendly conversation from the freezing minus twenty of Canada, to the sweltering forty-two degrees Celsius of the tropical Outback. When something like that happens to you, it makes you stop and realise how truly wonderful people are. The average human being is a very nice person to know. Characters a lot of them may be, but great human beings.

Some of the greatest human beings I have had the privilege of meeting are in the Royal Flying Doctor Service. All Australians know of this service, and indeed it is known all over the world, representing everything that is truly Australian. Even if people you meet can't speak English, their faces register recognition when you say the magic name. I grew up in the city, always hearing about the courageous acts of the RFDS in the vast Outback, and never dreaming that I would be so closely connected with the service later in my life.

As I explained in *From Strength to Strength*, when I went to Bullo in 1964 the only contact we had with the outside world was through our RFD radio sessions. These were for medical emergencies, but soon they also became a lifeline for all the families spread across the vast Australian bush. So messages were passed, then telegrams taken, gossip sessions took place between stations, and people travelling with two-way radios extended the service; so it grew and grew, until the Outback couldn't function without it.

Today, it remains vital for many of the still-isolated Outback areas. It is a very important part of my memories of the early days on Bullo. In our first year on the station, Marlee and Bonnie were aged four and two. I watched them as much as I could, and kept them close to the tin shed in which we lived, shouting at intervals from wherever I was, 'Children, where are you?' or, 'Children, what are you doing?' The replies came back regularly, and I knew they were within range, and all was well.

One morning I was going into the radio room for the morning session. I called out to ask the girls where they were, and what they were doing, and the reply came from Marlee, nothing much, just sitting. Satisfied, I continued into the radio room, and checked in for the session.

The station's call sign, S.O.V. (Sierra Oscar Victor), came to me over the crackle and static, and I started to read out the telegrams I wanted to send. I was halfway through one when I felt a tug at my sleeve. It was Marlee, saying, 'Mummy, Mummy.' I paused in the middle of reading and quickly said that unless it was important, she should wait until I had finished. I clicked the microphone on again and continued to read the telegram. Marlee persisted and said maybe Bonnie had broken her arm, and was that important. I let out a scream and dropped the microphone, as I swung around to look at Bonnie. Horror swept over me, as I looked at the expression on her little face, and the shape of the tiny forearm that was being carefully cradled by Marlee.

I screamed, 'Oh, Bon, you've broken your arm!'

The little eyes looked up at me, the bottom lip quivering, then the eyes moved to her older sister, who asked me, 'Is this really bad?'

The question was asked because their father always told them they could only cry if it was something really bad; they were not to cry over small things, they had to be brave. It was obvious Marlee had told Bon she could not cry until she had ascertained the status of a broken arm.

'Of course, this is very bad!' I said in a shocked voice. 'We will have to get a doctor straightaway!'

Marlee looked closely into her little sister's eyes, put her other arm gently on Bon's shoulder and said in a voice of complete and reassuring authority, 'It's all right, Bon, you can cry now.'

The quivering lip went slack and she really did cry. I made her comfortable on the bed, and my panicked brain thought, 'Doctor, I must get a doctor!'

Charles was not on the station; he had flown to Darwin early that morning. I jumped up from the bedside, grabbed the microphone, and started shouting, 'Sierra Oscar Victor— medical emergency, medical emergency!' The more I panicked, the louder Bon screamed.

Mr Bardwell's calm voice came through the static to assure me I didn't have to scream. I had left the button on when I dropped the microphone and he—indeed, the whole North on two-way radio—had heard all about Bon's broken arm. He went on to say he would arrange for the plane to come and collect Bon and bring her into Wyndham Hospital.

The X-ray revealed a greenstick fracture just above the wrist, and so a plaster cast went from her fingers to the elbow. Marlee and I had accompanied her to Wyndham, and Mr Bardwell called the Darwin tower, to have them contact Charlie in flight, and tell him to fly to Wyndham. We had to stay there for the next few days, to make sure the swelling did not continue and make the plaster too tight.

The next morning I was walking from the hotel room to the hospital, when a vision of black scowling thundered down the street, in the form of Mr Bardwell, to inform me that Bullo River was holding up the entire northern section of the Royal Flying Doctor Service, and what was I going to do about it?

I had no idea what he was talking about, but he soon explained. When I left Bullo, I had raced off in sheer panic with the children and had left the keys for the liquor store room on the radio desk. I had also left on the station an alcoholic cook! So it didn't take her long to get roaring drunk, and poor old John, our manager, came riding back that night, right into the thick of it.

He went into the radio room to check in for the last session that night. At this stage he did not know about Bonnie's accident. But he had just started to talk to Mr Bardwell when the drunk cook pounced on him. John dropped the microphone and hot-tailed it out the door, leaving the switch open. The result was a dreadful noise over the airways, and everything said in the radio room at Bullo was broadcast all over the RFD network. It was fortunate for John that not long after he returned to the room, and the cook pounced again, the sun set, and transmission after sunset is almost impossible to hear. But Mr Bardwell informed me quite enough had been heard, between John having a few too many swigs of rum, the cook returning, and the sun setting. All of it, he assured me, was against the rules in the RFDS code of conduct book on what you can do and say on the airwaves.

He demanded to know what I was going to do about it! I pacified him by saying Charles would fly out to the station immediately. Charles took off without delay, but John in the meantime had found the 'on' microphone and realised what he had done. When Charles arrived on the station the radio was off, the battery on charge, John had gone bush, and the cook was still drinking. Charles told the cook to pack, locked up what was left of the grog, left a note for John, and brought her back into town.

John, who was always on the radio up to that disastrous night, didn't go near it for months, and would not drive to town for a long time. He couldn't face all the ribbing he knew he would receive in the pub, and from friends in general.

Mr Bardwell seemed to blame me personally for this breach of radio etiquette, and I was never in his good books from that day on; we were always civil to each other, but he always reminded me if there was any breach of the RFD radio rules by me. According to Mr Bardwell, this was a daily occurrence!

But the service was always there, and helped in times of need, and even when the situation was laughable.

Charlie was getting his full share of come-uppances in our first year living 'close to nature'. While I was in Sydney recovering from a horse kicking me in the head, within weeks Charlie had his next medical emergency. He got through to the RFD base, and the doctor diagnosed a stockman as having acute appendicitis. But it was too late for the plane to pick him up that day, as it was approaching last light and we had no lighting facilities on the airstrip. So the pick-up was arranged for first light the next morning. Unlike Charlie, the pilot would not consider a landing guided only by a torch light balanced on someone's head, however many times Charlie assured the amazed pilot over the radio it was quite all right, he did it all the time. So Charlie had to face the night alone with a sick Aboriginal, with suspected acute appendicitis, moaning and groaning, in the medical room.

The tribal medicine man was administering his own style of cure, while most of the boy's relatives sitting outside the room were also moaning, humming and watching Charlie's every movement.

The doctor gave Charles instructions on what to do for the poor boy, but I am sure it went in one ear and out the other, as he tried to persuade them to come that night. He kept a cool cloth on the patient's head, and talked, and that was about the extent of his medical ability. The medicine man obviously didn't think it was enough, because he kept racing into the room, throwing dust and various things on the boy, and chanting. When he decided things weren't getting any better, he shocked Charlie into silence by rushing up and spitting in the boy's eyes. Charlie wasn't too up on medical procedure, but he quickly decided this would definitely not help, so he spent the night warding off the tribal doctor whenever he saw a spitting attack approaching. To get some sleep for the boy and himself, he finally had to lock the door.

The plane arrived at first light. The boy, having survived the night, Charlie's care and the medicine man, was whisked away to hospital where his appendix was removed. Despite the operation, he had a comfortable night in hospital, far from the medical madness of Bullo.

We had our fair share of starry-eyed young women applying for jobs as governess, with nothing more in their heads than trying to catch the eldest son—or the father, for that fact. One such female arrived, and of course there were no sons old enough, so she set her sights on Charlie. But this one didn't last too long, because medical problems got in the way.

She announced that she thought she might have to see a doctor, and could my husband take her to town. I told her, not necessary. We had a daily medical session on the radio, and she could talk to the doctor, and if her complaint was considered serious, the Flying Doctor's plane would come and take her to hospital.

Her problem, it seemed, was fluid retention; her hands and feet were swelling. She went on to inform me that she had tablets to control it, but since she had arrived she was experiencing too much swelling.

I told her it was because she had come from a cold climate into our hottest weather, and even people without this weakness experienced swelling of the feet until their bodies adjusted. I said not to worry, just to elevate her feet a few times a day, and at night.

She curtly thanked me for the information, but made it clear I didn't know what I was talking about. I made it clear that Charlie wouldn't be driving her to town, so she condescended to talk to the doctor.

I briefed her on using the radio: flip the switch 'on' to talk, flip it in the opposite direction to listen, and say 'over' when you finish speaking. Well, what a mess she made of those three simple instructions. She shouted at the microphone with the switch in the listening position, switched to speaking position to listen, and had the whole session in an uproar. Mr Bardwell managed to get a word in, and in a booming voice of authority told her not to touch another thing, and to go and get me to supervise her.

I had left her with the three simple instructions, hoping she would foul up, and was in the kitchen chuckling as she tried to have a conversation with the doctor at the hospital via Mr Bardwell at the RFD base.

'Hullo, are you there, doctor?'; a few too many clicks of the switch had her back to an open line for her to speak, so she couldn't hear the doctor, and on open air, broadcasting all over the North, she expressed her frustration at our communication set-up.

'Oh shit, I can't work this f..... thing! Is anyone there?'— click, click—two clicks instead of one click, so the doctor could answer, and she was back on the air with, 'What the f... is wrong with this bloody thing?'—click, click—'Doctor, are you there?'—click, click—'Oh, what a crappy set-up!'

I was rolling around the kitchen floor, roaring with laughter. She would now be the laughing stock of the North; everyone had heard about her fall from grace. A woman using that language wasn't accepted in the North in the 1960s, and over the RFDS radio it was sacrilege. If she ever made town, none of the women would let her anywhere near their sons!

The moment she only clicked once, Mr Bardwell pounced, and his booming voice instilled so much fear into her that she was still frozen when I came into the radio room. It had sunk into her brain by that point that all she had said, mumbling to herself, had gone out over the airways. Even though she was a thoroughly modern type from the 'big smoke', she knew she had not just stepped over the line, but plunged into irretrievable depths.

I smugly picked up the dropped microphone and politely

said, 'Sierra Oscar Victor, Mrs Henderson here, Mr Bardwell, over.'

'Mrs Henderson, would you please inform *that person* that swearing over radio channels is an offence by law. Please do not leave her unattended again, and supervise her medical call please, over.' The voice dripped disgust, and put the governess well and truly in her place.

I then controlled the switch, and held the microphone in front of her so she could answer the doctor's questions. Whenever she looked like lapsing into descriptive lingo, I cut the transmission. We were progressing as well as could be expected. I had warned her not to tell the doctor she knew everything about her complaint, but she continued to do so. It wasn't long before the doctor's voice resembled Mr Bardwell's.

Having patiently listened to her work through the history of her swelling feet and hands, the doctor finally got a chance to question her. 'How do the waterworks work?'.

She replied, 'Well, I really don't know. I have only been here for a few days.' She then turned to me and asked me how the water system worked.

I flicked the switch, not wanting the North to hear my reply, and said, 'Not the station's waterworks, you blithering idiot, yours! The doctor wants to know how often you go to the toilet!'

I left her sitting with her mouth open as I quickly flicked the switch and told the doctor I was trying to obtain this information for him; a grunt in reply indicated he wished me luck.

I turned to the governess, only to find she had stood up and was heading for the door. I told her the doctor was waiting for her answer, and she informed me that he was getting too personal for her liking, and she did not wish to continue the conversation.

I told the doctor, eliminating all the unacceptable language, that the patient didn't want to continue the conversation, and the doctor just moved to the next station on the list without comment.

A few days later, when she said she thought she should talk to the doctor again, I told her no way, and said I thought that someone of such delicate health shouldn't be in the Outback; she should have a job in the city, near medical help. So arrangements were made to get her to town as soon as possible, and despite much manoeuvring, mostly by her, and some by Charlie, I made sure she was driven to town by one of the stockmen, not by Charlie.

I heard later via the 'bush telegraph' that she was not readily accepted in town, her radio reputation having gone before her, and she soon left for the South, where her colourful language wasn't so shocking and people didn't keep ostentatiously asking about her waterworks!

I marked up one imaginary stroke for me, on the invisible scoreboard, recording my constant efforts to foil Charlie's attemped affairs.

But I must admit, he was willing to fly all over the Kimberleys to help out in emergencies, when the RFD had too many patients and not enough planes. And a few times, to help out in an emergency, he actually missed a prearranged *rendez-vous*; his sense of duty being so strong it prevailed even over affairs. Unfortunately for me, the RFD didn't call on him enough!

18

ET TU BRUTUS ET AL

We have, over the years, had a most interesting array of animals, but I think the most outstanding breed of dog is the Rottweiler.

Our first association with this dog came in the 1970s, when we bought Montejinni Station from the Crowsons, and Mrs Crowson asked us to take care of her Rottweiler/Doberman cross, a wonderful creature, aptly named Brutus. Very few dogs make me stop breathing and pause, but when Brutus walked into the room I did just that. Having just said I didn't mind taking care of the dog, in lumbered this half-horse. My heart dropped, my first thought was, Good heavens, what on earth have I let myself in for? We were told he didn't like men very much, but was a complete wuss when it came to women. Looking at the black shiny creature before me, I didn't think that dog could ever be called a wuss. It was the last word I would have used to describe that supreme powerhouse of muscle. But after my panic died down, I could see this massive animal had wonderful eyes.

I was relieved when Mrs Crowson went on to say he was gentle and good with children; I had been visualising locking Danielle, who was aged around eight, in a cage for our entire stay. But his owner was one hundred percent right; the

243

children fell madly in love with Brutus, and he with them. They were inseparable the whole time we lived at Montejinni. I never had to worry about their safety; Brutus was always there. I think virtually everyone and everything harmful went in the opposite direction when Brutus was sighted.

There was a lovely narrow creek, emptying into a great little swimming hole at the back of the house, and the children and Brutus and I would play whenever we had time, the girls throwing sticks and then racing Brutus, diving for them.

He never went into his run the entire time we were there; in fact, I was flat out stopping the children from taking him to bed. He got as close as he could, and then curled up on the mat between the beds.

After we finished the muster, we were going back to Bullo for The Wet. We pleaded with Charles to let us take Brutus back to Bullo with us, but I think Charles realised this dog was more than a match for him. And Charlie was well aware of the 'loves-women-and-children, hates-men' phobia Brutus had, so he flatly refused. His excuse was that Mrs Crowson was taking him back to Adelaide.

Marlee and I followed this up, because we were determined to have him if possible. But he went to Adelaide as planned, and we had to accept that the few short months we had with Brutus were all we were going to have as memories of him. Marlee called Mrs Crowson and said how much we all enjoyed taking care of Brutus, and we would have him any time, and went on to ask where she bought him.

It turned out her son had bred him, and he just happened to have a pure-bred male Rottie by Brutus's father, and a young female. We arranged to have the male puppy air-freighted to Darwin, and that was how Marlee got her first Rottie. She called him Cosmo. It must have been a strong trait of the father's line, because Cosmo wasn't too fond of men, either. In fact, he had a very distinct dislike for them, and unfortunately Charlie seemed to be top of his list.

The situation never improved. Marlee trained Cosmo to do tricks, eat on command, track, guard, but she couldn't persuade him to be friendly to Charlie, or to men in general. Whenever we had a party, it was difficult for Marlee to dance with anyone, as Cosmo would try to push between Marlee and her partner. It got to the point where he had to be locked in her room when she was dancing, or tied to a chair in the midst of the action, where he could still see her. This was very useful to Marlee if she didn't want to dance with a particular person; she just let Cosmo off the chain, and he made dancing so difficult that the poor boy would finally agree with Marlee that they had better stop. Of course, if it was someone she liked, Cos stayed well and truly anchored.

He was also taught to growl when you stopped scratching his chest. He did love having his chest scratched, so this soon developed as a trick. If Cosmo growled, he could have more scratching; it didn't take him long to get the picture. But often an unsuspecting visitor would have to be rescued.

When Cos found someone sitting in one of the lounge chairs, he would walk up to them, and very soon have his chest positioned where they could do nothing but scratch it. He'd just place one paw on the cushion on one side of the person's legs, and the other paw on the other side. Then he would slowly, so as not to scare the living daylights out of the potential scratcher, rise up on his hind legs, until he towered over them at his full height. There was no way the person could get out, short of standing on the cushion and jumping over the arm. But as far as I know, this never happened; people just stayed immobilised, and scratched, until rescued.

Each victim would set out to convince Cos they were his friend, and would start scratching his chest, which just happened to be blocking out most of their vision. He would assume an extremely satisfied expression which clearly indicated to the scratcher that they were doing the right thing. Sometimes they'd have quite a wait to be rescued from their predicament. If they tried to terminate the scratching, saying, 'Nice dog, that's enough, go away', Cosmo would look into their eyes, with a pleasant expression on his face but a low, deep, rumbling growl coming from the depths. To be on the safe side, they kept scratching. Immense relief would spread over the scratcher's face when one of the family appeared, and Cosmo would reluctantly relinquish his position of power.

For the rest of the visitor's stay, if Cosmo walked into the room and they happened to be sitting in a lounge chair, they would spring to their feet in a flash and remain standing until he left the room. Even though you told them it was a joke, and that if they could see his little tail, it was wagging all the time. One session in the lounge chair with Cosmo towering over you was enough for most people.

Cosmo's claim to heroism dated from when he rescued Marlee from a rather unsavoury type. We didn't employ this man; he arrived with a contractor as a labourer. The contractor was working on water tanks, away from the house, so we didn't see him or his workers much. But over the week, the few people who had reason to speak to this man remarked that he was not normal. I was about to discuss with Charles having him sent off the property, when his actions left no doubt that immediate action was required.

Her father had sent Marlee over to the Two Mile Bore, which is two miles straight across the river as the crow flies, but twelve miles by road via the river crossing in shallow water at six miles, where you can see the crocodiles.

Marlee was busy working on fence repairs, when she turned around and there he was standing behind her. He had swum the river, and his clothes were dripping wet. Marlee could see by the expression on his face that she was in trouble. She was a fair distance from the Toyota, where the shotgun was, and also her knife under the seat. She only had the pliers and fence strainers to defend herself. But she had forgotten Cosmo snoozing under a tree nearby. He had never had to save her from a dangerous situation, but she was in one now.

Shaking with fear, she tried to bluff her way out. 'Go back to work, now!' she growled at the labourer. His sickly smirk made her stomach turn; her fingers tightened around the pliers, and she braced herself for an attack.

'Go now!' she screamed at him. The fear in her voice brought Cosmo out of his slumber, and he launched at the labourer in a snarling, growling, hair-bristling charge, fangs glistening in the sun, and the growl changed to a gruesome roar. The smirk of power on the labourer's face turned to abject horror, and he turned and took off into the bush with Cos in hot pursuit.

Marlee sagged to the ground in relief, but not for long; she quickly called Cosmo, not wanting him out of range of her voice, or following the man into the river. Dogs were top choice on a crocodile's menu. As she called, she was running to the Toyota, and had the shotgun in her hands, ready for action. Cosmo came out of the trees, his hair still standing on end. Marlee gave him a quick hug, told him he was the best, and they both jumped into the utility and drove at high speed back to the homestead. Marlee told her father the story, the labourer was escorted off the property post-haste, and Charles had to admit Cosmo was the hero of the year.

After Cosmo came another beautiful Rottweiler puppy called Hunter; he, too, grew to be a smart dog, learned many tricks and enjoyed participating in all events.

Hunter used to drive all the way to Queensland with Marlee and Charlie each year. Marlee made a roof for shade, and put in a mattress so he could be comfortable. The jeep was packed with expensive tools and equipment, and when they stopped along the road for a meal they would park and leave the jeep seemingly unattended.

The light-fingered types that sometimes hang around these places would smile to themselves, and think, city slickers, I'll relieve them of some of that gear.

But while they were casually leaning up against the jeep with one hand busily ferreting among the gear, suddenly a big black mass would rise out of nowhere, and growl. One guy was so terrified, he froze in position, with his hand on the chain-saw, and didn't move until Marlee and Charlie appeared and told him he could go. Hunter didn't have to do anything, just the look of him scared most of the thieves half to death.

He also saved Marlee's life, this time in the yards. She was on the top rail, leaning across to open a gate, and a bull charged the panel she was standing on. The force of the impact knocked her off balance, and she fell into the yard almost at the bull's feet. Hunter was at her side in a flash, and went for the bull's nose, distracting it long enough for Marlee to scramble to her feet and up the rails to safety.

Donna and Hunter sang beautiful duets, Donna high soprano, while Hunter was deep, deep baritone. Hunter loved centre stage; he would pucker up his mouth, and let forth a beautifully controlled howl; all the time his eyes would look at you sideways, to gauge the effect this melodious sound was having on you. When you told him it was wonderful, he would take a deep breath, and increase the volume.

If he was lying on the floor in the dark, when the generator was off, and you started to walk towards him, he seemed to know you couldn't see him, and would warn you he was there, not with a growl, but with a sound that almost said, 'Look out, I'm here.'

When you said, 'It's okay, I can see you', he would go back to sleep with a grunt. If you couldn't see him and said, 'Where are you, Hunter?' he would stand up and you would feel a big head slip under your hand.

That dog could almost talk! He could do many tricks; Marlee taught him to blow bubbles under water, and to dive and pick up stones on the riverbed. When we took him to the beach in Queensland, he body-surfed on the small waves on the shore. He would walk out into the surf with Marlee and Charlie, and Charlie would hold him waiting for the right wave. When Charlie launched him on a wave, he'd hold his paws out in front of him, his back legs working double time, his ears flattened against his head, and his whiskers standing straight out. He looked for all the world like a seal in the foam, riding the crest of a wave.

He was so well trained, Marlee could put his plate of meat on the floor, and he would look at her face and wait for her to nod, or say it was 'okay' to eat. Although there were a few times this little trick backfired. On one occasion Marlee put his plate of meat on the kitchen floor, then raced off to answer the phone without saying 'okay'. She talked too long, hung up, and forgot poor old Hunter. I came into the kitchen to find him standing over the plate, guarding his dinner from all the other dogs, who had finished theirs and made it clear if Hunter wasn't going to eat his they would oblige. The saliva was dripping from his mouth as he stood guard. His eyes looked at me pleadingly: 'Please get my mistress!' Marlee came rushing back with me, and apologised profusely. But Hunter was more interested in the magic word 'okay', and he wolfed down the meat in record time before accepting praise for being an obedient dog.

Other times, when he didn't have to wait an hour for the 'okay to start' order, he would play games with the other dogs. He would leave half the meat on his plate. When one of the other dogs wandered by and stopped to eat it, Hunter would sit up and growl; they would quickly drop the piece of meat and scamper away. But by far his favourite game was with the crows. He would put a bone on the lawn, then sit in the shade, just under the arches of the front verandah. The crows would land some distance away from the bone, and 'case the joint', then slowly hop over, pausing and searching all the time, anticipation building. When the crow could almost touch the bone, Hunter would rush out of the shadows, barking and growling. The poor old crow, inches from the inviting snack, would squawk, hop and fly to a safe distance from the bone, then just watch. Hunter would retire to the shade, and the whole procedure would be repeated. Sometimes it would go on all morning, until someone got sick of the crow squawking and the bone was removed.

We lost Hunter last year; he died of cancer. He was part of the family for a long time, a tolerant and patient dog, kind to all the new puppies that came his way. We were very sad at his passing, but Marlee was particularly upset; he was such a faithful friend, and she missed him terribly. Franz decided she needed a puppy straight away. He called me from Darwin, saying he had found a beautiful Rottie puppy. I had reservations; I told him you had to be very careful buying Rotties and all ours had come from the South, from established and registered kennels. I told him to do a lot more research into the seller. Franz is very thorough, and when he called back the next night he bombarded me with facts. The dog had been bred South, great pedigree, sound in health, all injections, certificates for hip problems, the lot. I said, well, it seems like you have covered everything, and I knew he was set on this dog. He said the price was one thousand dollars, which was a lot, even more than we had paid for Hunter, but Franz reminded me that was many years ago.

So he brought home Bow, a beautiful black and tan ball of fluff with a wonderful face. When Franz handed him to me to take into Marlee, I could understand why he insisted on wanting him; he was a beautiful puppy.

It was love at first sight when Marlee and Bow met, and the house was full again with puppies. Franz had a German Shepherd puppy, Muzzie, I had my Rottie, Sumie, and now Marlee had Bow. The three pups had a wonderful time together.

Sadly, it didn't last. We started to notice Bow would not want to play, or would snap suddenly and savagely at one of the other pups if it came bounding up to him. Marlee finally took him to the vet. X-rays revealed he had hardly any hip joints. The only things that kept the top of the leg bone anywhere near the hip joint were the muscles. The vet assured Marlee that Bow was in pain most of the time. It just broke our hearts but we had to put him to sleep. He was only six-months old, and he would grow into a dog of one hundred pounds plus; his life would have been constant misery.

I tell this story to make people realise there are unscrupulous breeders out there, breeding dogs with chronic hip problems and other major faults, and they are getting away with selling these dogs for high prices. One litter in a few months makes them thousands of dollars. This is pure misery money; the puppy grows and there is heartbreak for the family who have to put their pet down, not to mention the large sum paid, which should guarantee a healthy puppy.

Please, if you are buying a puppy, check out the breeder carefully, ask advice from breeder associations, show judges; learn the format and things to look for from other breeders. Check and check again; check every detail. Always remember that an unscrupulous breeder is relying on your heart melting the moment you see that beautiful bundle of fluff with an angelic face peering out at you. So until you *know* the breeder is reliable, don't even go there so they can let the puppy's charm make a sale for them.

Some of these breeders are selling dogs into the Far East, for astronomical prices; not only do the dogs have breeding defects, and grow up in pain, but they are sold to people who do not know about pet care. In one case recently, a dog was rescued from a tenth-floor balcony where it had been chained night and day, in the sun, cold, all weathers. It had never left the balcony for one year! These breeders have to be stopped from trading in this despicable animal misery. You can start the ball rolling by not buying puppies from them and by urging your local M.P. for laws to be passed to prevent this uncontrolled profiteering.

19

BOOTS AND ALL

That just about brings me up to current times with friends, characters and animals. Well, not really, but I am running out of time and I must finish the book as the publishers are waiting. I am happy to say there are still lots of friends and animals around. All the old characters of Bullo River are gone, Uncle Dick, Max, Diesel Don, Fred the Gardener, Stumpy the Cook, to mention a few of our outstanding 'dedicated drinkers'. Today, on Bullo, the only resident characters are the animals; all the people are hard workers, serious about their work, young people... except for me, and I suppose the young people think *I'm* a bit of a character.

But amongst the animals we have characters galore. The present pets, close to the homestead, are Daisy and Pumpkin, the milking cows; Bazza, our new baby Bazadaise stud breeding bull; Aly, our new stallion; Boots, our old stallion; Muzzie, Franz's German Shepherd; Sumie, my Rottweiler; and Meow, the resident half-Burmese half-wild house cat.

Daisy and Pumpkin are the senior resident characters; they came over from Malanda in Queensland, in January 1988, so they are the kingpins around the garden. One is usually in the garden over The Wet, to be milked for house milk and to help feed any orphan calves. This year, Daisy was feeding four orphans. She is literally a milk machine; we stuffed the feed in one end and the four little hungry calves sucked milk out the 'udder'. Daisy stands quietly grazing as the four calves are going hammer and tongs at getting milk. When she is sick of them drinking, she just squats down under a tree for a snooze. The four calves try to burrow under her to find a teat. Daisy sits dozing, surrounded by four little backsides, tails up in the air, swishing back and forth in anticipation, while four little heads disappear under Daisy's legs, trying vainly to locate the milk supply.

Pumpkin had her last calf just after Christmas, almost on the front porch. Heavy rains made a large muddy stretch of ground at the front step, so Marlee dumped a few tonnes of sand there with the front-end loader. It promptly became the animals' sandpit. Boots rolls in the sand; the dogs dig and sleep there; Bazza just sits and surveys his domain; and Pumpkin decided it was the right place to have her calf. Within weeks, Marlee and Franz had found more orphans, so along with her own calf, Pumpkin is feeding three orphans. It is a wonderful picture, with the setting sun throwing a golden glow across the valley, to see the two old cows, adoringly followed by eight baby calves, in a straight line, bending and weaving, following the cows' every movement, as the two old friends casually stroll together.

Bazza is the latest addition to the menagerie. He is just coming up to two years old, and is our most expensive stud bull to date. We expect great things from Bazza, even if he doesn't know it. We hope his bloodline will bring to our herd the double-muscled hindquarters and faster-growing young animals that do well just on native grasses. A tall order for one small young bull, but if his offspring show any of his characteristics we can turn off our steers six months younger at the same weight as our steers now. This will give us more income yearly while still grazing the same number of cattle.

That's why Bazza lives in the garden; we keep him right under our noses until he is ready to work. Even then, I think we will bring the cows to him: surrounded as he is by strong personalities, he can't help developing into one himself. Marlee brushes him every day, so already he waits at the door for her to appear and pamper him. It is not unusual to find him sitting in the sandpit with Muzzie, Sumie and Boots. They all acknowledge each other, and the sandpit seems to be neutral territory. Elsewhere in the garden, the two dogs stay clear of both of them.

Sumie, my Rottie, and Muzzie, Franz's German Shepherd, share the inside of the house with another longtime resident, Meow, the cat. Well, when I say share, it is a broad term.

I call Meow our aerial cat; he lives up in the ceiling, and only comes down at night for his meal, and then that is eaten on top of a high cupboard. It was not always so; Mcow grew up with my Donna and Marlee's Hunter, and the cat loved these two, especially Donna. Many a time I would find him curled up between Donna's paws, fast asleep, with her chin resting on his back. When we lost the old dogs, new puppies appeared. Meow, getting on in years himself, thought he would be safer at elevated heights, so he took to the ceilings. But at night, when the dogs are in the bedrooms sleeping, Meow has the run of the house. The evidence is always there in the morning in the form of a paw mark on some surface, or a dead baby snake deposited somewhere strategic, just to remind us he is still on the job.

He is nowhere near as sprightly as he used to be, and sometimes during the day, when he has ventured to lower levels, he has been trapped by the puppies. They thought him a wonderful plaything, and I had to come running to Meow's yowls, as the puppies became too rough. A few times when springing to the safety of heights, the spring has been lacking, and he has had to be rescued from two now big and playful dogs, who are not quite sure what they do with this yowling bundle of fur. I have to scold them for being too rough, and carefully help Meow to the top of the cupboard, from where he disappears up into the ceiling while the dogs watch with a mystified expression.

I tell them Meow is too old and he doesn't want to play; they look at each other with an expression that says, 'what's old?', then bound away out the door at speeds just under Mach One, looking for the next adventure. They usually end up in the sandpit, always careful not to disturb Boots if he is sleeping. If the dogs get too close and disturb him, he will give them a nip; they learned very early in their puppy days that Boots can give quite a nasty nip.

Which brings us to Boots, the present reigning character on Bullo. He has to be a Charlie-in-horse-clothing; maybe that's why I like him so much . . .

Boots is very old now, and he resides in the garden so we can care for him. He is blind in one eye, his teeth are worn down almost to gum level, and it seems impossible to keep him up to weight. We are going to try a bit of stout with his feed, to get a bit of weight on him. But he is bright-eyed, his coat is shiny and he eats all day. And should a filly in season walk past, just watch the miraculous change. He will be standing under the tree, hound-dog expression, drooping, ears down, snoozing, looking for all the world like the next in line for the knackery, and some filly sashays by and gives a 'how-de-do' whinny.

The head shoots up, the ears prick, the bow goes out of

the sagging back, the neck arches, the tail elevates in a graceful curve of red cascading hair, and he starts swaggering in a graceful trot, as if he is lead horse at the Vienna Riding School. He races over to the fence and struts his stuff, whinnying and snorting and tossing his head. When the filly eventually moves on, he deflates like a balloon losing air, and finally gets back to the tree and continues his snooze. This transformation can happen many times a day.

Boots, apart from doing what comes naturally, being a stallion, must be the most pleasant-natured horse ever—and especially for a stallion. When we had our free-ranging chickens, apart from using Boots as a protective shelter from the chicken-hawks, they also joined him at his feed time. So, one stallion and thirty hens had a meal together. His feed bin was half of a forty-four-gallon drum, so as many chickens as possible would get into the drum around Boots' head and eat with him, while the rest would teeter around the rim, regularly falling in on top of everything, or off onto the ground.

Boots was so patient, he never hurt the hens, but every now and then when he let out a tremendous snort, all the hens in the bin would elevate a few feet, then stagger around the yard. The next lot would jump into the bin to eat, only to be similarly elevated by the next sonic-boom snort. By lunchtime, all the hens would have hearing impairments, and chicken communication and egg-laying arrangements would be done at very high decibels. A cry for help warning of an approaching, diving chicken-hawk would be so loud that it even put the chicken-hawk off target! Their hearing would return by afternoon, just in time for the next feeding session.

Feeding time is the only time Boots will try to bully you for his feed, even though he is gentle with the chickens, but if you hold up a clenched fist he will back off. He was fairly old when he came to Bullo, and his former owners told us about the fist. If he was naughty, he got a punch in the shoulder. Even to this day, if you hold up a clenched fist, you can see the muscles in his shoulder tighten, waiting for the punch. He is the only horse I know that stands outside the house, at the rope across the kitchen door, and 'weaves' to get in. Most racehorses stand in their stalls and 'weave' to get out! (Weaving is a rocking action where the horse sways from side to side at a barricade; most stabled horses get the 'weaving' habit.)

Boots is very fond of coming into the house, and over The Wet, when it's very hot, you can't keep him out unless you barricade every door. He can walk through the house and not knock anything over. He always heads for the kitchen, and food. In this department, Boots definitely thinks he is human. He will eat eggs, bacon, Vegemite and bread, ham and tomato sandwiches. He drinks coffee, chocolate milk; loves chocolate in any form, from bars to cakes. One of our cooks set out morning tea for some guests on the kitchen bench, then went to get the guests. Boots sneaked in the back door, and while everyone was chatting around the swimming pool, he wiped out scones, cream, jam, cake and sandwiches. He knocked over the milk and lapped it up off the tiles, and lapped and sprayed the sugar all over the remaining mess. The only thing left intact was the pot of tea; Boots doesn't like black tea.

I caught him raiding the kitchen one morning. Jackie was thawing out three quiches for lunch, and they were on the bench, still with clear plastic covering them, and poor old Boots couldn't work out why he wasn't tasting any food. He had dug a hole in the quiche filling as he vainly tried to get some of it into his mouth, but the plastic hadn't broken. He had such a mystified look on his face. I led him out the door, leaving three quiches with strange-shaped bare patches in the middle, which mystified Jackie until I told her we'd had a visit from Boots.

If he isn't fed on time, he makes life difficult for you in any way he can. I was late feeding him one day, and he came looking for me in the house; he found me in the office, on the phone. He has been around long enough to know that a lot of my life is spent holding that strange contraption. To get my attention, he picks up papers and pens and generally pushes things around and off the desk. To keep him in line, I tap him on the nose to stop him from destroying anything. So my conversation proceeds while a silent game of tag goes on with my right hand raised ready to slap Boots's nose, and him trying to grab anything off my desk that's out of reach of the raised hand.

This game was in progress one day when I was on the phone talking to the bank manager; Boots was bored with the snatching game, and was looking out the double doors, when he spotted a filly. He took the deepest of breaths, and let out a welcoming whinny to the filly, a paddock away. In the closed room, the noise was deafening, as it reverberated off every wall. Even old Boots stopped short with a 'Good heavens! Was that me?' expression on his face. The filly stopped and replied, and Boots this time launched into a longer response. Of course, conversation on the phone was impossible, so I had to wait until Boots decided he might mosey on over to the fence, and have a chat.

When silence returned, I asked the bank manager if he was still there.

'What on earth was that?' he asked. I told him it was our stallion calling to another horse. He wanted to know was I telephoning from a stable. No, I told him, from my office.

'You have a horse in your office?' I suppose sitting in Pitt Street, Sydney, this would seem strange. I told him Boots often came into the office. I smiled as I put down the receiver; I could just see the entry in the Bullo River diary file at the bank: *Spoke to Mrs Henderson at 9:15 a.m.; conversation interrupted by Boots, the stallion, whinnying in office, calling to filly—not on the phone!*

Boots is a flagrant exhibitionist, demands to be the centre of attention, loves to eat all day, would probably drink beer all day if given the opportunity, and will try to chat up and chase any filly that passes by...

Sounds just like my Charlie!

I wonder... no, not possible... yet...?